SOLARO

STUDY GUIDE

ence 7

SOLARO Study Guide is designed to help students achieve success in school. The content in each study guide is 100% curriculum aligned and serves as an excellent source of material for review and practice. To create this book, teachers, curriculum specialists, and assessment experts have worked closely to develop the instructional pieces that explain each of the key concepts for the course. The practice questions and sample tests have detailed solutions that show problem-solving methods, highlight concepts that are likely to be tested, and point out potential sources of errors. ***SOLARO Study Guide*** is a complete guide to be used by students throughout the school year for reviewing and understanding course content, and to prepare for assessments.

Rao,Gautam,1961 –
SOLARO STUDY GUIDE – Science 7 Ontario

1. Science – Juvenile Literature. I. Title

Castle Rock Research Corp.
2410 Manulife Place
10180 – 101 Street
Edmonton, AB T5J 3S4

1 2 3 PP 15 14 13

Publisher
Gautam Rao

Contributors
Ken Boyko
Johanne Estephan
Ruby Grewal
Susan Oreski
Maureen Orr
Melissa Tesche

Dedicated to the memory of Dr. V. S. Rao

SOLARO STUDY GUIDE

Each ***SOLARO STUDY GUIDE*** consists of the following sections:

Key Tips for Being Successful at School gives examples of study and review strategies. It includes information about learning styles, study schedules, and note taking for test preparation.

Class Focus includes a unit on each area of the curriculum. Units are divided into sections, each focusing on one of the specific expectations, or main ideas, that students must learn about in that unit. Examples, definitions, and visuals help to explain each main idea. Practice questions on the main ideas are also included. At the end of each unit is a test on the important ideas covered. The practice questions and unit tests help students identify areas they know and those they need to study more. They can also be used as preparation for tests and quizzes. Most questions are of average difficulty, though some are easy and some are hard—the harder questions are called *Challenger Questions*. Each unit is prefaced by a ***Table of Correlations***, which correlates questions in the unit (and in the practice tests at the end of the book) to the specific curriculum expectations. Answers and solutions are found at the end of each unit.

Key Strategies for Success on Tests helps students get ready for tests. It shows students different types of questions they might see, word clues to look for when reading them, and hints for answering them.

Practice Tests includes one to three tests based on the entire course. They are very similar to the format and level of difficulty that students may encounter on final tests. In some regions, these tests may be reprinted versions of official tests, or reflect the same difficulty levels and formats as official versions. This gives students the chance to practice using real-world examples. Answers and complete solutions are provided at the end of the section.

For the complete curriculum document (including specific expectations along with examples and sample problems), visit http://www.edu.gov.on.ca/eng/curriculum/

SOLARO STUDY GUIDE *Study Guides* are available for many courses. Check www.castlerockresearch.com for a complete listing of books available for your area.

For information about any of our resources or services, please call Castle Rock Research at 1.800.840.6224 or visit our website at http://www.castlerockresearch.com.

At Castle Rock Research, we strive to produce an error-free resource. If you should find an error, please contact us so that future editions can be corrected.

CONTENTS

Key Tips for being Successful at School

KEY TIPS FOR BEING SUCCESSFUL AT SCHOOL

KEY FACTORS CONTRIBUTING TO SCHOOL SUCCESS

In addition to learning the content of your courses, there are some other things that you can do to help you do your best at school. You can try some of the following strategies:

- **Keep a positive attitude:** Always reflect on what you can already do and what you already know.
- **Be prepared to learn:** Have the necessary pencils, pens, notebooks, and other required materials for participating in class ready.
- **Complete all of your assignments:** Do your best to finish all of your assignments. Even if you know the material well, practice will reinforce your knowledge. If an assignment or question is difficult for you, work through it as far as you can so that your teacher can see exactly where you are having difficulty.
- **Set small goals for yourself when you are learning new material:** For example, when learning the parts of speech, do not try to learn everything in one night. Work on only one part or section each study session. When you have memorized one particular part of speech and understand it, move on to another one. Continue this process until you have memorized and learned all the parts of speech.
- **Review your classroom work regularly at home:** Review to make sure you understand the material you learned in class.

- **Ask your teacher for help:** Your teacher will help you if you do not understand something or if you are having a difficult time completing your assignments.
- **Get plenty of rest and exercise:** Concentrating in class is hard work. It is important to be well-rested and have time to relax and socialize with your friends. This helps you keep a positive attitude about your schoolwork.
- **Eat healthy meals:** A balanced diet keeps you healthy and gives you the energy you need for studying at school and at home.

How to Find Your Learning Style

Every student learns differently. The manner in which you learn best is called your learning style. By knowing your learning style, you can increase your success at school. Most students use a combination of learning styles. Do you know what type of learner you are? Read the following descriptions. Which of these common learning styles do you use most often?

- **Linguistic Learner:** You may learn best by saying, hearing, and seeing words. You are probably really good at memorizing things such as dates, places, names, and facts. You may need to write down the steps in a process, a formula, or the actions that lead up to a significant event, and then say them out loud.
- **Spatial Learner:** You may learn best by looking at and working with pictures. You are probably really good at puzzles, imagining things, and reading maps and charts. You may need to use strategies like mind mapping and webbing to organize your information and study notes.
- **Kinesthetic Learner:** You may learn best by touching, moving, and figuring things out using manipulatives. You are probably really good at physical activities and learning through movement. You may need to draw your finger over a diagram to remember it, tap out the steps needed to solve a problem, or feel yourself writing or typing a formula.

Scheduling Study Time

You should review your class notes regularly to ensure that you have a clear understanding of all the new material you learned. Reviewing your lessons on a regular basis helps you to learn and remember ideas and concepts. It also reduces the quantity of material that you need to study prior to a test. Establishing a study schedule will help you to make the best use of your time.

Regardless of the type of study schedule you use, you may want to consider the following suggestions to maximize your study time and effort:

- Organize your work so that you begin with the most challenging material first.
- Divide the subject's content into small, manageable chunks.
- Alternate regularly between your different subjects and types of study activities in order to maintain your interest and motivation.
- Make a daily list with headings like "Must Do," "Should Do," and "Could Do."
- Begin each study session by quickly reviewing what you studied the day before.
- Maintain your usual routine of eating, sleeping, and exercising to help you concentrate better for extended periods of time.

CREATING STUDY NOTES

MIND-MAPPING OR WEBBING

Use the key words, ideas, or concepts from your reading or class notes to create a mind map or web (a diagram or visual representation of the given information). A mind map or web is sometimes referred to as a knowledge map. Use the following steps to create a mind map or web:

1. Write the key word, concept, theory, or formula in the centre of your page.
2. Write down related facts, ideas, events, and information, and link them to the central concept with lines.
3. Use coloured markers, underlining, or symbols to emphasize things such as relationships, timelines, and important information.

The following examples of a Frayer Model illustrate how this technique can be used to study vocabulary.

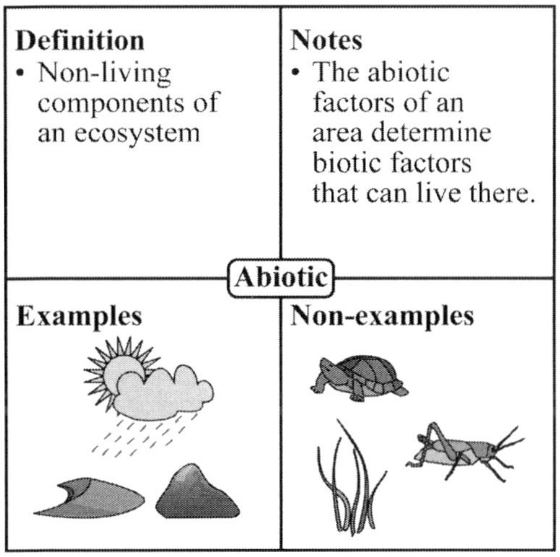

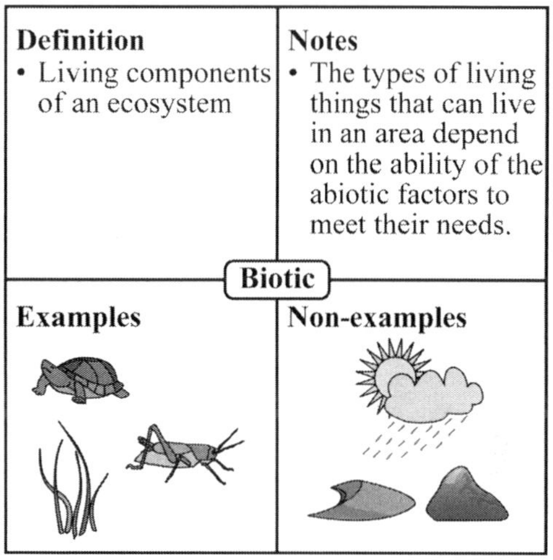

INDEX CARDS

To use index cards while studying, follow these steps:

1. Write a key word or question on one side of an index card.
2. On the reverse side, write the definition of the word, answer to the question, or any other important information that you want to remember.

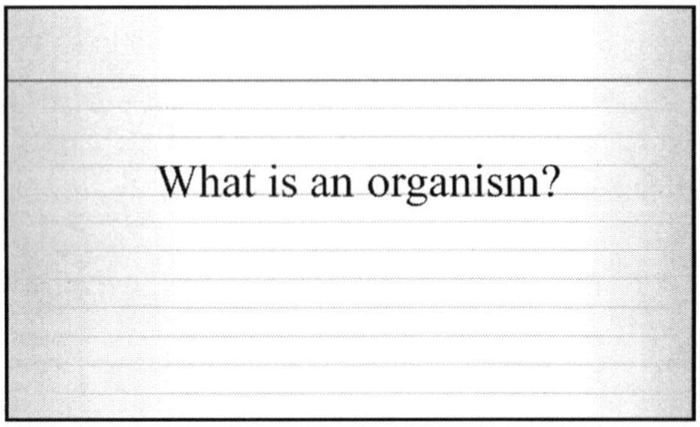

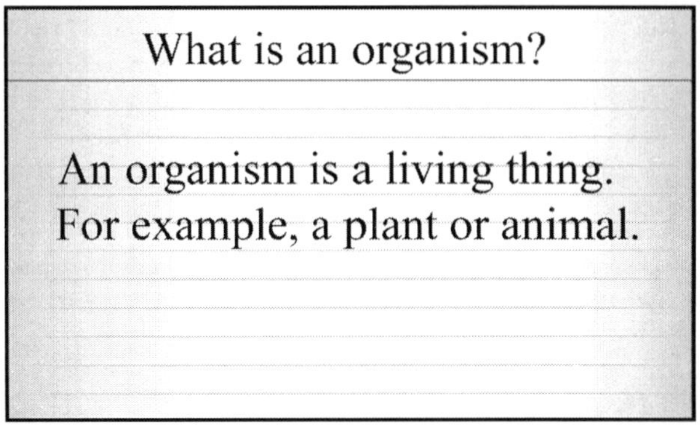

SYMBOLS AND STICKY NOTES—IDENTIFYING IMPORTANT INFORMATION

Use symbols to mark your class notes. The following are some examples:

- An exclamation mark (!) might be used to point out something that must be learned well because it is a very important idea.
- A question mark (?) may highlight something you are not certain about
- A diamond (◊) or asterisk (*) could highlight interesting information that you want to remember.

Sticky notes are useful in the following situations:

- Use sticky notes when you are not allowed to put marks in books.
- Use sticky notes to mark a page in a book that contains an important diagram, formula, explanation, or other information.
- Use sticky notes to mark important facts in research books.

Memorization Techniques

- **Association** relates new learning to something you already know. For example, to remember the spelling difference between dessert and desert, recall that the word *sand* has only one *s*. So, because there is sand in a desert, the word *desert* has only one *s*.
- **Mnemonic** devices are sentences that you create to remember a list or group of items. For example, the first letter of each word in the phrase "Every Good Boy Deserves Fudge" helps you to remember the names of the lines on the treble-clef staff (E, G, B, D, and F) in music.
- **Acronyms** are words that are formed from the first letters or parts of the words in a group. For example, RADAR is actually an acronym for Radio Detecting and Ranging, and MASH is an acronym for Mobile Army Surgical Hospital. HOMES helps you to remember the names of the five Great Lakes (Huron, Ontario, Michigan, Erie, and Superior).

- **Visualizing** requires you to use your mind's eye to "see" a chart, list, map, diagram, or sentence as it is in your textbook or notes, on the chalkboard or computer screen, or in a display.
- **Initialisms** are abbreviations that are formed from the first letters or parts of the words in a group. Unlike acronyms, an initialism cannot be pronounced as a word itself. For example, GCF is an initialism for **G**reatest **C**ommon **F**actor.

Key Strategies for Reviewing

Reviewing textbook material, class notes, and handouts should be an ongoing activity. Spending time reviewing becomes more critical when you are preparing for a test. You may find some of the following review strategies useful when studying during your scheduled study time:

- Before reading a selection, preview it by noting the headings, charts, graphs, and chapter questions.
- Before reviewing a unit, note the headings, charts, graphs, and chapter questions.
- Highlight key concepts, vocabulary, definitions, and formulas.
- Skim the paragraph, and note the key words, phrases, and information.
- Carefully read over each step in a procedure.
- Draw a picture or diagram to help make the concept clearer.

KEY STRATEGIES FOR SUCCESS: A CHECKLIST

Reviewing is a huge part of doing well at school and preparing for tests. Here is a checklist for you to keep track of how many suggested strategies for success you are using. Read each question, and put a check mark (✓) in the correct column. Look at the questions where you have checked the "No" column. Think about how you might try using some of these strategies to help you do your best at school.

Key Strategies for Success	Yes	No
Do you attend school regularly?		
Do you know your personal learning style—how you learn best?		
Do you spend 15 to 30 minutes a day reviewing your notes?		
Do you study in a quiet place at home?		
Do you clearly mark the most important ideas in your study notes?		
Do you use sticky notes to mark texts and research books?		
Do you practise answering multiple-choice and written-response questions?		
Do you ask your teacher for help when you need it?		
Are you maintaining a healthy diet and sleep routine?		
Are you participating in regular physical activity?		

Life Systems: Interactions in the Environment

LIFE SYSTEMS: INTERACTIONS IN THE ENVIRONMENT

Table of Correlations

Specific Expectation		Practice Questions	Unit Test Questions	Practice Test 1	Practice Test 2
7LS1:STSE	Assess the impacts of human activities and technologies on the environment, and evaluate ways of controlling these impacts;				
7LS1.1	*assess the impact of selected technologies on the environment*	1, 2	1	38	
7LS1.2	*analyse the costs and benefits of selected strategies for protecting the environment*	3, 4	2		39
7LS2:Skills	Investigate interactions within the environment, and identify factors that affect the balance between different components of an ecosystem;				
7LS2.1	*follow established safety procedures for investigating ecosystems*				
7LS2.2	*design and construct a model ecosystem, and use it to investigate interactions between the biotic and abiotic components in an ecosystem*	5, 6	3	39	
7LS2.3	*use scientific inquiry/research skills to investigate occurrences that affect the balance within a local ecosystem*	12, 13	4, 5	40	40
7LS2.4	*use appropriate science and technology vocabulary, including sustainability, biotic, ecosystem, community, population, and producer, in oral and written communication*	31, 32	6, 7	41	41
7LS2.5	*use a variety of forms to communicate with different audiences and for a variety of purposes*				
7LS3:Concepts	Demonstrate an understanding of interactions between and among biotic and abiotic elements in the environment.				
7LS3.1	*demonstrate an understanding of an ecosystem as a system of interactions between living organisms and their environment*	7, 8	8		42
7LS3.2	*identify biotic and abiotic elements in an ecosystem, and describe the interactions between them*	9, 10, 11	9, 10	42	43
7LS3.3	*describe the roles and interactions of producers, consumers, and decomposers within an ecosystem*	14, 15, 16, 17	11, 12	43, 44	44, 45
7LS3.4	*describe the transfer of energy in a food chain and explain the effects of the elimination of any part of the chain*	18, 19, 20	13, 14	45, 46	46
7LS3.5	*describe how matter is cycled within the environment and explain how it promotes sustainability*	21, 22	15	47	47
7LS3.6	*distinguish between primary succession and secondary succession within an ecosystem*	23, 24, 25	16, 17	48	48
7LS3.7	*explain why an ecosystem is limited in the number of living things that it can support*	26, 27	18	49	49
7LS3.8	*describe ways in which human activities and technologies alter balances and interactions in the environment*	28, 29	19	50	50
7LS3.9	*describe Aboriginal perspectives on sustainability and describe ways in which they can be used in habitat and wildlife management*	30			

7LS1.1 assess the impact of selected technologies on the environment

Technology's Impact on the Environment

To assess the environmental impact of a specific technology, the impact of the manufacturing, daily usage, and disposal of this technology need to be considered.

Manufacturing computers, for example, requires a lot of energy. Most of this energy is produced by burning fossil fuels, which contributes to the greenhouse effect and climate change. Along with the energy required, the manufacturing process uses a lot of materials and chemicals. Because computer technology changes so quickly, computers quickly become outdated. These outdated machines are thrown out, resulting in large piles of computer equipment in landfills. It is unknown if the chemicals in the discarded computers leak out once they end up in the landfills. New recycling facilities reduce the amount of electronic materials that end up in the landfills, but the recycling process also requires energy from fossil fuels.

1. Which of the following events is **not** an indirect environmental consequence of the increasing use of computers?
   A. Discarded computers might leak toxins into the landfill.
   B. The use of computers can cause repetitive strain injuries.
   C. The production of computers uses a lot of energy from fossil fuels.
   D. Computers use electricity while they are turned on, even if they are on stand-by.

Use the following information to answer the next question.

Electric cars are becoming more common because people believe that they are better for the environment than regular gasoline-powered vehicles.

2. The **most likely** environmental cost of using electric cars is that they
   A. use traditional sources of electricity, such as nuclear and coal-burning plants
   B. do not produce as much carbon dioxide emissions as gasoline-burning cars
   C. require fewer parts because of their smaller sizes
   D. are more efficient than gasoline-burning cars

7LS1.2 analyse the costs and benefits of selected strategies for protecting the environment

Analyzing Strategies for Protecting the Environment

Although most people would agree that protecting the environment is a good thing, the costs and benefits of an environmental strategy should be analyzed before the strategy is used.

Many people, for example, use recycling as a strategy to protect the environment. Recycling materials has an obvious environmental benefit because it reduces the amount of natural resources that need to be taken from the environment. But recycling can also take the focus away from other strategies, such as reducing and reusing materials. This is a cost of recycling, because reducing and reusing are even better for the environment than recycling. Recycling facilities require electricity and energy, while reusing materials and reducing the amount of materials used do not.

Use the following information to answer the next question.

Recycling is one common strategy for protecting the environment.

3. Which of the following statements describes one environmental drawback to recycling?

A. It takes a lot of extra effort to recycle material instead of discarding it as garbage.

B. Not all materials can be recycled, so a lot of material still ends up in the landfill.

C. It takes the emphasis away from other strategies, such as reducing and reusing.

D. It creates extra strain on the environment because it requires special facilities.

4. An effect that recycling has on the environment is that it

A. increases pollution

B. saves valuable raw materials

C. puts more waste into landfills

D. uses more natural resources than using landfills

7LS2.2 design and construct a model ecosystem, and use it to investigate interactions between the biotic and abiotic components in an ecosystem

7LS3.1 demonstrate an understanding of an ecosystem as a system of interactions between living organisms and their environment

7LS3.2 identify biotic and abiotic elements in an ecosystem, and describe the interactions between them

Ecosystems: Interactions in the Environment

All living things need certain things to survive, such as energy, water, air, and shelter. **Organisms** live in ecosystems that help them meet these needs. All the living and non-living things in an area and the interactions between them make up an **ecosystem**. An ecosystem can be very small, such as the inside of your mouth, or very large, such as Earth. For example, the pond shown below is an ecosystem.

A pond ecosystem

The grasses, insects, fish, and frog are a few of the organsims in the pond ecosystem. The living parts of an ecosystem are called **biotic**, after the Greek word "bios," which means life.

The air, water, rocks, sunlight, and open space are some of the non-living, or **abiotic**, parts of the pond ecosystem.

One biotic part of an ecosystem interacts with the other biotic parts and the abiotic parts of the ecosystem to meet their needs. For example, a frog in the pond ecosystem will eat insects for energy, use water to keep its skin moist, breathe the air, and use the plants and rocks as shelter. These are just a few of the interactions that occur in a pond ecosystem; there are many other interactions taking place at the same time.

Model Ecosystems

Scientists use model ecosystems to study the interactions between the living and non-living parts of an ecosystem. A model ecosystem helps the study of these interactions because the changes made to the model will only affect the living things in that ecosystem. For example, if John wants to investigate the relationship between the growth of a tomato plant and the amount of water given to the plant, he could set up a greenhouse. The greenhouse serves as a model ecosystem because it has both living and non-living parts that interact. John could alter either or both of these parts to study how these changes affect the rest of the ecosystem. Other examples of model ecosystems include composters, aquariums, and terrariums.

Use the following information to answer the next question.

Kathleen wants to set up a model ecosystem inside an empty two-litre pop bottle. She finds instructions on the Internet and follows them exactly.
She cleans the bottle, making sure not to leave soap residue behind, and then she adds some dirt and pond water, including a tadpole. She puts the lid on the bottle and puts it on her windowsill. Her tadpole does not survive.

5. Kathleen's tadpole **most likely** did not survive because Kathleen

A. did not add decomposers, so no nutrients could be recycled

B. put the lid on the bottle, preventing the carbon dioxide-oxygen cycle

C. did not add secondary consumers, so the tadpole did not learn survival instincts

D. left the bottle on the windowsill, and heat from the sun caused the water to evaporate

Use the following information to answer the next question.

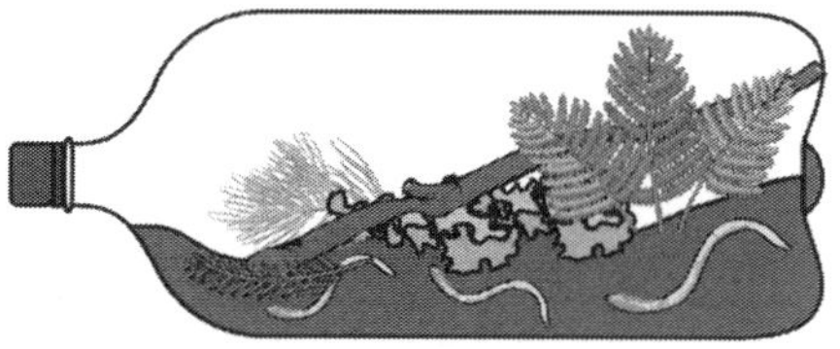

This is a terrarium. A terrarium is an example of an ecosystem.

Open Response

6. Identify two community members of this terrarium ecosystem, and describe the role of each.

____

____

Use the following information to answer the next question.

The pitcher plant is the provincial flower of Newfoundland. When filled with water, the pitcher-shaped leaves of this plant trap small insects. The plant digests these insects to obtain nitrogen. Several other organisms live in the plant, such as microorganisms, and they consume the bodies of the insects. In turn, mosquito larvae consume these microorganisms.

7. The pitcher plant and the organisms that live in the pitcher plant comprise a small ecosystem because
   A. only the living organisms in an area and their interactions are included
   B. materials but not energy are transferred between living organisms and their environment
   C. all the living organisms in an area and the abiotic factors with which those organisms interact are included
   D. it is regulated by the external environment and involves transfer of both energy and matter between biotic and abiotic factors

Use the following information to answer the next question.

When Sanchez stopped to look at a rotting log that lay across his path, he made four observations.

I. Droplets of water had formed in the cracks of the log.
II. Ants were transporting leaves into their log burrows.
III. Clumps of soil covered the bottom of the log.
IV. Mold had grown on the end of the log.

8. Sanchez knew that two biotic factors in this ecosystem are shown by observations
   A. I and II **B.** I and III
   C. II and III **D.** II and IV

Use the following information to answer the next question.

Abiotic and biotic factors within an ecosystem affect one another. Both biotic and abiotic factors can dictate what a landscape looks like and its features.

9. Some biotic components in a grassland ecosystem are
   A. water, soil, and air
   B. trees, mice, and soil
   C. soil, trees, and water
   D. hawks, grass, and earthworms

Use the following information to answer the next question.

No organism is totally independent of its environment. Both biotic factors and abiotic factors influence every organism in an environment.

10. Which of the following environmental factors is biotic?
   A. Vegetation **B.** Minerals
   C. Climate **D.** Soil

11. Which of the following interactions occurs between an abiotic and a biotic component of a forest ecosystem?
 A. Rain falls on a shrub
 B. A bear catches a salmon
 C. A stream washes away some soil
 D. A woodpecker bores a hole in a tree

7LS2.3 use scientific inquiry/research skills to investigate occurrences that affect the balance within a local ecosystem

Investigating Environmental Events

Good research skills make it easier to learn how an environmental event affects the balance of an ecosystem. You can learn about environmental events from different types of media, such as newspapers, television, radio, and Internet news pages. The Internet has a lot of information, but it is important to check the accuracy of the information you find. Anyone can publish a website, claiming their facts to be true. Start your research with government websites and well-known environmental organizations. The library is another good place to do some research.

Use the following information to answer the next question.

Simon, an environmentalist, wants the government to let a forest fire burn. Lightning started the forest fire in a patch of boreal forest in northern Ontario.

12. Which of the following arguments would Simon **least likely** use to support his case?
 A. Fires are a natural part of the forest ecosystem.
 B. Fires kill old and weak trees, keeping the forest's trees at different ages.
 C. Fires will kill any invasive species living in the forest, making survival easier for native species.
 D. Fires help some trees release their seeds and germinate, and they create space for new plants to grow.

Use the following information to answer the next question.

Zebra mussels were introduced to the Great Lakes in the late 1900s. They have spread rapidly throughout the lakes. Zebra mussels feed extensively on plankton and filter water at a considerable rate. Thus, they play an important role in making water clear. Zebra mussels from a river enter into a lake by water currents.
The lake contains a large population of bottom feeding fish, large fish, small fish, zooplankton, and plants.

13. Which of the following living things will **most likely** benefit from the spread of zebra mussels?
 A. Zooplankton **B.** Water plants
 C. Small fish **D.** Large fish

7LS3.3 describe the roles and interactions of producers, consumers, and decomposers within an ecosystem

The Members of an Ecosystem: Producers, Consumers, and Decomposers

Many different organisms live in an ecosystem. These organisms can be divided into three categories based on the role they play in the ecosystem: producers, consumers, and decomposers.

Producers

A **producer** is an organism that makes its own food. Most producers, including plants and algae, make their food using energy from the sun. Producers use this energy to turn carbon dioxide and water into oxygen and food. Producers make their food in the form of sugar. If they do not use up all their food, the sugar is stored for later use.

Consumers

A **consumer** is a living thing that cannot make its own food. A consumer needs to eat, or consume, other organisms in order to gain the energy it needs to survive. All animals are consumers. By eating producers, such as plants, consumers gain the energy stored within the producer's body. They can also gain energy by eating other consumers. A consumer stores any energy that it does not use for living within its body.

There are three types of consumers, based on what they eat:

- Herbivores eat only plants. Some herbivores include elephants, cows, and caterpillars.
- Carnivores, sometimes called meat-eaters, eat only other animals. Carnivores include tigers, sharks, and seals.
- Omnivores eat both plants and animals. Examples of omnivores are bears, raccoons, and humans.

A **scavenger** is a special consumer. Scavengers do not usually kill or gather their own food. Instead, scavengers feed on the leftover parts of another consumer's meals. Vultures and coyotes are examples of scavengers.

Decomposers

A **decomposer** is an organism that breaks down, or decomposes, dead plant and animal material. They decompose both producers and consumers. When decomposers break down dead material and wastes, they return important nutrients and chemicals to the soil to be used again. There is a limited amount of these nutrients and chemicals, so they must be recycled. Some examples of decomposers include earthworms, bacteria, and fungi. Some decomposers are so small that you need a microscope to see them.

Use the following information to answer the next question.

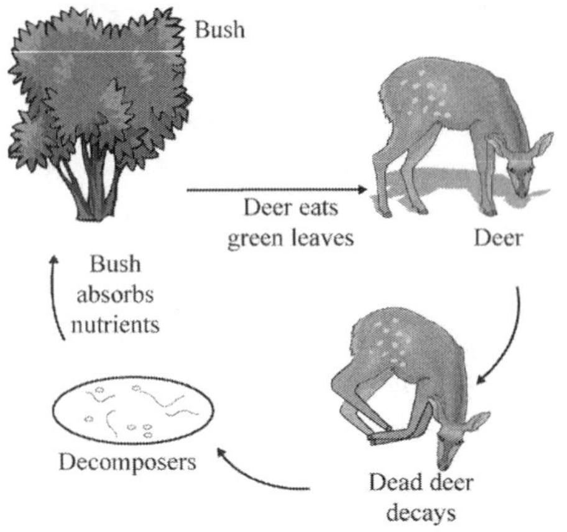

The Carbon Cycle

14. Decomposers help the carbon cycle by

A. releasing the carbon in the dead plant and animal bodies

B. taking in carbon from the animals that they decay and passing it along to their offspring

C. taking in the carbon dioxide that animals breathe out and using it to make food for themselves

D. mixing the carbon in their bodies with the oxygen given off by plants to make carbon dioxide, which goes into the air

Use the following information to answer the next question.

Consumers can be primary, secondary, or tertiary. Primary consumers are first level consumers. They obtain energy from producers.

15. Which of the following groups of animals is a primary consumer?

A. Predators **B.** Carnivores

C. Herbivores **D.** Scavengers

16. In a typical interaction between a consumer and a decomposer, the decomposer

A. kills and eats the consumer

B. produces its own food, which the consumer eats

C. recycles the remains of the consumer when the consumer dies

D. gets its energy from the consumer, which produces its own food

Use the following information to answer the next question.

A black bear in northern Ontario was studied to determine its feeding habits. The results are shown in the following graph.

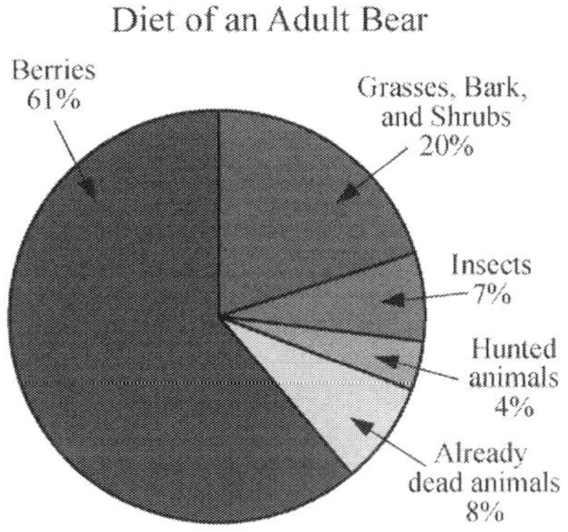

17. Which of the following pairs of terms **best** describes this bear's role in the ecosystem?

A. Producer, herbivore

B. Producer, omnivore

C. Consumer, carnivore

D. Consumer, omnivore

7LS3.4 describe the transfer of energy in a food chain and explain the effects of the elimination of any part of the chain

Energy Transfer in Food Chains

A producer captures energy from the sun and stores the energy in its body. This energy stays in the producer until a consumer eats the producer. The producer's energy then transfers to the consumer. This transfer of energy can be shown by a special flow chart called a **food chain**. The arrows in a food chain point from the organism storing the energy to the organism that consumes it.

The following food chain represents a series of relationships in Ontario's boreal forest:

The grass in the food chain is the producer. The grasshopper is the **primary consumer**, which feeds directly on the producer. The toad is the **secondary consumer**, and it eats the primary consumer. The snake is the **tertiary consumer**, which eats the secondary consumer.

Disrupting the foodchain

All of the organisms in a food chain are linked, so the elimination of any part of the chain affects the rest of the organisms in that chain. For example, when a farmer applies a pesticide to kill all of the grasshoppers in an area, the pesticide affects the rest of the food chain as well. In the absence of grasshoppers, the amount of grass increases. Without the grasshoppers as a food source, the number of toads and snakes decreases.

Use the following information to answer the next question.

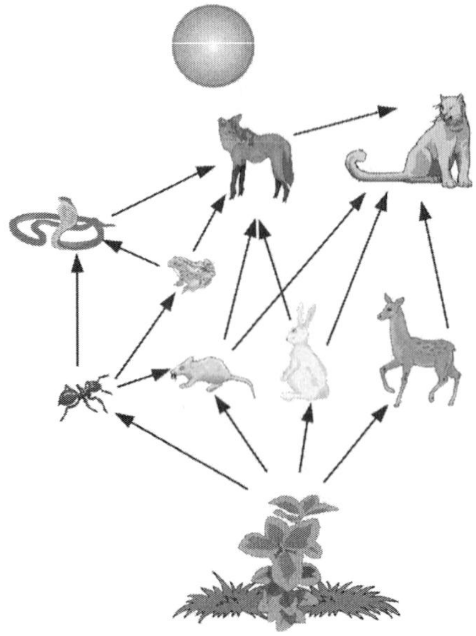

Food Web

18. Overgrazing by the deer population will lead to

A. a decrease in the rabbit population

B. an increase in the insect population

C. a decrease in the cougar population

D. an increase in the mouse population

Use the following information to answer the next question.

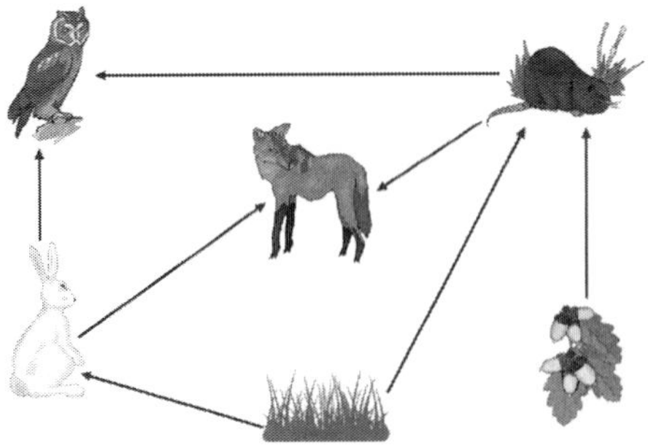

A forest food web

19. What affect will the introduction of a deer population have on the given forest?

A. The rat population will go up.

B. The owl population will go up.

C. The fox population will go down.

D. The rabbit population will go down.

Use the following information to answer the next question.

Bindu, a biologist, made the following observations while hiking through a park.

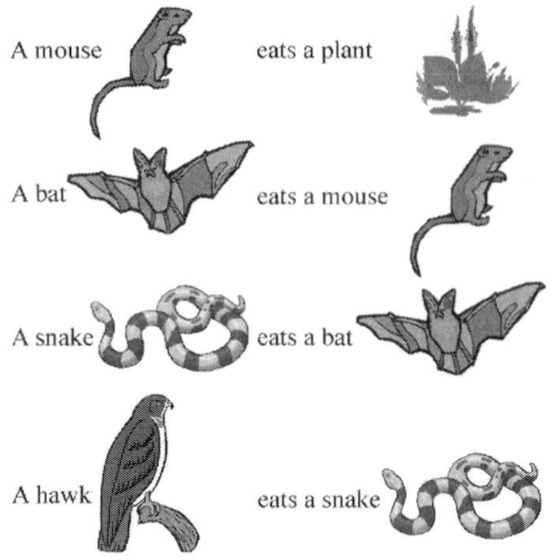

20. Which of the following situations would **most likely** occur if all the bats were removed from this park?

A. The plant population would fall, and the snake population would rise.

B. The plant population would rise, and the mouse population would fall.

C. The mouse population would rise, and the snake population would fall.

D. The hawk population would rise, and the mouse population would rise.

7LS3.5 describe how matter is cycled within the environment and explain how it promotes sustainability

Matter Cycles Within the Environment

There is a limited amount of matter on Earth. Some types of matter, such as carbon, nitrogen, and water, are recycled within the environment by natural processes. These natural cycles, without human interference, contribute to environmental **sustainability**.

THE CARBON CYCLE

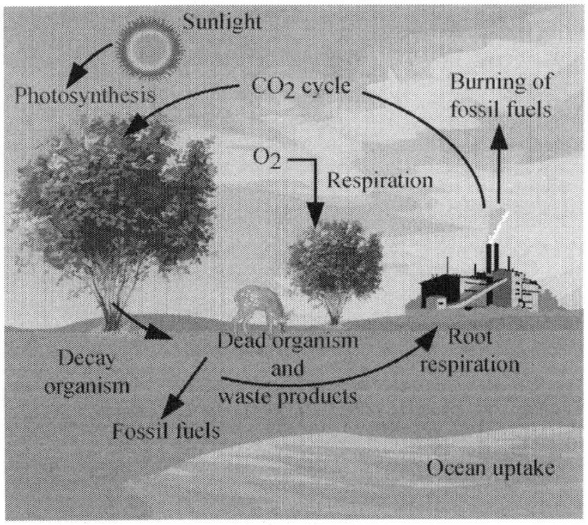

Carbon is the base of all life on Earth because all living tissues are formed from carbon. Carbon cycles through the environment through the processes of **photosynthesis** and **respiration**. Producers take carbon dioxide out of the atmosphere when they create their own food through photosynthesis. The carbon turns into sugar, which becomes part of the plant tissues.

Some of the sugar produced in photosynthesis is used by the plant in a process called respiration. In respiration, cells use oxygen to release the energy stored in the sugars. Using sugars produces carbon dioxide, which is released back into the environment. Respiration occurs in all the living cells of the plants, including the roots and leaves.

When a consumer, such as the deer in the diagram, eats a producer, the sugar stored in the producer's body is passed on to the consumer. In order to use the sugars from the producer's tissues, the consumer's cells respire and produce carbon dioxide. When the consumer exhales, it releases carbon dioxide into the atmosphere. When producers and consumers die, decomposers break down their remains. The decomposers release the carbon from these remains into the atmosphere for use again.

Some ancient plant and animal remains were trapped under layers of rocks before they were decomposed. Over millions of years, these remains changed into fossil fuels, such as coal, oil, and gas. Fossil fuels are carbon-based, and when factories or vehicles burn these fuels, they release carbon dioxide into the atmosphere. The oceans absorb some of the carbon dioxide from the atmosphere, and some of the carbon dioxide is absorbed by plants, which begins the cycle again.

THE NITROGEN CYCLE

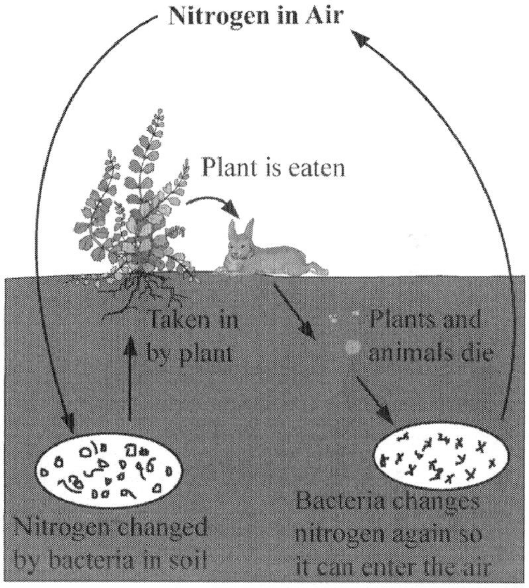

Nitrogen is important in the formation of plant and animal tissues. However, plants do not take in nitrogen from the air. Instead, plants take in nitrogen through their roots.
Special bacteria in the soil take nitrogen out of the air and turn it into a form that plants can use. Plants use the nitrogen to form plant tissue, which consumers take in when they eat plants.

Consumers then use the nitrogen to form their own tissues. When the consumers die, decomposing bacteria release the nitrogen into the air, beginning the cycle again.

The Water Cycle

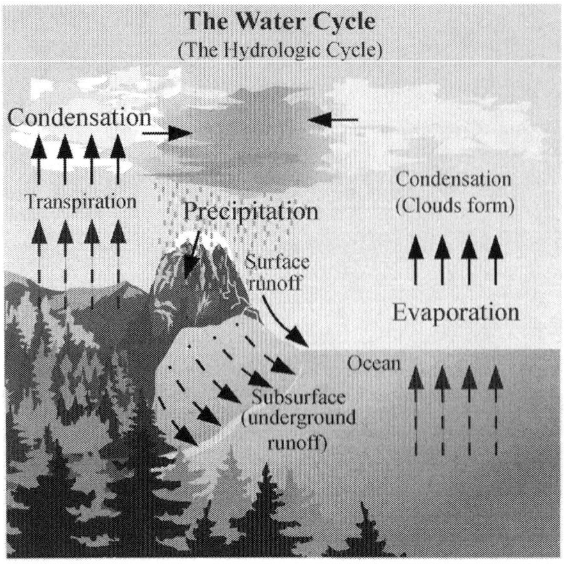

Water, which is essential to all forms of life, continuously cycles through the environment. Water exists in the atmosphere. When there is enough water in the atmosphere, the atmosphere releases the water, which falls to the ground and the bodies of water. This process is called **precipitation**.

The water on the ground moves along the surface as runoff, and some of the water seeps into the ground. In the ground, the water flows toward lower bodies of water as subsurface runoff.

Plants absorb the underground water. They also release water back into the atmosphere through **transpiration**. Similarly, animals take in water by drinking it, and they release it into the atmosphere when they respire and sweat.

The water released by plants and animals joins the water that evaporates from the ground and water bodies. This water collects as clouds in the atmosphere as **condensation**, preparing to begin the cycle again. It can take one water molecule anywhere from a couple of days to millions of years to complete a full cycle.

Natural Interactions

These matter cycles do not operate separately from each other. Often, one interaction can involve several of these cycles at one time.

A grizzly bear eats salmon.

For example, when a grizzly bear catches a salmon to eat, it will take in water, carbon, and nitrogen from the salmon. While the bear eats the salmon, it will respire and perspire, releasing both carbon and water into the atmosphere. Any pieces of the salmon that might drop to the forest floor will be decomposed by a variety of bacteria, which release carbon, nitrogen, and other nutrients into the soil.

Research has shown that the grizzly-salmon interaction is very important to some forest ecosystems because of the role it plays in the cycling of matter. There are many, many other examples of natural interactions that aid in the cycling of matter, promoting sustainability.

Use the following information to answer the next question.

The nitrogen cycle involves both biotic and abiotic factors of the ecosystem.

21. Which of the following factors of an ecosystem does **not** participate in the nitrogen cycle?

A. Plants **B.** Animals

C. Minerals **D.** Atmosphere

Use the following information to answer the next question.

Cellular respiration is the process by which cells release energy by turning oxygen and glucose into carbon dioxide and water.

22. The process of respiration is an important part of the

A. water cycle **B.** carbon cycle

C. element cycle **D.** nitrogen cycle

7LS3.6 distinguish between primary succession and secondary succession within an ecosystem

Succession

Ecosystems change naturally over time. Biotic communities are slowly and predictably replaced with new biotic communities until the ecosystem reaches a final stable community, called a **climax community**. These natural changes occur so slowly that it might seem like they are not changing at all. This process of gradual and orderly replacement of communities is known as succession.

Primary Succession

A pioneer community grows on a lava field

Primary succession refers to the changes that take place when plants grow in a new environment for the very first time. This might happen on newly exposed surfaces, such as when a landslide exposes a side of a valley, or on newly deposited surfaces, such as the side of a volcano after an eruption. The first group of plant species to settle on the surface is called the **pioneer community**.

After a pioneer community has populated a new environment, the species in the community change and new species replace some of the older species. These changes can usually be predicted, and they happen in a number of stages. Eventually, a community temporarily stops changing and this is the climax community.

Secondary Succession

Secondary succession refers to the natural changes that occur in an environment that has already been populated by a pioneer community. Secondary succession usually begins as a result of a natural disturbance, such as fire, flood, or disease. The natural disturbance can occur at any stage during a primary succession in a community. It starts secondary succession by reducing the number of species in the community, making the space needed to establish new species.

A forest-fire damaged area

Fireweed shows secondary succession

Often started by lightning, forest fires are common natural disturbances in forest ecosystems. The picture on the top shows a forest shortly after a fire. The fire initiates secondary succession, and plant species like fireweed, shown in the bottom photo, begin to fill the spaces that were created by the fire.

Use the following information to answer the next question.

In the process of succession, one community grows to replace another community within an ecosystem until a stable community is established.

23. What name is given to this stable living community?

A. Climax community

B. Primary community

C. Pioneer community

D. Secondary community

Use the following information to answer the next question.

A forest fire burned down all the plants and animals in a region. After the first rains, life in the region was re-established. This phenomenon is known as secondary succession.

24. Which of the following organisms is **most likely** to reappear first during secondary succession?

A. Small plants **B.** Large trees

C. Animals **D.** Grasses

Use the following information to answer the next question.

Pioneer plants are the first inhabitants of a barren or sterile region. Pioneer plants are followed by the development of other plants, finally forming a habitat. This process is known as primary succession.

25. The primary function of the pioneer plants is to

A. form humus

B. form new soil

C. multiply vegetatively

D. add nutrients to the soil

7LS3.7 explain why an ecosystem is limited in the number of living things that it can support

Limits in an Ecosystem

Organisms can survive in an ecosystem only when their needs for food, water, air, and kind and amount of space for living are met. However, in any ecosystem, there are only certain amounts of each of these resources. Recall that there is a limited amount of matter on Earth and that matter continuously cycles through an ecosystem. Because the resources in an ecosystem are limited, they can only support a certain number of plants and animals, including humans.

A red-tailed hawk

For example, a meadow may have enough food and water to support many red-tailed hawks, but hawks require a large area for flying and hunting and they require large, old trees for shelter. In this case, the meadow's size limits the number of hawks it can support.

Use the following information to answer the next question.

Kareem starts an ant farm in January. He begins with 20 ants in his ant farm. Kareem cares for his ants in exactly the same way every week. At the end of each month, he counts the number of ants in his farm. He graphs his data in the chart below.

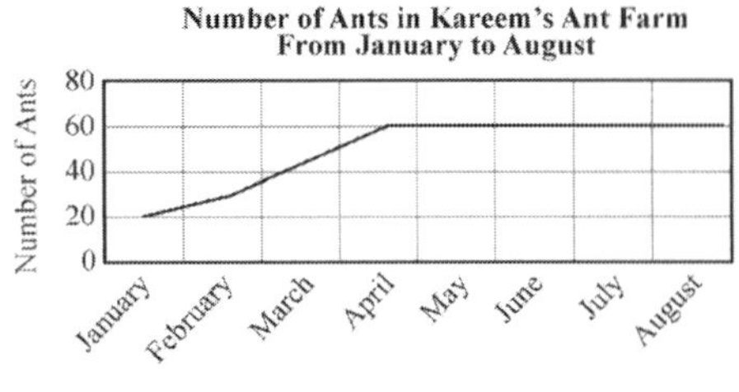

26. The number of ants in Kareem's ant farm **most likely** stopped increasing after April because

A. the ants ran out of oxygen to breathe

B. there was not enough food for more than 60 ants

C. the ants were escaping because the farm was too crowded

D. the temperature of the farm was too hot because there were too many ants

Use the following information to answer the next question.

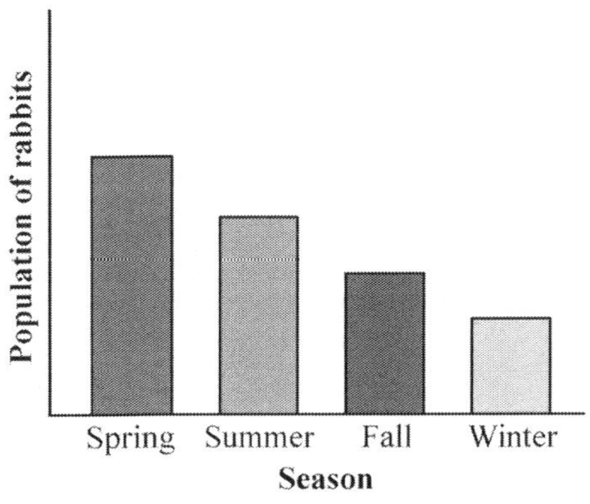

Seasonal rabbit populations

27. Which limiting factor **most likely** affects the rabbit population during the winter?

A. Food **B.** Space

C. Oxygen **D.** Sunlight

7LS3.8 describe ways in which human activities and technologies alter balances and interactions in the environment

Human Impact on the Environment

Humans are part of most ecosystems. Just like other organisms, humans can exist in an ecosystem when it meets their needs for food, water, air, and space. Unlike other organisms, humans have the ability to alter an ecosystem in order to meet their needs and wants.

Recall that ecosystems are complex, with many natural interactions, balances, and cycles that sustain the ecosystem. When humans alter the ecosystem, they directly or indirectly alter these natural processes, which often has negative impacts on the ecosystem. Humans have begun to realize their impact on ecosystems, and many are trying to reduce their impacts and undo some of the negative impacts of the past.

Positive Impacts

Many different projects have been started to protect the environment from negative human impacts. Parks have been set up to protect plants and animals. Species that are at risk of becoming extinct are studied and attempts are made to alter the natural balance in their favour.

Controlling the caribou-wolf interaction should protect the caribou population.

Some caribou populations in Yukon, for example, are decreasing for a variety of reasons. Wolves are one of the major predators of caribou, and they often benefit directly from human activities in their territory. Human activities, such as logging and road construction, make it easier for wolves to hunt caribou. The government hopes to increase the number of caribou by altering the natural food chain in their ecosystem through planned wolf-killings, which should control the size of the wolf population. Careful planning and research goes into making sure that the wolf population remains healthy and ensuring that the role of the wolf continues in the natural food chain.

Negative Impacts

Some human practices have several negative impacts on the environment, such as clear-cutting trees in a forest.

Removing the trees from a forest stops the trees from carrying out photosynthesis. This alters the carbon cycle, decreasing the amount of carbon dioxide taken from the atmosphere and the amount of oxygen returned to the atmosphere.

Trees are also important for the water cycle. Their leaves and needles transpire, returning water into the atmosphere. Their root systems keep water in the soil and decrease surface runoff. The removal of all the trees in an area greatly impacts the water cycle.

After a forest is clear-cut, the species present change. Grasses and shrubs begin to grow in the clear-cut area. Sometimes, forestry companies use herbicides to control these grasses and shrubs, and they replant the trees they have taken. Despite their efforts, they can never restore the original ecosystem and its species balance. Many of the animals in the forest have to find new homes and food sources.

A clear-cut forest

Some negative human impacts on the environment were accidental or unforeseen. For example, the introduction of non-native species to an ecosystem can have a devastating impact. Purple loosestrife, a hearty weed plant, was brought to Canada from Europe in the 1800s. Since this time, it has damaged many of Ontario's wetland ecosystems.

When purple loosestrife begins to grow near a wetland, it soon takes over and replaces the native plants. This reduces the available food, shelter, and nesting sites for the hundreds of species of amphibians, reptiles, insects, fish, and mammals that depend on healthy wetland ecosystems for survival.

Purple loosestrife

Use the following information to answer the next question.

> Ashley, a developer, wants to build a housing development on two sides of a marshland. She wants to connect the developments on both sides of the marshland so that the residents can cross from one side to the other by vehicle. Ashley develops some options for discussion.

28. Which of the following options would cause the **least** amount of impact on the marshland ecosystem?

A. Drain the marshlands and install a paved road.

B. Build an elevated bridge that allows the water to flow underneath.

C. Build a road through the marshlands from one side from the other.

D. Lay down logs through the middle and only allow vehicles with four-wheel drive to cross.

29. A copper smelting factory, located several hundred metres from the seashore, causes a reduction in the population of marine turtles. The turtles are **most likely** affected by

A. air pollution

B. soil pollution

C. water pollution

D. noise pollution

7LS3.9 describe Aboriginal perspectives on sustainability and describe ways in which they can be used in habitat and wildlife management

Traditional Knowledge and Managing the Environment

The First Nations and Aboriginal populations of Canada have lived within Canada's ecosystems for centuries. Over this time, they have observed the changing seasons and natural cycles of the ecosystems, and they have set good examples of environmental stewardship in their interactions within these systems. Decisions about how to use the land to meet their needs were made to ensure a good quality of life for the next seven generations—these decisions were made with sustainability in mind.

Some Canadians now recognize the stewardship and value of this traditional knowledge for making wildlife and habitat management decisions. A partnership between the Anishinabek Nation and the Ontario Ministry of Natural Resources recognizes the value of this traditional knowledge. This relationship will try to bring more cooperation and collaboration between the two groups in the management of Ontario's many natural resources.

30. The Aboriginal method of managing the environment so that the ecosystem will provide a good quality of life for the next seven generations is based on the concept of environmental

A. sustainability **B.** degradation

C. protection **D.** activism

7LS2.4 use appropriate science and technology vocabulary, including sustainability, biotic, ecosystem, community, population, and producer, in oral and written communication

Communicating in Science

It might seem that science has its own language. In a way, it does. When you speak and write about science, you need to use the proper terminology. The important terms for this unit are on the following list. It is important that you understand these terms and that you can use them properly. If you need help understanding these terms, refer to the other lessons in this unit or use the glossary in the back of this *Key*.

Important Terms in Life Systems

- biotic
- abiotic
- producer
- consumer
- population
- ecosystem
- community
- decomposer
- sustainability

31. Which of the following tables identifies an example of a species, a population, and a community?

A.

Species	Population	Community
beavers	school of fish	pond

B.

Species	Population	Community
school of fish	pond	beavers

C.

Species	Population	Community
beavers	pond	school of fish

D.

Species	Population	Community
school of fish	beavers	pond

Use the following information to answer the next question.

Erica studies a ____*i*____ of frogs in a field near her university. The use of pesticides in the area affects the frogs, snakes, and other ____*ii*____ components of the ecosystem. The overuse of pesticides concerns Erica because she believes that it is decreasing the ____*iii*____ of the ecosystem.

32. Which of the following tables contains the terms that **best** complete the given sentences?

A.

i	*ii*	*iii*
community	biotic	viability

B.

i	*ii*	*iii*
population	abiotic	viability

C.

i	*ii*	*iii*
community	abiotic	sustainability

D.

i	*ii*	*iii*
population	biotic	sustainability

ANSWERS AND SOLUTIONS

LIFE SYSTEMS: INTERACTIONS IN THE ENVIRONMENT

1. B	8. D	15. C	22. B	29. C
2. A	9. D	16. C	23. A	30. A
3. C	10. A	17. D	24. D	31. A
4. B	11. A	18. A	25. B	32. D
5. B	12. C	19. D	26. B	
6. OR	13. B	20. C	27. A	
7. C	14. A	21. C	28. B	

1. B

While computer use can cause repetitive strain injuries, this is not an environmental consequence. The correct answer is B.

2. A

An environmental cost of electric cars is the pollution created during the generation of the electricity used to power the cars. The lower emissions, higher efficiency, and smaller size are all environmental benefits of electric cars.

3. C

Recycling does take away some emphasis from other environmental strategies, such as reducing and reusing, that could further help to conserve natural resources. The correct answer is C.

Although it does take extra effort to recycle instead of discarding the materials, that is not an environmental drawback. As well, even though only some materials can be recycled, it is still beneficial to the environment. The environmental benefit of recycling outweighs the strain created by recycling facilities.

4. B

Recycling helps the environment by saving valuable raw materials.

5. B

All ecosystems require oxygen. By putting the lid on the bottle, Kathleen prevented oxygen from entering the system. This is the most likely reason the tadpole did not survive. The correct answer is B.

Not adding decomposers to the system should not kill the tadpole because the decomposers would only be required once the tadpole died. Although the heat may cause the water to evaporate, the lid was on, so the water would condense on the side of the bottle. A secondary consumer would not have increased the tadpole's survival chances because it would have eaten the tadpole.

6. OR

Answers should include:

- Plants—remove carbon dioxide in the bottle, and produce oxygen, **OR** provide food for animals.
- Worms—eat the dead and rotted plants, **OR** help to return chemicals to the soil for plants to use.

7. C

The pitcher plant is an example of an aquatic ecosystem. An ecosystem includes all of the biotic factors (living organisms) in an area and the abiotic factors (non-living parts) with which the biotic factors interact. The correct answer is C.

The interaction between biotic and abiotic factors involves an exchange of both materials (e.g., nitrogen) and energy (e.g., the mosquito larvae consume the microorganisms to obtain energy to grow).

The pattern and rate of exchange of matter and energy, however, is self-regulated by the ecosystem. This means that it is not regulated by an external environment. For example, the number of microorganisms living in one pitcher plant depends on the number and frequency of insects trapped in the pitcher-shaped leaves. The population of microorganisms similarly affects the survival and growth of mosquito larvae. The volume and nutrient content of the trapped water are the abiotic factors in this ecosystem. If the interaction of biotic and abiotic factors in an area is sufficient to support survival of the organisms, then the factors together comprise an ecosystem.

8. D

Biotic components of an ecosystem are living, and abiotic components are non-living. Observations II and IV deal with living components, and I and III deal with non-living components. The correct answer is D.

9. D

The term biotic refers to the living components of an ecosystem. Therefore, hawks, grass and earthworms are all biotic, so the correct answer is D.

Soil, air, and water are all non-living, or abiotic, components of an ecosystem.

10. A

A biotic component of the environment is a living thing. The only living thing listed is vegetation. The correct answer is A.

Minerals, the climate, and soil are all abiotic factors.

11. A

The biotic components of an ecosystem are living, and the abiotic components are non-living.
The example of the rain (abiotic) falling on a shrub (biotic) is the only example of an interaction between abiotic and biotic components. The correct answer is A.

12. C

Although a forest fire might kill any invasive species, it would probably not kill all of them. A forest fire would also kill a number of native species in the forest. The correct answer is C.

An environmentalist would support letting the fires burn because natural forest fires do have value. These fires are part of the ecosystem because they help keep the trees at different ages, clear off old and weak trees, and create space for new plants. As well, some plants release their seeds as a result of forest fires.

13. B

When the water becomes clearer, light will easily penetrate the water. Thus, water plants will grow more rapidly. They will benefit from the entry of zebra mussels into the lake. The correct answer is B.

Zooplankton feed on plankton, which will be consumed by zebra mussels, so their population might decrease. The small fish population might decrease because they also feed on plankton, which will be eaten by zebra mussels. Large fish feed on small fish. Since the population of small fish might decrease, the population of large fish might also decrease. As a result, the zooplankton, small fish, and large fish will not benefit from the presence of the zebra mussels.

14. A

Decomposers release the carbon in dead plants and animals as they decay. This carbon goes into the air, water, and soil. The correct answer is A.

15. C

Herbivores are primary consumers because they obtain their energy from producers. The correct answer is C.

Carnivores, predators, and scavengers are not primary consumers; they are secondary and tertiary consumers.

16. C

Decomposers break down dead and decaying matter, recycling the nutrients and organics. The correct answer is C.

Neither consumers nor decomposers are able to produce their own food. Decomposers do not kill organisms.

17. D

A producer makes its own food using the sun's energy. Bears are not producers. A carnivore feeds only on meat, and this bear ate berries and other plant material. Therefore, the bear is a consumer and an omnivore. The correct answer is D.

18. A

The food web is a combination of different food chains. Therefore, different consumers in the food web will consume the same food item. As a result, a change in one consumer may indirectly affect the other consumers at its level.

In this food web, both the rabbit and deer populations feed on plants. Therefore, overgrazing by the deer population will reduce the plant population, and as a consequence, the rabbit population will also decrease. The correct answer is A.

Because the insects and mice also depend on plants for food, there will be a decrease in their populations as well. The cougars do not depend on plants for food, so the overgrazing by the deer population will not affect the cougar population.

19. D

A food web is a combination of different food chains. Therefore, different consumers in the food web may consume the same food item. As a result, a change in one consumer might indirectly affect the other consumers at its level.

Both deer and rabbits eat plants. Introducing deer to this food web will decrease the available food for the rabbits. Since there will be less food available to support them, the rabbit population will go down. The correct answer is D.

20. C

In the given food chain, the bats eat the mice. If the bats were removed, the mice would not be eaten. This means that there would be more mice. Since the snakes eat the bats, if the bats were removed, there would be less food for the snakes. As a result, the snake population would decrease. Therefore, if the bats were removed from this park, the mouse population would rise and the snake population would fall. The correct answer is C.

Since the bat is not directly linked to the plant or hawk populations in the given food chain, the removal of the bat would not have a direct impact on their populations.

21. C

Minerals do not contain major nitrogen deposits. They are not a large player in the nitrogen cycle. The correct answer is C.

22. B

When organisms breathe in air, they respire carbon dioxide. As a result, respiration is an important part of the carbon cycle. The correct answer is B.

23. A

The final community in a succession of communities is called the climax community. The correct answer is A.

24. D

In secondary succession, the first organisms to appear are simple plants, such as grass. The correct answer is D.

After simple plants populate the ecosystem, the soil will begin to gain nutrients. Once the soil has enough nutrients, even small plants will begin to appear. Then, as the soil gains more nutrients, large trees will begin to appear. Animals will not appear until after the ecosystem has enough vegetation to support itself.

25. B

Pioneer plants have the capacity to occupy an otherwise sterile or barren area. Through their activities, the plants help in the formation of soil, leading to favourable changes in the environment, and eventually, the development of newer and varied life forms. The correct answer is B.

26. B

The most likely reason the ant farm is limited in the number of the ants it can support is because there is not enough food for more than 60 ants.
Kareem should increase the amount of food he puts in the farm if he wants the number of ants to increase. The correct answer is B.

If there was enough oxygen to support 60 ants in April, oxygen is not the limiting factor. If the ants were able to escape, it is likely that all of the ants would escape. Since there were still 60 ants in the farm, it is unlikely that any were escaping.
The temperature of an ant farm would not change significantly because of the number of ants in the farm.

27. A

Rabbits are herbivores, which means that they eat plants. Since very few plants survive during the winter, rabbit's food availability decreases during the winter season. Therefore, food is a limiting factor during the winter for the rabbit population. The correct answer is A.

The change of seasons does not affect the space or oxygen available. Also, rabbits do not need sunlight to survive.

28. B

Building a bridge to allow the water to flow underneath will have the least impact on the marshland environment because it will cause the least amount of disruption to the marshland. The correct answer is B.

Each of the other alternatives involves disrupting the movement of water through the wetlands, which would have significant negative impacts.

29. C

A copper smelting factory can cause air, soil, water, and noise pollution. Since these turtles are marine animals, the pollution of the water is most likely responsible for the decline in their population. The correct answer is C.

30. A

Environmental sustainability refers to the ability of the ecosystem to keep going indefinitely; this is the basis for the Aboriginal's seven-generation method of management. The correct answer is A.

Environmental degradation is the destruction of the environment, and it would not allow the ecosystem to provide for future generations. While environmental protection and activism are methods for ensuring sustainability, they are not the basis for the management decisions.

31. A

A species is a group of animals that can successfully breed and produce fertile offspring. A population is all the organisms of a single species in an area. A community is all the organisms of every species living in an area.

In this example, the beavers are the species, a school of fish is the population, and the pond is the community. The correct answer is A.

32. D

The frogs in the area would be considered a population. A community refers to all the species living in an area. The frogs and snakes are biotic components of the ecosystem; abiotic means non-living. Sustainability is the ability of an ecosystem to continue thriving and support life. Viability is the ability to grow and reproduce. Therefore, the table that best completes the given statement is

i	*ii*	*iii*
population	biotic	sustainability

The correct answer is D.

UNIT TEST — LIFE SYSTEMS: INTERACTIONS IN THE ENVIRONMENT

1. What type of pollution is prevented by the regular inspection of gaseous emissions from cars and other vehicles?

A. Water **B.** Noise

C. Land **D.** Air

Use the following information to answer the next question.

Integrated Pest Management (IPM) is a method of controlling insect pests of agriculture that uses a combination of strategies to reduce the environmental impacts of pest controls. There are six main components to pest control:

- Acceptable pest level—What is the amount or level of pests that is tolerable?
- Preventive practices—Do the crops match local growing conditions? Would crop rotation help?
- Monitoring—Monitor pest populations to avoid over-treating and to treat at the right time.
- Mechanical controls—Remove pests using strategies such as trapping or removal by hand.
- Biological controls—Use natural predators of the pest to keep pest numbers down.
- Chemical controls—Use synthetic and natural pesticide sprays.

2. Which of the following scenarios is **not** an example of IPM?

A. A farmer sprays his field with pesticides twice each year, in May and July.

B. A greenhouse gardener examines his plants individually and removes the aphids by hand.

C. A farmer alternates the crops in his fields to reduce the amount of available food for the pests.

D. A gardener sprays his plants with pesticides only when he finds at least 20 slugs in the traps that he checks each week.

Use the following information to answer the next question.

A model ecosystem can be used to study the interactions between the biotic and abiotic components of an ecosystem because many of the variables can be controlled. A model ecosystem allows experimental manipulation of these components without disrupting environmental balances.

3. Chris wants to study the interaction between decomposers and different types of decaying matter. The model ecosystem **best** suited to Chris' study is

A. a greenhouse **B.** a composter

C. an aquarium **D.** a terrarium

Use the following information to answer the next question.

Purple loosestrife is a common garden plant that was brought from Europe in the 1800s. It spread to many of the wetlands across North America, choking out many of the native plants. Since very few animals eat purple loosestrife, the wetlands are left with little or no wildlife.

4. The **best** method for an environmentalist to control this weed would be to

A. find a species of herbivore that will eat the weed and introduce it to the damaged wetlands

B. dig out each plant by hand, burn it, and send the ashes to a landfill

C. jail the people who brought it and have them remove the weeds

D. spray all wetlands with chemicals to kill the plants

Use the following information to answer the next question.

The lamprey is an eel-like fish that is a parasite in the Great Lakes. A parasite is an organism that lives in a close relationship with another organism and causes harm to it.
Until the canals joined the Great Lakes together, lampreys lived only in Lake Ontario. Now, lampreys live in all of the Great Lakes, and they damage all of the native fish species.

5. Lampreys are considered a harmful invasive species because they alter the balance of the ecosystems by

A. out-competing native fish species for limited food resources

B. out-competing native fish species for space in the lakes

C. disrupting the mating of native fish species

D. injuring and killing the native fish species

Use the following information to answer the next question.

Deer, moose, and wolves live and interact with each other in a certain area.

6. Which of the following statements **best** explains the reason these animals have a relationship with each other?

A. They are all organisms.

B. They are all part of a population.

C. They are all part of a community.

D. They are all part of an ecosystem.

7. Which of the following tables matches each role with an organism that carries out that role?

A.

Role	Organism
Producer	Moss
Consumer	Raspberry bush
Decomposer	Mushroom

B.

Role	Organism
Producer	Mushroom
Consumer	Deer
Decomposer	Moss

C.

Role	Organism
Producer	Moss
Consumer	Deer
Decomposer	Mushroom

D.

Role	Organism
Producer	Raspberry bush
Consumer	Mushroom
Decomposer	Moss

8. In a land ecosystem, the main source of energy is

A. the sun

B. a producer

C. a herbivore

D. the oxygen cycle

9. Which of the following components of an ecosystem is biotic?

A. Temperature **B.** Omnivore

C. Moisture **D.** Sunlight

Use the following information to answer the next question.

The number of organisms that can exist within an area depends on biotic and abiotic factors.

10. Which of the following factors is an example of an abiotic factor that can affect a rabbit population?

A. Availability of food

B. Availability of water

C. Number of parasites

D. Number of predators

11. In a food chain, rabbits belong to which trophic level?

A. Producers

B. Decomposers

C. Primary consumers

D. Secondary consumers

12. What would be the **most likely** result if all the decomposers were absent from Earth?

A. No one on Earth would die.

B. Earth would be filled with dead matter.

C. The number of producers on Earth would increase.

D. The number of consumers on Earth would decrease.

Use the following information to answer the next question.

13. Which of the following organisms in the given food web is a producer?

A. Bush **B.** Goat

C. Worm **D.** Human

14. If the producers are removed from a forest ecosystem, the **most likely** outcome is that

A. no change will take place

B. only the carnivores will survive

C. only the herbivores will survive

D. both herbivores and carnivores will disappear

Use the following information to answer the next question.

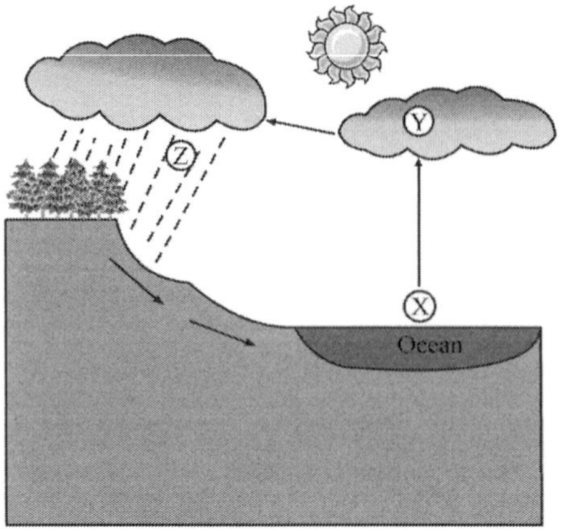

Water cycle

15. The process in the water cycle illustrated at letter *Z* is called

A. evaporation **B.** precipitation

C. transpiration **D.** condensation

Use the following information to answer the next question.

Any change that takes place in a sterile or barren area that leads to the establishment of a successful community is called primary succession. When a new community develops in an area where an earlier community has been damaged or destroyed, it is called secondary succession.

16. Which of the following situations may bring about secondary succession?

A. Forest fire

B. Lava sediments

C. Shifting sand dunes

D. Newly exposed sea floor

17. After new, barren ground is exposed, the first species to appear in the area is referred to as a

A. climax species

B. primary species

C. pioneer species

D. secondary species

18. Which of the following factors does **not** limit the number of plants that can grow in a forest?

A. Food | **B.** Water
C. Oxygen | **D.** Sunlight

19. Sometimes forestry companies burn sections of a forest on purpose. Which of the following reasons does **not** explain why these companies burn forests intentionally?

A. To get rid of stands of insect-infested trees

B. To remove dead and decaying trees before they fall down

C. To prevent larger, more dangerous fires from spreading into a new area

D. To allow trees that need extreme heat to release and germinate their seeds

ANSWERS AND SOLUTIONS — UNIT TEST

1. D	6. C	11. C	16. A
2. A	7. C	12. B	17. C
3. B	8. A	13. A	18. C
4. B	9. B	14. D	19. D
5. D	10. B	15. B	

1. D

The gases that vehicles release are toxic, which means that they are poisonous. These gases are released into the air. When they mix with the air, the air quality declines. Emission checks, carried out by environmental authorities, maintain vehicular standards and their aim is to reduce the overall amount of air pollution. The correct answer is D.

2. A

A farmer who sprays twice a year has not incorporated any of the other components required by IPM. Before spraying, the farmer should monitor and evaluate if spraying is needed. The correct answer is A.

Removing aphids by hand is an example of mechanical control. Crop rotation is a preventive practice. Trapping before spraying is a part of monitoring and determining acceptable pest levels.

3. B

Decomposers are organisms that break down dead and decaying matter. A composter would be well suited to studying decomposers. The correct answer is B.

A greenhouse, aquarium, or terrarium would be better suited for studying interactions between producers and consumers.

4. B

An environmentalist would most likely support digging out the plants by hand, burning them, and sending the remains to a landfill. Burning the plants prevents their seeds from spreading. The correct answer is B.

Environmentalists would probably not want to introduce another new species to the wetland because that would risk further disrupting the wetland's natural balance. As well, they would probably not support spraying the wetlands with chemicals because that would be damaging to the other plants and animals. Jailing the people who brought the weeds and making them remove it would be impossible because the people who introduced purple loosestrife lived more than a century ago.

5. D

Lampreys damage the native fish in the lakes. In other words, they injure and kill the native fish species, making them a dangerous species when they invade new bodies of water. The correct answer is D.

Lampreys attach themselves to obtain food from the native fish. They are not competing with the other fish for food or space. They do not usually disrupt the mating patterns of the native fish.

6. C

When several different species live in the same area, they make up a community. In this case, the deer, moose, and wolves make up a community. The correct answer is C.

7. C

Producers are organisms that make their own food, such as moss and raspberry bushes. Consumers, like deer, eat other organisms. Decomposers, like mushrooms, act on dead and decaying matter. Therefore, the table that correctly matches the roles with an organism that carries out that role is table C.

8. A

The sun is the main source of energy for land ecosystems. The correct answer is A.

Producers use the energy from the sun to provide energy to consumers, including herbivores. The oxygen cycle helps organisms use the energy from the sun.

9. B

Omnivores are living, or biotic, components of the ecosystem. They are consumers that eat both plant and animal matter. The correct answer is B.

Moisture, temperature, and sunlight are non-living, or abiotic, components of the ecosystem.

10. B

Abiotic factors are non-living influences, such as water and other components of the physical environment. The correct answer is B.

Food is predominantly organic matter, either living or formerly living. Both predators and parasites are living creatures.

11. C

The position of an organism in the food chain is known as its trophic level. Animals are consumers because they eat producers or other consumers. Animals that consume plants, such as rabbits, are known as primary consumers. The correct answer is C.

12. B

Decomposers break down dead matter and recycle the materials into the environment. If all the decomposers were absent from Earth, then the planet would be filled with dead matter. The correct answer is B.

13. A

Bushes are producers. They provide energy for consumers in food webs. Goats, worms, and humans are all consumers. The correct answer is A.

14. D

If the producers are removed from an ecosystem, the herbivores will not have a food source and will die. If the herbivores die, the carnivores will not have a food source either, and they will also die. The correct answer is D.

15. B

The process represented by the letter *Z* shows water returning from the atmosphere to Earth's surface. This process is called precipitation. The correct answer is B.

Evaporation is the conversion of water from liquid to vapour. This process is represented by letter *X*. Transpiration is the movement of water by vascular plants, which is not pictured on this diagram. Condensation is the conversion of vapour to liquid form and is represented by the letter *Y*.

16. A

Forest fires destroy already existing forest communities, but they do leave behind some organisms. If left undisturbed, these surviving organisms will form a new community that should proceed through the stages of succession. This gives rise to a new community in an area formerly occupied by another community. Because these successional changes were brought on by a disturbance, this is an example of secondary succession. The correct answer is A.

Shifting sand dunes, the appearance of new lava sediments, and new exposure of sea floor would all represent completely new surfaces. The changes on these new surfaces that lead to the development of a biotic community are examples of primary succession.

17. C

The first species to settle a previously unsettled area is called a pioneer species. The correct answer is C.

Primary and secondary species are those present in any serial stages of succession, and a climax species is a species present in the final stage of succession.

18. C

Oxygen does not limit the number of plants in an ecosystem (though it can limit the number of animals) because plants use carbon dioxide and produce oxygen.

The plants in a forest compete for food and water. Sunlight can also limit the number of plants because some plants will shade out others, limiting the number of plants that can grow in the area.

19. D

Fires are not usually set on purpose to get cones to release seeds and germinate. Often, intense heat from the sun is enough to get the cones to open. The correct answer is D.

Fire is a natural part of the forest ecosystem. Humans often use fire to alter the balance of the forest ecosystem and get rid of insect infested trees, to prevent larger, uncontrolled fires, and to remove dangerous dead and decaying trees.

NOTES

Structures and Mechanisms: Form and Function

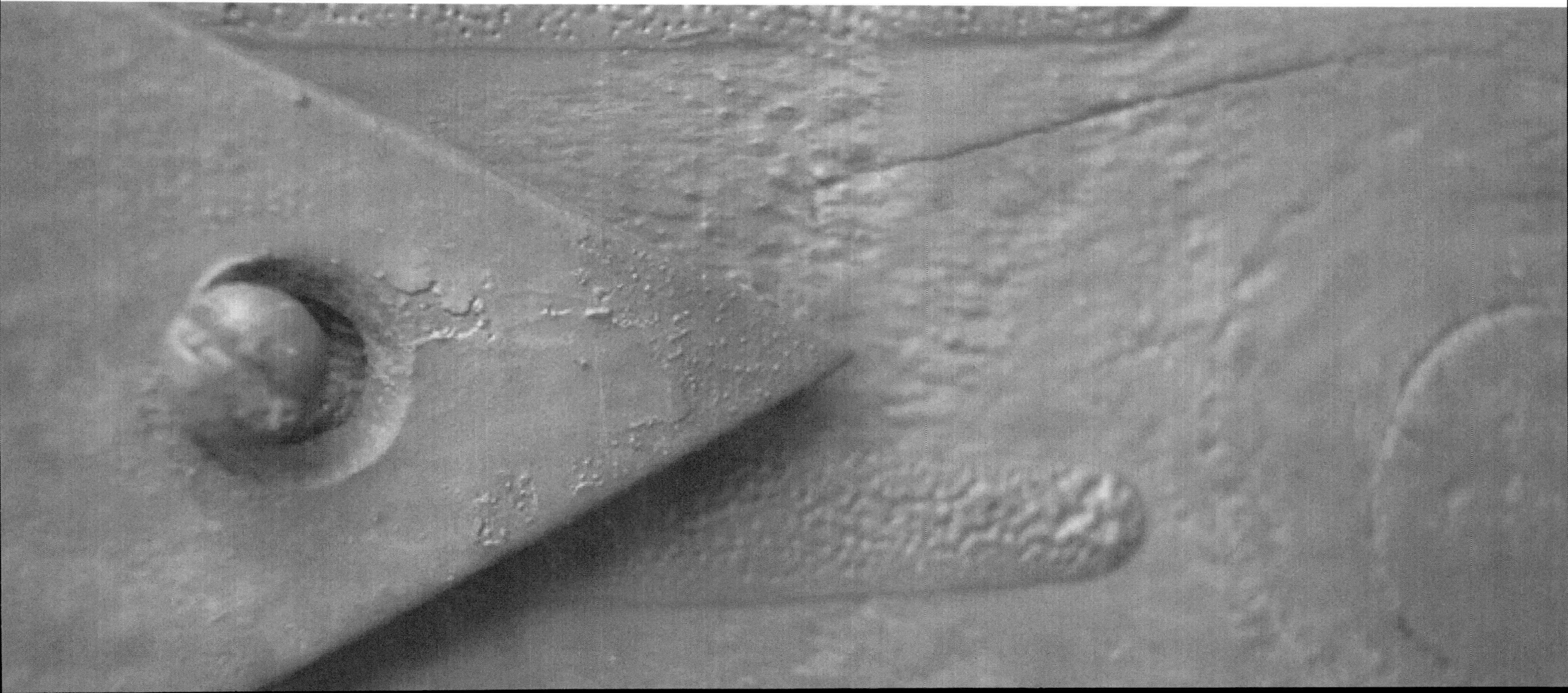

STRUCTURES AND MECHANISMS: FORM AND FUNCTION

Table of Correlations

Specific Expectation		Practice Questions	Unit Test Questions	Practice Test 1	Practice Test 2
7SM1:STSE	Analyse personal, social, economic, and environmental factors that need to be considered in designing and building structures and devices;				
7SM1.1	*evaluate the importance for individuals, society, the economy, and the environment of factors that should be considered in designing and building structures and devices to meet specific needs*	1, 2, 3	1	13	
7SM1.2	*evaluate the impact of ergonomic design on the safety and efficiency of workplaces, tools, and everyday objects, and describe changes that could be made in personal spaces and activities on the basis of this information*	4, 5	2		14
7SM2:Skills	Design and construct a variety of structures, and investigate the relationship between the design and function of these structures and the forces that act on them;				
7SM2.1	*follow established safety procedures for using tools and handling materials*	6			
7SM2.2	*design, construct, and use physical models to investigate the effects of various forces on structures*	7, 8, 9	3, 4	14	15
7SM2.3	*investigate the factors that determine the ability of a structure to support a load*	16, 17, 18	5, 6	15	16
7SM2.4	*use technological problem-solving skills to determine the most efficient way for a structure to support a given load*	19, 20	7	16	17
7SM2.5	*investigate methods used by engineers to ensure structural safety*	21	8	17	18
7SM2.6	*use appropriate science and technology vocabulary, including truss, beam, ergonomics, shear, and torsion, in oral and written communication*	31, 32	9, 10	18	19
7SM2.7	*Use a variety of forms (e.g., oral, written, graphic, multimedia) to communicate with different audiences and for a variety of purposes*				
7SM3:Concepts	Demonstrate an understanding of the relationship between structural forms and the forces that act on and within them.				
7SM3.1	*classify structures as solid structures, frame structures, or shell structures*	24, 25	11	19	20
7SM3.2	*describe ways in which the centre of gravity of a structure affects the structure's stability*	26, 27	12	20	21
7SM3.3	*identify the magnitude, direction, point of application, and plane of application of the forces applied to a structure*	10, 11, 12	13, 14	21	22, 23
7SM3.4	*distinguish between external forces and internal forces acting on a structure*	13, 14, 15	15, 16	22	24
7SM3.5	*describe the role of symmetry in structures*	28	17	23	25
7SM3.6	*identify and describe factors that can cause a structure to fail*	22, 23	18	24	26
7SM3.7	*identify the factors that determine the suitability of materials for use in manufacturing a product*	29, 30	19		

7SM1.1 evaluate the importance for individuals, society, the economy, and the environment of factors that should be considered in designing and building structures and devices to meet specific needs

Factors to Consider When Designing Structures and Devices

You interact with a number of different **structures** every day. For example, you live in a house, study in a school, ride in a car or bus, sit in a chair, and wear shoes. Each of these structures was designed for a purpose. When designing a structure, the purpose of the structure is only one of the many factors that designers need to consider. Some of the other factors that need to be considered include:

- Intended lifespan—How long will the user want it to last?
- Ease of use—Is it complicated to use? Could it be simplified?
- Aesthetics—Does it look good? Does it fit in, or stand out, from its surroundings?
- Efficiency—How well does it serve its function? Could it be faster? Stronger? More effective?
- Legal requirements—Does it meet government standards? Does it meet building codes?
- Cost—Is it expensive to build? Are the materials expensive? Is there a lot of labour involved? Can it be mass produced?
- Safety and health—Will the builders be safe? Will people be safe when they use it? Will it affect the user's health negatively?
- User preferences—What do the users want to see the structure do? Do they have suggestions that might improve the design?
- Effect on the environment—Does the manufacturing and building process hurt the environment? Does it use a lot of non-renewable resources? Does it produce any pollution?

Each of these factors can impact individual people, the economy, the environment, and society in general. Engineers and builders have to evaluate the wants and needs of all these groups. They must consider each of these factors to create the best possible structure or device.

1. Brick is a construction material commonly used to build houses, but it has the undesirable property of being weak under tension. An engineer would choose **not** to use brick when designing a skyscraper because bricks

A. cost too much for such a tall building

B. will not last long because they break under tension

C. are too heavy, so a brick skyscraper would collapse from its weight

D. are used only for aesthetic appeal since they cannot support any tension

Use the following information to answer the next question.

Adam has the task of designing the plans for a huge lumber storage facility.

2. Which of the following factors should Adam consider **most carefully** when he designs the facility?

A. Colour, environmental impact, and function

B. Cost, environmental impact, and function

C. Cost, aesthetic appearance, and function

D. Colour, cost, and function

Open Response

3. List five factors that a company should consider when designing a product or structure.

____

____

____

____

____

7SM1.2 evaluate the impact of ergonomic design on the safety and efficiency of workplaces, tools, and everyday objects, and describe changes that could be made in personal spaces and activities on the basis of this information

ERGONOMIC DESIGN

Ergonomics is the science of the relationship between the design of a structure and the affect on the human body of using this structure. Ergonomic designs reduce the stress and fatigue of the human body when it interacts with its environment. They increase the safety, comfort, and efficiency of an object, benefiting the user. This is important at work, school, home, and even in recreational activities. Many everyday objects, such as furniture, computer equipment, home and building tools, and even cooking equipment, come in ergonomic designs.

For example, the employees of a company that equips its office with comfortable, ergonomic chairs, desks, and computer keyboards and mice are less likely to suffer repetitive stress injuries. As a result, the employees may be happier, healthier, and more productive than the employees that work in an office without ergonomic equipment. The same idea can be applied to schools, where students spend a lot of time in desks and at computers. Ergonomics can also benefit the lives of the elderly and people with disabilities.

An ergonomic keyboard

A traditional keyboard

Consider the images of the two keyboards above. The keyboard on the left has an ergonomic design. The curved keyboard fits more naturally to the shape and angle of the user's hands and wrists, reducing the strain on the hands, wrists, and back while typing. In contrast, the straight keyboard on the right, which is not ergonomically designed, was designed without considering the comfort or safety of the intended users. As a result, users can develop soreness and possibly even repetitive strain injuries, such as carpal tunnel syndrome.

4. Which of the following statements **best** explains ergonomics?
   A. Using scientific information about the environment to understand the impact of structures.

   B. Applying scientific information about different forces to the design of structures.

   C. Using scientific information about the human body for the design of structures.

   D. Communicating scientific information using experimental results.

Use the following information to answer the next question.

Ergonomists design and evaluate systems in order to make them more efficient for human use.

5. What is the **most important** factor that an ergonomist would consider when designing a computer keyboard to be more ergonomic?
   A. Increasing the colour selection of keyboards to maximize its aesthetic appearance.
   B. Elevating sections of the keyboard to minimize muscle strain in the wrist.
   C. Increasing the size of the keyboard to minimize eye strain.
   D. Decreasing the size of the keyboard to minimize cost.

7SM2.1 follow established safety procedures for using tools and handling materials

Safety Procedures in Construction

Building and testing structures can be hazardous work. Safety is extremely important in the construction and manufacturing industries, and anyone who uses tools or handles building materials must follow the established safety procedures. Safety equipment in the construction industry is referred to as Personal Protective Equipment, or PPE. Some examples of PPE include: hardhats, safety glasses, gloves, steel-toed boots, and flame-retardant coveralls.

It is important to read all safety signs

Even the building materials can pose dangers to the builders who are using the materials. It is important to read all labels for safety and handling information.

Use the following information to answer the next question.

Personal protective equipment, or PPE, should be used when building and testing structures.

6. In the given picture, which of the following protective equipment is the **most important** for the worker to use?
   A. Fall protection harness
   B. Fire extinguisher
   C. Safety glasses
   D. Hard helmet

7SM2.2 design, construct, and use physical models to investigate the effects of various forces on structures

7SM3.3 identify the magnitude, direction, point of application, and plane of application of the forces applied to a structure

7SM3.4 distinguish between external forces and internal forces acting on a structure

Forces

A **force** is any push or pull that acts on an object to change its movement or its shape. The actual effect of a force acting on a structure depends on the following factors:

- Magnitude—the size of the force
- Direction—the position toward which the force pulls or pushes
- Point of Application—the exact spot on the object on which the force acts
- Plane of Application—the horizontal or vertical nature of the force

For example, a man pushing a wheelchair exerts a push force with enough magnitude, or strength, to make the wheelchair move. The man applies the force to the back of the wheelchair at the handlebars in the forward direction along the horizontal plane. As a result, the wheelchair gains speed in the forward direction. In contrast, the man could pull the wheelchair in the backward direction. The wheelchair would then gain speed in the backward direction.

The man exerts a push force on a wheelchair.

External Forces

External forces are forces that act from outside of the structure. A force is also called a load. There are two types of loads: static and dynamic.

A static force is an unchanging force that acts on a structure at all times. The weight of an object on Earth is due to the force of gravity, which is a static force. The stress on a structure caused by its own weight is called a static load.

A dynamic force is an external force that changes in size or direction. These forces are called dynamic loads, and they can change very quickly. A dynamic load is any force that causes an impact, such as a gust of wind or an earthquake. External forces produce internal forces, or stress, within a structure.

Internal Forces

Internal forces are forces that one part of the structure exerts on other parts of the structure. These forces act within a structure. There are four types of internal forces:

- Compression
- Tension
- Shear
- Torsion

Compression is a pushing force within a structure caused by an external force. It is the force you feel when you push your hands together. Compression forces occur when an external load pushes on part of a structure, which then pushes on the other parts of the structure. A structure may be shortened or crushed if it cannot withstand the compression forces acting within it. For example, when you sit on a chair, your weight exerts a force on the seat of the chair, which then exerts an internal force on the legs of the chair.

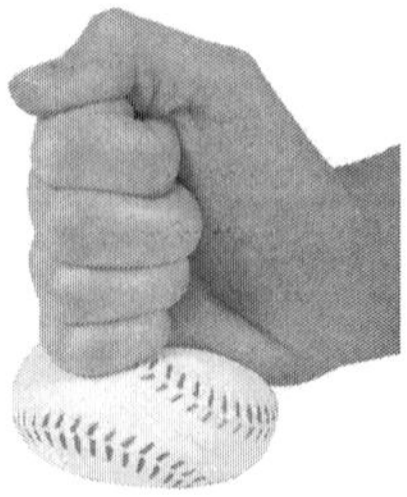

The ball is crushed by a compression force.

Tension is a pulling force within a structure caused by external forces acting in different directions. It is the force you feel when you try to pull your linked hands apart. Tension forces stretch a material by pulling its ends apart. A structure may pull apart and break if it cannot withstand the tension forces acting on it. For example, the cables that hold up a suspension bridge experience tension as the weight of the bridge pulls one end of the cable down while the support beam pulls the other end of the cable up.

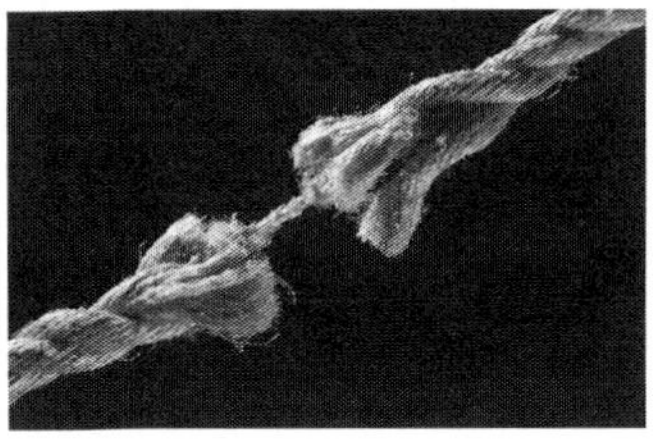

A rope pulls apart because of tension.

Shear is a force that pushes part of an object in the opposite direction of another force. It is the force you feel when you slide your hands against each other in opposite directions. Shear forces bend or tear a material by pressing parts in opposite directions at the same time. A structure may bend or tear if it cannot withstand the shear forces acting on it. For example, a nail used to hold up a picture frame experiences shear as the weight of the frame pulls the nail down while the wall holds the nail up.

The pin holding a scissors' blades together experiences shear.

Torsion is a twisting force. It is the force you feel when you twist your linked hands. Torsion forces twist a material by turning the ends of a structure in opposite directions. A structure may twist and break if it cannot withstand the torsion forces acting on it. For example, a plastic ruler experiences torsion if you twist the ends of the ruler in opposite directions.

The blades of the fan experience torsion.

Considering Forces When Designing Structures

Architects, engineers, and builders need to study and understand the various forces that will act on the structures they design and build. To help do this, they design, construct, and test models of their structures. Then, they can understand the effects of forces, such as compression, tension, torsion, and shear, that will be placed on the structures.

Use the following information to answer the next question.

John and Emily have a friendly game of tug of war.

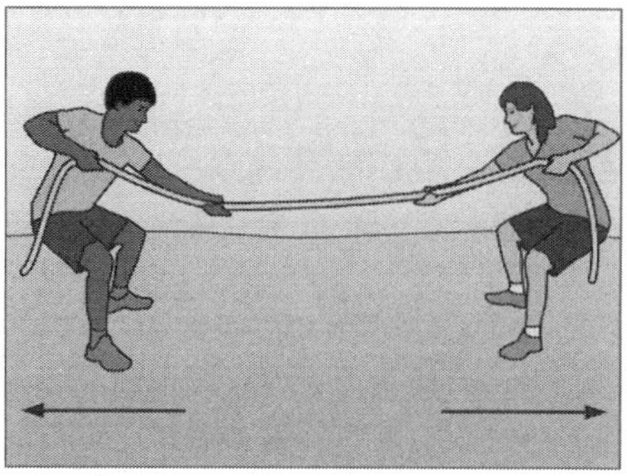

7. The force acting within the rope is called
   A. shear **B.** torsion
   C. tension **D.** compression

Use the following information to answer the next question.

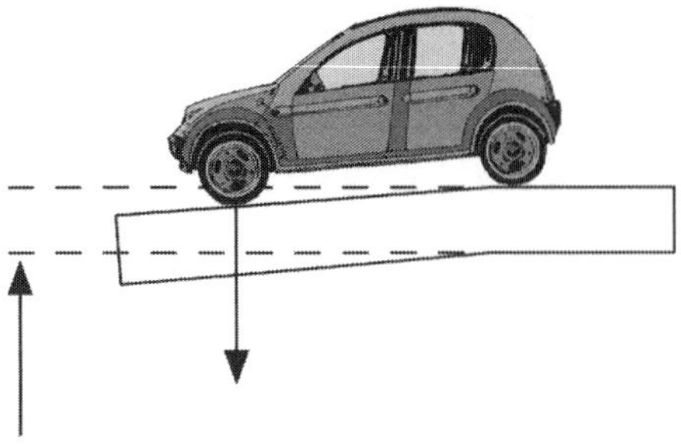

A force

8. In the diagram, the force acting within the road is called

A. torsion **B.** shearing

C. static load **D.** compression

Use the following information to answer the next question.

Scissors

Monica investigates the forces acting on everyday objects. She picks up a pair of scissors and opens the scissors' blades.

9. The force that acts on the pin of the scissors is called

A. shear **B.** torsion

C. tension **D.** compression

Use the following information to answer the next question.

A boat moves at a constant velocity of 20 kph in a straight line. Suddenly, a strong wind starts blowing in the direction opposite to the boat's direction of motion, as shown in the figure.

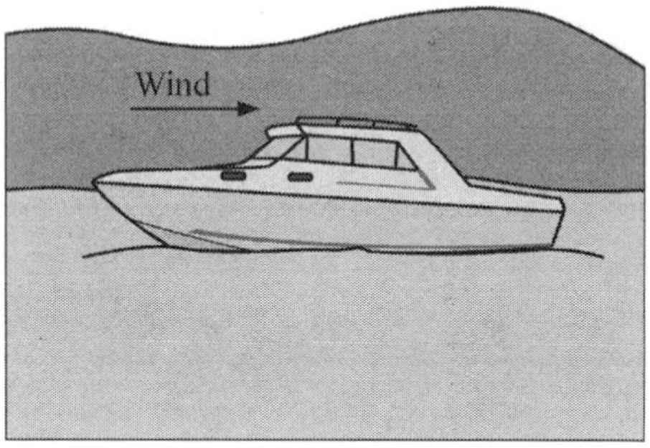

10. In order for the boat to continue at the same velocity, the sailor must apply

A. no force

B. less force than before

C. more force than before

D. the same force as before

Use the following information to answer the next question.

A bolt holds two pieces of a wooden shelf together, as shown in the diagram.

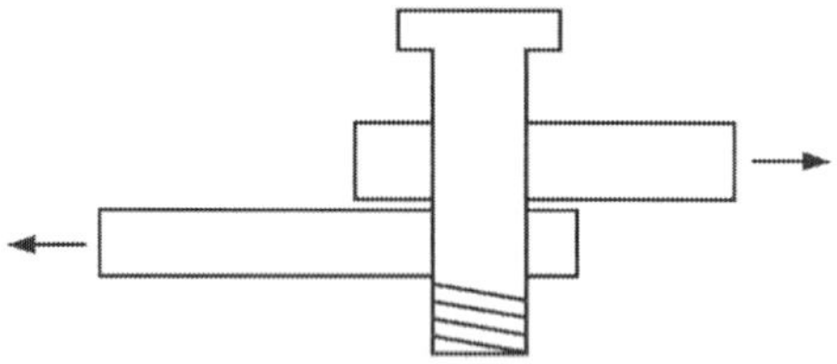

11. The plane of application of the force on the bolt is

A. perpendicular to the bolt

B. right diagonal to the bolt

C. left diagonal to the bolt

D. parallel to the bolt

Use the following information to answer the next question.

Adler, Chatwin, Jacob, and Lee pull a rope in a tug of war. Adler and Chatwin pull in one direction, while Jacob and Lee pull in the other direction. The sizes of force that Adler, Chatwin, and Jacob use to pull the rope are shown in the given figure.

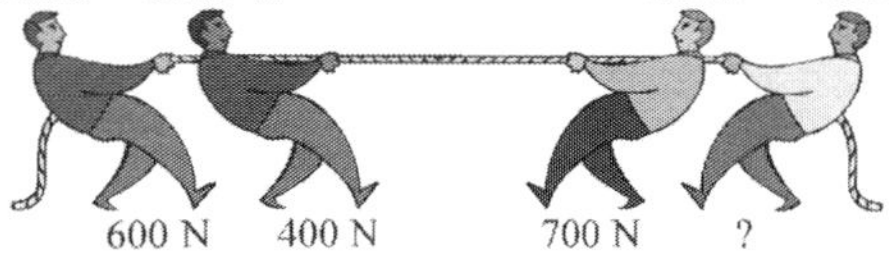

12. If the rope does not move, what is the size of the force that Lee uses to pull the rope?
A. 1 000 N **B.** 700 N
C. 300 N **D.** 0 N

Use the following information to answer the next question.

A yo-yo experiences a variety of forces.

13. The string on a fully extended yo-yo experiences
A. compression force
B. tension force
C. torsion force
D. shear force

Use the following information to answer the next question.

In 1941, the Tacoma Narrows Bridge in Washington collapsed when winds caused the bridge to move and twist.

14. The wind force that acted on the bridge is an example of a
A. static load
B. tension force
C. dynamic load
D. compression force

15. As part of her engineering project, Annie built and tested a model bridge.
When Annie placed a one-kilogram mass in the centre of the bridge, it collapsed.
This indicates that the
A. internal forces were greater than the external forces
B. external forces were greater than the internal forces
C. combined internal and external forces were too small to support the bridge
D. combined internal and external forces were too much for the bridge to support

7SM2.3 investigate the factors that determine the ability of a structure to support a load

Factors in Load-Bearing Structures

Many structures are designed to support specific **loads**. These structures are called load-bearing structures. However, there are a number of factors that affect how much force a structure can support. Some of these factors are:

- the weight of the load
- the weight of the structure itself
- the strength and structural characteristics of the materials used to build the structure

As well, there are many different types of strength. A material that has high tensile strength, or the ability to withstand tension, may have a low compressive strength, or the ability to withstand compression. The reverse is also true. Often, you can increase the strength of a material by reinforcing it. This can be done by welding or gluing layers of the material together.

16. Welding, gluing, and melting material together are all methods of increasing a material's

A. flexibility **B.** strength

C. stability **D.** ductility

Use the following information to answer the next question.

Engineers must choose their building materials carefully. Some characteristics that engineers look at include:

- Strength—the ability of a material to resist an applied force.
- Durability—the ability of a material to endure a stress or force over time.
- Workability—the ease with which a material can be worked or changed.
- Maintainability—the ease with which a material can be maintained or fixed.
- Deformability—the measure of the extent to which a material can deform or bend without breaking.

17. Derek designs a bridge that needs to withstand heavy loads, and he needs to choose some materials to build the bridge. Which two of the following characteristics are the **most important** for him to consider?

A. Workability and maintainability

B. Durability and deformability

C. Strength and deformability

D. Workability and durability

Use the following information to answer the next question.

Rope is made from fibres that are wound together. Some ropes can support heavy loads, such as firefighters who rappel down a rope from a helicopter to fight remote forest fires.

18. Which of the following structural properties is **most important** for determining whether a rope can support a person rappelling down from a helicopter?

A. Ductility

B. Malleability

C. Tensile strength

D. Compressive strength

7SM2.4 use technological problem-solving skills to determine the most efficient way for a structure to support a given load

ENGINEERING FOR EFFICIENCY

Engineers require good technological problem solving skills. As they create new structures and devices, they need to think creatively. The following steps are important in good technological problem solving:

- careful planning
- purposeful selection of tools and materials
- testing and retesting
- modifications of a product or process
- communicating about the solution
- recommending changes and improvements

By following these steps, an engineer can determine the most efficient way for a structure, such as a chair, shelf, or bridge, to support a given load.

Use the following information to answer the next question.

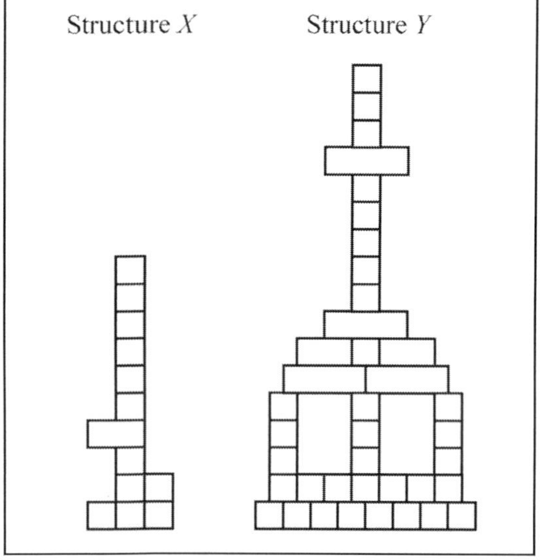

19. Structure *Y* is more stable than structure *X* because it has a

A. larger mass

B. higher peak

C. thicker foundation

D. wider base of support

Use the following information to answer the next question.

Arjun wants to build a chair for his little brother who weighs 16 kg. He builds four different chairs out of newspaper and masking tape. He then tests each chair to see which chair will be best for his brother. He recorded the results in the chart below.

	Do all four feet of the chair touch the floor?	**Does the chair swivel or wobble when weight is added to it?**	**How much weight does the chair hold?**
Chair one	Yes	Yes	25 kg
Chair two	Yes	No	42 kg
Chair three	No	Yes	6 kg
Chair four	No	Yes	17 kg

20. Which of Arjun's chairs is the safest for his little brother to use?

A. Chair one **B.** Chair two

C. Chair three **D.** Chair four

7SM2.5 investigate methods used by engineers to ensure structural safety

7SM3.6 identify and describe factors that can cause a structure to fail

Why Structures Fail

Engineers design structures to withstand the forces that act upon them. A structure that withstands these forces is stable. In contrast, a structure that cannot withstand these forces is said to fail. A structure might fail because of one of many factors:

- bad design
- faulty construction
- foundation failure
- extraordinary load

If the design of a structure does not take into account all the forces that will act on it, it is likely to fail. The design of the Tacoma Narrows Bridge in Washington, for example, failed to take into consideration the force of the wind. Four months after being opened, the bridge collapsed because of torsion forces created by the wind.

Bad design can cause a bridge to fall.

Sometimes, the design of the structure is good, but mistakes might occur during the construction process. For example, if the frame is not joined together properly or defective building materials are used, the structure could fail. If the ground beneath the structure fails to support the structure, it will also fail.

The structure might also fail if it is used improperly or if the load exceeds the maximum load. For example, a balcony in Chicago built to hold 30 people collapsed when more than 50 people stood on it.

Engineering for Safety

When engineers design new structures and devices, their top priority is safety. There are many practices that engineers follow to ensure the safety of their products.

- Following building codes—the government has developed many different building codes for engineers to follow. This ensures that all engineers are following a minimum standard of safety.
- Careful design and testing—models of new products are built and tested to ensure they will stand up to their intended uses. If the products fail their tests, they are redesigned.
- Incorporating sensors—many devices have computerized sensors built into them. These sensors detect unusual loads and stress on the device and give warnings if the device might fail. Some sensors indicate when repairs are needed, and some can even stop the device from working if there is danger that the device might fail.
- Ensuring a margin of safety—engineers often design products to carry much heavier loads than they will actually need to bear. This prevents the user from accidentally overloading the device.

Use the following information to answer the next question.

> The following factors to must be considered when building a house:
>
> I. Reinforce the roof rafters to provide additional support
> II. Build reinforced walls to allow for movement of the ground
> III. Perform soil tests to ensure a solid foundation
> IV. Add extra insulation in the attic to prevent heat loss

21. Which two of these factors are the **most important** to consider when building a house in northern Canada?

A. Factors I and II

B. Factors I and IV

C. Factors II and III

D. Factors II and IV

Use the following information to answer the next question.

After many rides through the river valley, Shaun notices that his mountain bike has developed a crack in the frame. He takes his bike into a repair shop, and the mechanic tells him that the crack is a result of structural fatigue.

22. If the crack is due to structural fatigue, it was **most likely** caused by

A. wear and tear from the many bike rides through the river valley

B. over-inflation of the tires on the bike

C. a bike accident with a tree

D. a manufacturing defect

Use the following information to answer the next question.

Structures are built to withstand a specific maximum load. The largest load that the structure would typically have to support determines the maximum load. Sometimes, structures are subjected to loads far beyond what they were designed to support.

23. A load that exceeds a structure's maximum load is called

A. an extraordinary load

B. a superordinary load

C. an ordinary load

D. a massive load

7SM3.1 classify structures as solid structures, frame structures, or shell structures

Classifying Structures

A structure is any object that gives support. A structure gives support by resisting both the internal and external forces that act upon it. There are three basic types of structures:

- solid structures
- frame structures
- shell structures

Solid Structures

A solid structure is usually made from a solid piece of material. A solid structure has little or no space within it. It relies on its own mass to resist the forces that act upon it. For example, a dam consists of solid materials that limit the flow of water in a stream or river.

A dam is a solid structure

Frame Structures

A house is a framed structure

A frame structure comprises parts fastened together to provide shape and support. There is usually space between the components of a frame structure. A frame structure also provides strength to materials that cannot function as structures on their own. Although frame structures are not as strong as solid structures, they are lighter and use less building materials. For example, a house consists of several components, such as beams, trusses, and drywall, fastened together to form a framed structure.

Shell Structures

A shell structure consists of materials moulded into a shape to enclose a space. Shell structures can be made from strong materials, such as brick, concrete, and stone, if there are strong forces acting on the structure. Light materials, which may not provide as much strength but are lighter and more flexible, can also make up shell structures. For example, a soccer ball consists of soft materials stitched together to enclose an empty space.

A soccer ball is a shell structure

24. Which type of structure depends on its entire mass to withstand the forces that act on it?

A. Solid structure

B. Shell structure

C. Beam structure

D. Frame structure

Use the following information to answer the next question.

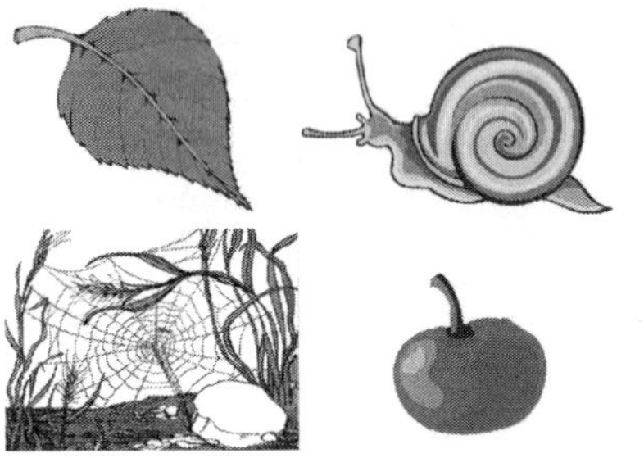

Four structures found in nature

25. Which two of the given structures are examples of frame structures?

A. Leaf and apple

B. Leaf and spider web

C. Apple and snail shell

D. Snail shell and spider web

7SM3.5 describe the role of symmetry in structures

7SM3.2 describe ways in which the centre of gravity of a structure affects the structure's stability

Centre of Gravity

In order to provide support, a structure must be stable. This means that the structure must be able to resist the force due to gravity. As a result, when engineers design structures, they need to identify where its **centre of gravity** occurs. Even though gravity acts equally on all parts of the structure, think of the centre of gravity as the point in the structure where gravity pulls the structure downward. A stable structure will have a low centre of gravity located over top of its base.

A structure constructed without considering its centre of gravity is likely to be unstable. A structure built with a high centre of gravity could easily tip over. To avoid building unstable structures, engineers design buildings and towers with wider bases than tops, like the pyramids in Egypt and the CN tower in Toronto.

Both the pyramids and the CN tower have wider bases than tops.

A structure will also be unstable if its centre of gravity is not located over its base. Consider the centre of gravity in a child's high chair. Draw an imaginary line down the middle of the chair. The chair will have approximately the same mass on both sides of the line. If mass is added to one side of this line, the chair's centre of gravity will move toward the added mass. If the centre of gravity moves to a point where it is no longer over the chair's base, it is likely to tip over in the direction of the mass.

Symmetry in Structures

Symmetry occurs when the mass that composes a structure is arranged equally around a line down the centre of the structure. This line down the centre of the structure is called the line of symmetry.

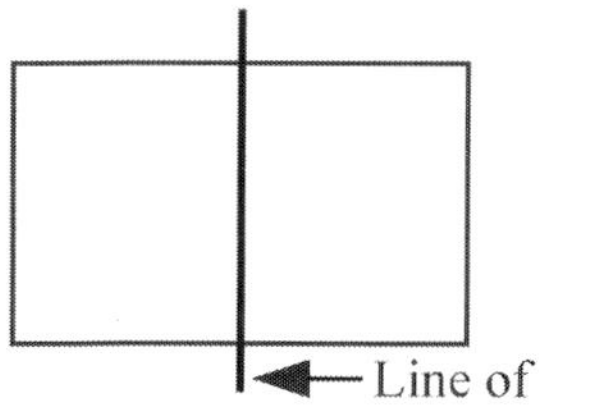

A balance is symmetrical

If the mass of a structure is distributed symmetrically around its line of symmetry, then the centre of gravity will occur along the line of symmetry. You can see this principle when you balance a basketball on your finger. The basketball balances when your finger is at the centre of the bottom of the ball. At this point, your finger aligns with the ball's centre of gravity. The mass of the ball is the same on both sides of your finger, and the ball is stable on your finger. If you move your finger out of alignment with the centre of gravity, the mass of the ball will no longer be evenly distributed, and the ball will no longer be stable.

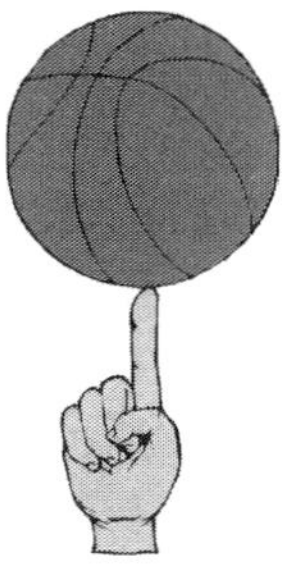

Engineers use symmetry to build stable structures. Buildings that are not symmetrical are not as stable as symmetrical buildings.

Asymmetrical Building

Symmetrical Building

Symmetry also plays a role in the aesthetic appeal of a structure. Structures that are considered beautiful are often symmetrical.

A butterfly's body is symmetrical.

The Taj Mahal is symmetrical.

26. In a symmetrical structure, gravity acts

A. only on the bottom part of the structure

B. unevenly on all parts of the structure

C. only on the top part of the structure

D. evenly on all parts of the structure

27. Which of the following properties would **not** be considered in designing the most stable office building?

A. The structure should be symmetrical.

B. The structure should have a solid foundation.

C. The top of the structure should be wider than the base.

D. The mass of the structure should be evenly distributed around the centre of gravity.

28. Which of the four structures is the **least** stable?

A.

B.

C.

D.

7SM3.7 identify the factors that determine the suitability of materials for use in manufacturing a product

THE SUITABILITY OF MATERIALS

It is important to choose appropriate materials when designing a product. There are many factors that determine the suitability of a material to use in a product, such as:

- Aesthetics—Does the material look good?
- Strength—Will the material resist the forces to which it will be exposed?
- Availability—Is the material hard to get? Is there a lot of it available?
- Cost—How much does the material cost? How much will it cost to ship it if it cannot be purchased locally?
- Disposal—What will happen to the material when the product is disposed of? Is it biodegradable? Is it toxic?
- Resistance to heat, cold, and water—Will the material hold up against the temperatures to which it will be exposed? Can it be exposed to varying temperatures?

Use the following information to answer the next question.

Tom designs a house for his family. He can use a variety of building materials in the construction of the house, but he wants to use materials that are natural, strong, and cheap.

29. Which of the following pairs of materials **best** satisfies Tom's criteria?

A. Mud and stone

B. Metal and glass

C. Wood and grass

D. Concrete and clay

Use the following information to answer the next question.

Annick studies a chart that lists 4 materials that can be used to make running shoes.

Material	1	2	3	4
Strength	High	Low	High	Low
Aesthetic Appeal	Medium	Medium	Low	High
Cost	Low	Low	High	High
Durability	High	Medium	High	Low

30. Which of the four materials should Annick use to make a pair of running shoes?

A. Material 1 **B.** Material 3

C. Material 3 **D.** Material 4

7SM2.6 use appropriate science and technology vocabulary, including truss, beam, ergonomics, shear, and torsion, in oral and written communication

Communicating in Science

It might seem that science has its own language. In a way, it does. When you speak and write about science, you need to use the proper terminology. The important terms for this unit are on the following list. It is important that you understand these terms and that you can use them properly. If you need help understanding these terms, refer to the other lessons in this unit or use the glossary in the back of this *Key*.

Important Terms in Structures and Mechanisms

- truss
- shear
- beam
- torsion
- tension
- ergonomics
- compression

Use the following information to answer the next question.

A transporting truck carries a large load located on one side of its flatbed trailer.

31. The load on the one side of the trailer bed causes the bed to experience an internal force called

A. torsion **B.** tension

C. shearing **D.** compression

Use the following information to answer the next question.

To provide structural support for roofs, engineers design triangular shaped ___*i*___ by joining together many ___*ii*___.

32. Which of the following charts identifies the terms that **best** complete the given statement?

A.

i	*ii*
trusses	beams

B.

i	*ii*
frames	trusses

C.

i	*ii*
beams	frames

D.

i	*ii*
beams	trusses

ANSWERS AND SOLUTIONS
STRUCTURES AND MECHANISMS: FORM AND FUNCTION

1. B	8. D	15. D	22. A	29. A
2. B	9. A	16. B	23. A	30. A
3. OR	10. C	17. C	24. A	31. A
4. C	11. D	18. C	25. B	32. A
5. B	12. C	19. D	26. D	
6. C	13. B	20. B	27. C	
7. C	14. C	21. B	28. A	

1. B

Bricks are weak under tension. In other words, brick structures will crack as a result of tension forces created in the bricks when forces are exerted in opposite directions on the ends of the bricks. As a result, bricks are used for structures that are wider than they are tall. This keeps the tension forces small enough to keep from cracking. A skyscraper is a building that is taller than it is wide, so the tension forces on the building would cause the bricks to crack. The correct answer is B.

Bricks are inexpensive and are strong under compression. These are desirable properties when choosing materials to build a house. As well, while bricks are heavy, their weight is not the property that causes tall brick structures to fail.

2. B

The most important factors to consider in designing a structure are the cost, environmental impact, and function of the structure. The correct answer is B.

The colour and aesthetic appearance of a structure are secondary factors; these factors will improve the look of the structure, but they are not vital to the construction of the structure.

3. OR

Any five of:

- Function of product (forces it may need to withstand)
- Efficiency
- Ease of use (ergonomic design)
- Aesthetics
- Cost of production
- Intended lifespan of product
- Effect of product on the environment (disposal of product, production of materials)
- Safety, health, and legal requirements

4. C

Ergonomics is the application of scientific information about the human body for the design of structures and devices. The correct answer is C.

5. B

In this situation, the most important consideration for ergonomists is the safety of the keyboard design for human use. Therefore, the most important consideration is minimizing the strain of the keyboard on the human body. The most likely strain caused by using the keyboard is on the hands and wrist. The correct answer is B.

Increasing the size of the keyboard may help certain segments of the population with visual impairment, but it would not apply to the majority of users, since most users do not look directly at the keyboard while typing. Minimizing the cost and maximizing aesthetic product appeal are important in the design of products, but they are not ergonomic issues.

6. C

In this situation, the worker requires safety glasses to prevent debris from coming into contact with his eyes. The correct answer is C.

7. C

Tension acts within structures when it is pulled in different directions. As John and Emily pull on the ends of the rope, a tension force acts within the rope. The correct answer is C.

8. D

The weight of the car pushes down on the road. As a result, the top of the road pushes down on the road beneath it. This pushing force within the road surface is called compression. The correct answer is D.

9. A

A shear force pushes part of an object in the opposite direction of another force. When the scissors blades open, both of the blades exert a pushing force on the pin that holds them together. These forces act in the opposite direction of one another, so the pin experiences a shear force. The correct answer is A.

Torsion is a force that results in a twist in the object. Tension is the force that results from the object being pulled in opposite directions. Compression is a force that acts to push objects together.

10. C

Without the wind blowing, the sailor needs to apply a certain amount of force to make the boat move. The sailor does this by rowing a paddle in the water. If the wind begins to blow against the direction of the boat, it will apply a force opposing the movement of the boat. In order to move the boat at the same velocity as before, the sailor must apply more force to overcome the force of the wind. The correct answer is C.

If the sailor applies the same amount of force or less force than he applied before, the boat will slow down. If the sailor does not apply any force at all, the boat will certainly come to a stop.

11. D

The bolt experiences shear forces from the shelf which act parallel to the bolt. The correct answer is D.

12. C

The combined forces that Adler and Chatwin use to pull the rope is equal to the combined forces that Jacob and Lee use. The force that Adler and Chatwin use to pull the rope is:

$$\begin{aligned} \text{rope} &= 600\text{ N} + 400\text{ N} \\ &= 1\ 000\text{ N} \end{aligned}$$

Therefore, the combined force that Jacob and Lee use to pull the rope is also 1 000 N. Therefore, the force that Lee pulls the rope with is:

$$\begin{aligned} \text{rope} &= 600\text{ N} + 400\text{ N} \\ 1\ 000\text{ N} &= 700\text{ N} + \text{Lee's Force} \\ 1\ 000\text{ N} - 700\text{ N} &= \text{Lee's Force} \\ 300\text{ N} &= \text{Lee's Force} \end{aligned}$$

Therefore, Lee uses 300 N of force to pull the rope.

13. B

As the mass of the yo-yo drops, it pulls on the string, creating a tension force within the string.

Compression forces result when an object or substance is pushed or squeezed inwards. Torsion forces result from twisting. Shear forces are created when two objects are forced against each other in the same plane.

14. C

The wind force that acted on the bridge was a dynamic force. A dynamic force is an external force that moves or changes. The correct answer is C.

A static load refers to the weight of the bridge itself. Tension and compression forces are examples of internal forces. The wind force itself is an external force; however, the wind force may cause these internal forces. In this case, the wind caused internal torsion forces as the bridge twisted.

15. D

External forces, such as the weight of a one-kilogram mass, can cause internal forces in a structure, such as compression and tension. When the combined external and internal forces acting on a structure are greater than the structure's ability to withstand the forces, the structure will fail. The correct answer is D.

16. B

Welding, gluing, and melting materials together reinforces the material to provide additional material strength. The strength of a material refers to the material's ability to resist an applied force.
The correct answer is B.

Flexibility refers to the ability to easily bend a material. Stability refers to the ability to recover from changes or forces. Ductility describes how much a material can be deformed before it fractures.

17. C

The bridge needs to support a large load, so it needs materials that can resist applied forces. As well, the bridge will need to use materials that can be deformed to take shape without breaking. Thus the most important factors for Derek to consider are the material's strength and deformability. The correct answer is C.

18. C

The rope experiences tension forces when a person rappels down, so it needs high tensile strength to withstand these tension forces. The correct answer is C.

Ductility and malleability refer to the ability of a material to be bent and squished without breaking. Compressive strength is the amount of compression, or squeezing, that a material can withstand.

19. D

A structure with a wide base is more stable than a structure with a narrow base. The compression force from above the base spreads out among the blocks of the base, making the structure more stable. The correct answer is D.

20. B

The safest chair is the most stable chair that can hold the weight of Arjun's brother without his brother falling off. The most stable chair is the chair that has all four feet touching the floor and does not wobble or swivel when weight is added to it. Of the chairs, chair two best meets this criteria, so it is the most stable chair and can support the weight of Arjun's brother. The correct answer is B.

A chair with all four feet touching the ground is stable (this eliminates chairs three and four). A chair that does not swivel or wobble is also stable (this eliminates chair one). As well, chair three cannot hold the weight of Arjun's brother.

21. B

In northern Canada, a house needs to withstand the cold and snowy climate of the long winters. Therefore, the roof rafters should be reinforced to provide additional support in the event of a heavy load of snow on the roof. As well, it is important to add extra insulation in the attic to prevent heat loss during the cold winter. The correct answer is B.

It is not necessary to build reinforced walls that allow for movement of the ground as earthquakes are very rare in northern Canada. It is also not essential to test soil as the soils in northern Canada are permanently frozen material (permafrost). This ensures a solid foundation.

22. A

Structural fatigue occurs when a material is forced to withstand maximum forces over time, causing it to slowly break down. Riding a bike often, particularly on bumpy paths, will cause structural fatigue in the bike. The correct answer is A.

The over-inflation of the tires would not affect the frame of the bike. If the crack were the result of an accident with a tree, the force would have to exceed the maximum force. This would not be a result of structural fatigue. If the crack in the frame resulted from a manufacturing defect, it would have been present when the bike was purchased. This would have been the result of a bad design, not an excessive force.

23. A

A load that exceeds the typical load that a structure is designed to withstand is called an extraordinary load. The correct answer is A.

24. A

A solid structure has little or no space inside it, and it relies on its own mass to resist the forces that act upon it. The correct answer is A.

25. B

Frame structures have frameworks made up of parts fastened together. There is usually space between the components of a frame structure. The leaf and spider web are examples of frame structures. The correct answer is B.

The apple is an example of a solid structure. A solid structure has little or no space inside.

The snail shell is an example of a shell structure. Shell structures have a moulded shape enclosing a space.

26. D

In a symmetrical structure, all parts of the structure distribute evenly around the centre of gravity. Thus, the force of gravity acts evenly on all parts of the structure. The correct answer is D.

27. C

If there is more mass above the centre of gravity than below it, the base will not support the weight, making the structure unstable. The base of the structure should be wider than its top in order for the structure to be stable. The correct answer is C.

If the structure is built on a solid foundation, it will resist the force of compression. As well, a symmetrical structure will have its mass evenly distributed around the centre of gravity. A stable structure will also have its mass evenly distributed around the centre of gravity because the gravity will act evenly on all of the parts of the structure.

28. A

A symmetrical structure is more stable than an unsymmetrical structure. All of the structures above are symmetrical except for structure I. Therefore, structure I is the least stable. The correct answer is A.

29. A

Mud and stone are natural, strong, and cheap materials. They best satisfy Tom's criteria. The correct answer is A.

Wood and grass are natural, and can be cheap, but grass is not a strong building material. Concrete and clay are strong, but concrete is neither natural nor cheap. Metal and glass are also strong, but neither are cheap or natural.

30. A

When designing a running shoe, a designer will consider of the materials strength, aesthetic appeal, cost, and durability. A desirable material should have high strength, low cost, high aesthetic appeal, and high durability.

Material 1 has high strength, low cost, and high durability. Therefore, it fulfils three of the four criteria. The aesthetic appeal is only medium, but of the four materials given, Material 1 fulfils the most criteria, so it is the best suited for making a running shoe. The correct answer is A.

Material 2 has low cost, but that is the only criteria it fulfils.

Material 3 has high strength and durability, but it only fulfils two of the criteria.

Material 4 has a high aesthetic appeal, but it only fulfils one of the criteria.

31. A

Torsion is an internal force that creates a bend or twist in an object. If the load is on one side of the trailer bed, it will cause the bed to twist, resulting in a torsion force in the bed. The correct answer is A.

Tension forces result from pulling the object in opposite directions. Shearing forces are forces that act parallel to the face of the material. Compression forces result from a squeezing of the object.

32. A

Engineers design trusses to provide structural support for roofs. Trusses are triangular shaped supports made of many beams joined together. The correct answer is A.

UNIT TEST — STRUCTURES AND MECHANISMS: FORM AND FUNCTION

Use the following information to answer the next question.

An R-value describes the insulating properties of a material. The higher the R-value, the greater the insulation.

1. Earl is designing his winter cabin for heat efficiency. Which of the following factors is the **least important** for him to consider when he chooses his insulating material?

A. Cost **B.** Colour

C. Weight **D.** R-value

2. Ergonomically designed chairs would be **most beneficial** for which segment of the population?

A. Athletes

B. Dancers

C. Office workers

D. Construction workers

Use the following information to answer the next question.

Bob and Marley are learning to rock climb. They learn that they will be attached to one another by a safety rope as they climb.

3. Which of the following properties of rope will Bob and Marley be **most concerned** about when selecting their safety rope?

A. The compression force that the rope can withstand

B. The tension force that the rope can withstand

C. The diameter of the rope

D. The colour of the rope

Use the following information to answer the next question.

4. A man stands on a piece of wood held up at each end by a brick. The forces that act on the piece of wood are

A. friction and shear

B. tension and shear

C. compression and shear

D. compression and tension

Use the following information to answer the next question.

Freezing rain is a common occurrence in Canada. In 1998, a severe ice storm left millions of people in the dark when several electrical towers toppled under the weight of several inches of ice that accumulated over 80 hours of steady freezing rain.

5. In order to prevent a similar disaster, which of the following plans of action should the local governments and industry take?

A. Bury electrical cables underground so the weight of ice and snow will no longer be a concern.

B. Construct electrical towers that are taller so the weight of the ice and snow is further spread out.

C. Design electrical towers that can withstand greater static loads than what they can currently handle.

D. Build electrical towers that can withstand greater dynamic loads than what they can currently handle.

6. Wind loads can affect the stability of a structure because they

A. cannot be accounted for when designing the structure

B. apply a varying pressure on a surface

C. are the most destructive of all loads

D. differ in different parts of the world

Use the following information to answer the next question.

Different types of roofs serve the same function—to protect the inhabitants from the weather.

7. Which of the given roof types is **best** suited for a snowy, mountainous climate?

A. Roof P **B.** Roof Q

C. Roof R **D.** Roof S

8. Which of the following factors will **not** have to be considered when deciding the type of foundation to use in a structure?

A. Soil characteristics of the area

B. Type of load the building will have

C. Direction of the load on the building

D. The area available for the foundation

Use the following information to answer the next question.

Rebecca accidentally tore her paper in half during her writing class.

9. Which type of force did Rebecca exert to tear the paper?

A. Shear **B.** Torsion

C. Tension **D.** Compression

Use the following information to answer the next question.

The following bridge is constructed using box-like structures that support the load of the bridge.

10. Which of the following terms best describes the bridge, according to the way it supports its load?

A. Arch bridge

B. Beam bridge

C. Cable bridge

D. Suspension bridge

11. Which of the following objects **best** represents a shell structure?

A. Airplane body **B.** Roof truss

C. Goal post **D.** Fence

12. A structure will be the **most** stable if mass is added

A. to the right of the centre of gravity

B. to the left of the centre of gravity

C. above the centre of gravity

D. below the centre of gravity

Use the following information to answer the next question.

Trevor competes in the Science Olympics at his school. He has built a bridge out of plastic drinking straws and tape.
The judges put a one-kilogram weight on the middle of the bridge. Trevor's bridge has no problem bearing the load, so the judges put a second one-kilogram weight on top of the first.

13. By adding a second weight to the bridge, the judges have changed the

A. plane of application of the force

B. point of application of the force

C. magnitude of the force

D. direction of the force

Use the following information to answer the next question.

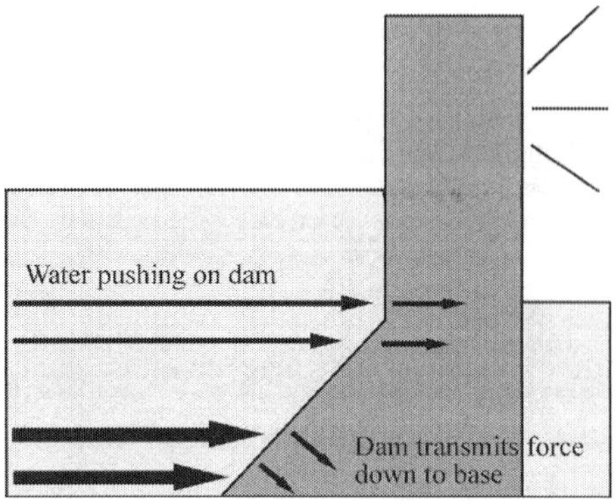

14. Which of the following statements **best** explains the reason that dams are built with triangular bases?

A. The dam is cheaper to build with a triangular base.

B. Triangular bases provide symmetry and make the dam aesthetically pleasing.

C. The load of the water is greater deep in the water, so the larger base is needed to withstand the greater load.

D. The load of the water is greater at the top of the water, so the larger base provides stability to the top of the dam.

15. A heavy weight placed at the centre of a bridge causes the bridge to bend in the middle. The forces that act on the bridge are
   - **A.** tension and shear
   - **B.** shear and compression
   - **C.** compression and torsion
   - **D.** tension and compression

Use the following information to answer the next question.

A load of books on a shelf causes the shelf to bend after a period of time.

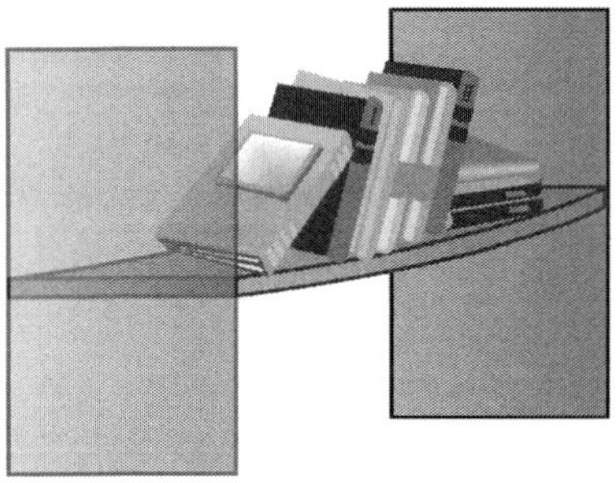

16. If the shelf breaks, it is **most likely** due to
   - **A.** bad design
   - **B.** foundation failure
   - **C.** faulty construction
   - **D.** extraordinary load

Use the following information to answer the next question.

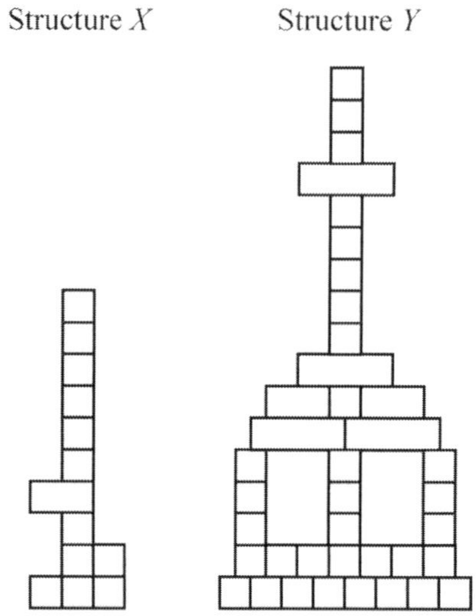

17. Structure *Y* is more stable than Structure *X* because it
   - **A.** has more mass
   - **B.** is more symmetrical
   - **C.** has a thicker foundation
   - **D.** is made from more blocks

18. The Leaning Tower of Pisa started to lean soon after construction started. The tower leans because of
   - **A.** an extraordinary load
   - **B.** a foundation failure
   - **C.** a lack of symmetry
   - **D.** a dynamic load

Use the following information to answer the next question.

Erica works for a sportswear company. She needs to choose the materials for a new sports bag.

19. Which of the following factors would make a material unsuitable for use in Erica's product?

A. High aesthetic appeal

B. Easy to dispose of

C. Widely available

D. Low durability

ANSWERS AND SOLUTIONS — UNIT TEST

1. B	6. B	11. A	16. D
2. C	7. A	12. D	17. B
3. B	8. C	13. C	18. B
4. D	9. A	14. C	19. D
5. D	10. B	15. C	

1. B

In this situation, the most important consideration in building a winter cabin is having materials with a high R-value to keep the cabin as warm as possible. The cost and weight of the insulation are also important factors. The colour of the insulation is the least important factor, since it is put in the walls and ceilings and is not seen. The correct answer is B.

2. C

An ergonomic chair is designed to reduce the fatigue and discomfort of the user. This type of chair would be most beneficial for the segment of the population that spends most of their time sitting in a chair. Office workers would benefit the most from ergonomic chairs. The correct answer is C.

3. B

Rock climbers use a safety rope in case one of the climbers slips. If this were to happen, the rope would be pulled on both ends. This type of force is called tension. Therefore, when selecting ropes, rock climbers are most concerned with how much tension force the rope can withstand. The correct answer is B.

Compression occurs when the material is squeezed together. The amount of compression the rope can withstand is called compressive strength. Neither compressive strength, the diameter of the rope, nor the colour of the rope would be as important as how much tension the rope can withstand.

4. D

A compression force acts to compress or shorten the object on which it acts. A tension force acts to expand or lengthen the object on which it acts. When these two forces act on a structure at the same time, they strengthen or cancel each other out, depending on their direction and magnitude. In this case, these two forces act together to strengthen the piece of wood, making it strong enough to support the man in the middle of the wood. The correct answer is D.

5. D

The accumulation of ice is a dynamic load. The best way to prevent the structural failure of electrical towers is to design towers to withstand greater dynamic loads. The correct answer is D.

Burying the electrical cables underground is expensive and makes it difficult to access them for repairs. The static load of an electrical tower is the weight of the electrical tower itself. Therefore, they are designed to withstand their static loads. Increasing the height of the electrical towers will make them less stable, not more stable.

6. B

Wind loads apply different amounts of pressure on the surface of a structure. This leads to tension or torsion forces within the structure. The correct answer is B.

7. A

The roof of a building in a snowy climate should be steeply sloped to prevent snow from piling up. It should also be constructed from materials that are strong enough to withstand the compressive force that can result from snow collecting on the roof. The roof type that best shows these properties is Roof P. The correct answer is A.

8. C

The foundation of a structure has to withstand the compressive force from the structure. The compressive force is only in a downward direction. Therefore, the direction of the load on the building is not an important factor when deciding what type of foundation should be used. The correct answer is C.

9. A

Rebecca exerted a force that caused the paper to move in opposite directions, causing the paper to tear. A force that acts to push the parts of an object in opposite directions is a shear force. The correct answer is A.

10. B

Recall that a beam is a box-like structure that supports a load. The bridge in the picture is a series of beams that support the bridge's load. Therefore, the bridge is called a beam bridge, which supports its load from within the bridge deck. The correct answer is B.

An arch bridge is a bridge in which the underside of the structure forms an arch, or half-circle, which supports the bridge's load. Both cable and suspension bridges use materials that hold up the bridge's load from above, rather than supporting the load from within or below the bridge.

11. A

A shell structure has a moulded shape that encloses an empty space. The body of an airplane is moulded and encloses the interior of the plane. The correct answer is A.

Roof trusses, goal posts, and fences are all examples of frame structures.

12. D

The most stable structure is one in which its base is wider than its top. Therefore, a structure that has mass added below its centre of gravity will be the most stable. The correct answer is D.

Adding mass above or to either side of the centre of gravity will cause the structure to become less stable.

13. C

Magnitude is the measure of how much force is applied to the structure. By increasing the weight on the bridge, the judges have increased the magnitude of the force on the bridge. The correct answer is C.

The second weight placed on top of the first weight does not change the point of application, the plane of application, or the direction of the force.

14. C

Water pressure increases with the depth of the water. At the bottom of a body of water, the water is "piled up," so its pressure is greater than higher in the body of water. This places a greater load on the dam at the bottom than at the top. Therefore, a dam must withstand a greater pressure at the bottom than at the top, so many dams are built with triangular bases. The wide bottom withstands the greater load of the water deep below the surface, while the top of the dam can be built thinner to reduce the amount of costly materials used while still being able to resist the load of the water at the top. The correct answer is C.

15. C

The weight in the centre of the bridge exerts a compression force on the bridge. The bending of the bridge pulls on the bridge supports at both ends, causing tension forces to act on the bridge. The correct answer is C.

Shear forces (a push in opposite directions) and torsion forces (a twisting in the structure) are not significant forces in this situation.

16. D

The shelf bends because of the weight of the books. If the shelf breaks, it is because the load of the books is too large for the shelf to support. When a structure experiences a force larger than the maximum load it can support, the force is called an extraordinary load. The correct answer is D.

17. B

Symmetry is a balanced arrangement of mass distributed evenly around its centre. If a line is drawn down the centre of structure *Y*, the mass on both sides of the line is equal. This means that the structure will be stable. The correct answer is B.

18. B

The building site of the tower had weak and unstable soil. In addition, the tower had an insufficient foundation of only three metres, which could not withstand the compressive forces. Therefore, the tower started to lean because of a foundation failure. The correct answer is B.

19. D

Durability describes the material's ability to stand up to wear and tear. Low durability is not usually a desirable property for any product. Erica should look for a material with high durability. The correct answer is D.

Matter and Energy: Pure Substances and Mixtures

MATTER AND ENERGY: PURE SUBSTANCES AND MIXTURES

Table of Correlations

Specific Expectation		Practice Questions	Unit Test Questions	Practice Test 1	Practice Test 2
7ME1:STSE	Evaluate the social and environmental impacts of the use and disposal of pure substances and mixtures;				
7ME1.1	*assess positive and negative environmental impacts related to the disposal of pure substances and mixtures*	1, 2	1	25	
7ME1.2	*assess the impact on society and the environment of different industrial methods of separating mixtures and solutions*	3	2		27
7ME2:Skills	Investigate the properties and applications of pure substances and mixtures;				
7ME2.1	*follow established safety procedures for handling chemicals and apparatus*	4		26	
7ME2.2	*use scientific inquiry/experimentation skills to investigate factors that affect the solubility of a substance and the rate at which substances dissolve*	19, 20, 21, 22	3, 4	27	28
7ME2.3	*investigate processes used for separating different mixtures*	16, 17	5	28	29
7ME2.4	*use scientific inquiry/experimentation skills to investigate the properties of mixtures and solutions*	26, 27, 28	6, 7	29	30
7ME2.5	*use appropriate science and technology vocabulary, including mechanical mixture, solution, solute, insoluble, saturated, unsaturated, and dilute, in oral and written communication*	31, 32	8	30	31
7ME2.6	*use a variety of forms to communicate with different audiences and for a variety of purposes*				
7ME3:Concepts	Demonstrate an understanding of the properties of pure substances and mixtures, and describe these characteristics using the particle theory.				
7ME3.1	*distinguish between pure substances and mixtures*	5, 6	9	31	32
7ME3.2	*state the postulates of the particle theory of matter*	7, 8, 9	10, 11	32	33
7ME3.3	*use the particle theory to describe the difference between pure substances and mixtures*	10, 11	12	33	
7ME3.4	*distinguish between solutions and mechanical mixtures*	12			34
7ME3.5	*describe the processes used to separate mixtures or solutions into their components, and identify some industrial applications of these processes*	13, 14, 15	13, 14	34	35
7ME3.6	*identify the components of a solution*	18	15	35	
7ME3.7	*identify solutes and solvents in various kinds of solutions*	23	16		36
7ME3.8	*describe the concentration of a solution in qualitative terms and in quantitative terms*	24, 25	17	36	37
7ME3.9	*describe the difference between saturated and unsaturated solutions*	29	18	37	
7ME3.10	*explain why water is referred to as the universal solvent*	30	19		38

7ME1.1 assess positive and negative environmental impacts related to the disposal of pure substances and mixtures

Environmental Impacts of Pure Substances and Mixtures

Before a pure substance or a mixture can be used, researchers need to determine how to dispose of the material. Since some substances are harmful to people or the environment, their disposal depends on their properties.

The properties of a pure substance cannot be changed before the substance is discarded. Therefore, the method of disposal needs to account for the possible harmful effects of the substance. For example, nuclear power stations use uranium, a pure substance, to generate electricity. When the power plant has finished using the uranium, it cannot recycle it because uranium remains radioactive for thousands of years. Instead, the uranium has to be disposed of in sealed containers in chambers that are buried 500–1 000 metres underground.

When power plants dispose of the uranium waste, they must carefully choose a location where the uranium will not affect the environment. Some of the factors that the nuclear power plants consider before disposing of used uranium are the stability of the ground, the type of rock in the disposal area, the location of underground water, and the human and animal populations in the area.

Unlike pure substances, mixtures can be separated into the simpler substances that they contain before they are discarded. Therefore, the method of disposal will involve steps where the mixture is changed into less harmful substances.

Sewage is an example of a mixture that contains harmful substances. Industrial plants that create sewage use filters to remove the solid materials from the liquid parts of the sewage. Then, they use chemicals to treat and remove additional harmful substances from the liquid parts.

When the remaining sewage mixture no longer contains harmful substances, it can be reused. The harmful solid substances that were removed can be further treated or buried in special landfills. These landfills are designed to prevent the harmful substances from entering into the environment.

1. A group of people buried their garbage after having a picnic. Several years later, the garbage was dug up. Which of the following pieces of garbage **most likely** changed over time?

A. Milk carton **B.** Plastic cup

C. Pop can **D.** Apple

2. Which of the following types of energy creates a waste disposal problem?

A. Wind **B.** Tidal

C. Solar **D.** Nuclear

7ME1.2 assess the impact on society and the environment of different industrial methods of separating mixtures and solutions

Impacts of Industrial Separation Processes

It is often necessary to separate a mixture into its components, either to remove harmful components or to access useful components. Industrial processes have been developed for separating mixtures on a large scale. These processes can have both positive and negative impacts on society and the environment.

Positive Impacts

- Creates jobs
- Removes harmful components
- Access to marketable components

Negative Impacts

- Requires large facilities
- Factories require a lot of energy
- Generates large amounts of pollution

For example, oil refineries are built to separate the oil removed from the ground, called crude oil, into its various components. Some of the harmful components are removed, and the rest is divided into its useful components, including tars, propane, diesel, gasoline, and jet fuel. Oil refineries provide many products that are necessary every day, such as gasoline, and they try to minimize and remove the harmful components in these products. As well, oil refineries are good for the economy because they provide jobs for many people.

However, oil refineries are often large, sprawling complexes. They use up a lot of land, and they produce odours and noises that are offensive to people. For this reason, they are often located away from populated areas. Refineries require a lot of energy and water to perform their separation techniques, and they produce a lot of air and water pollution.

Oil refineries produce a lot of pollution.

Not all industrial separation methods produce as much pollution as oil refineries. Maple syrup production involves the evaporation of the water component in maple tree sap. This concentrates the sugar in the sap. In this process, the only substance that is released into the environment is the water. However, a lot of energy is used during the evaporation process. For 40 litres of sap, 39 litres of water must boil off to make maple syrup. Unfortunately, producing and using heating fuel pollutes the air and water.

3. To help protect the environment, oil refineries and power plants need to minimize the amount of sulfur and nitrogen oxide gases released into the atmosphere because these gases can cause

A. acid rain

B. foul odours

C. topsoil erosion

D. excessive moss growth

7ME2.1 follow established safety procedures for handling chemicals and apparatus

Safety in Chemistry

It is important to follow established safety procedures when handling chemicals and apparatus. Some of the most important safety rules are:

- Always wash your hands after handling chemicals
- Make sure all bottles and chemicals are properly labelled
- Read and follow all univeral warning symbols on containers
- Never remove chemicals or other materials from the laboratory
- Never return chemicals that are not used to their original container or bottle
- Never touch your face, mouth, body, or eyes when handling chemicals or laboratory equipment

The following symbols are warning labels that may appear on the storage containers for materials in the chemistry laboratory in your school. You will also see them on the containers for many different chemicals that you use at home. Each of these symbols has a definition that accompanies it here, but these definitions are not present on the containers. It is very important that you can recognize what they mean so that you can handle these chemicals properly.

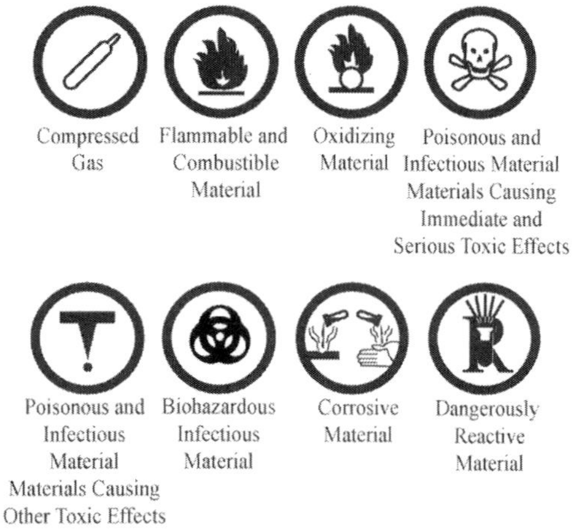

Look for a full list of safety procedures in your science lab or ask your teacher if you are unclear.

Use the following information to answer the next question.

Marc carries out an experiment in his school laboratory using a strong acid. He wears a lab coat to protect his clothes and arms, and he wears safety gloves to protect his hands.

4. What other precaution should Marc take during his experiment to be even safer?

A. Stand back farther from the flask

B. Wear safety goggles over his glasses

C. Have someone help him pour the liquid

D. Put paper towel down on the counter in case he spills

7ME3.1 distinguish between pure substances and mixtures

Pure Substances and Mixtures

Everything is made of matter. However, matter can be divided into two categories: pure substances and mixtures. The properties of pure substances and mixtures can be investigated in the laboratory.

Pure Substances

A **pure substance** is matter that contains only a single substance. A pure substance cannot break down into a simpler substance. Examples of pure substances include distilled water, sugar, and copper pipes.

Mixtures

A **mixture** is matter that is made up of two or more pure substances mixed together. Chocolate chip cookie dough is a mixture of flour, sugar, eggs, salt, and cocoa. Mixtures also occur in nature, such as soil and salt water.

Chocolate chip cookie

Use the following information to answer the next question.

Arnold created the following chart to classify materials as either pure substances or mixtures.

Pure Substances	Mixtures
Distilled water	Oatmeal raisin cookies
Carbon dioxide	Fruit salad
Salt	Copper pipe
	Paint

5. Which of the materials did Arnold classify **incorrectly**?

A. Oatmeal raisin cookies

B. Carbon dioxide

C. Distilled water

D. Copper pipe

6. Which of the following objects is a pure substance?

A. Chocolate chip cookies

B. Salad dressing

C. Gravel

D. Salt

7ME3.2 state the postulates of the particle theory of matter

Particle Theory of Matter

The particle theory of matter states that:

- All matter is made up of tiny particles that are in constant motion.
- Matter occurs in three different states: solid, liquid, and gas.
- The speed of the particle's motion determines the state in which the matter occurs. The faster the particles move, the more energy the particles have.
- The energy of the particles in matter is measured as its temperature. Therefore, the state of matter relates directly to its temperature: matter is solid at lower temperatures. As the temperature increases, the matter changes from solid into liquid, and then from liquid into gas.

Solids

The particles in solid matter are packed closely together. They are packed too tightly to move past each other, so instead they vibrate in place. As a result, solids keep their shape.

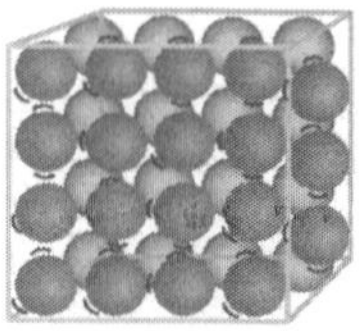

Particles in a solid

Liquids

The particles in liquid matter are not packed as tightly as they are in solids. They have enough space to move past each other, so they move faster than the particles in a solid. Therefore, liquids can flow as their particles move past one another.

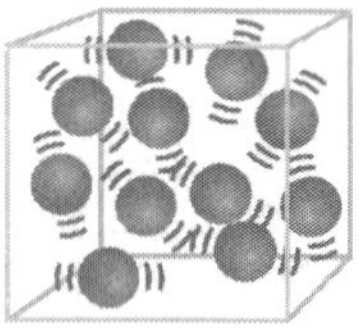

Particles in a liquid

Gases

The particles in gaseous matter have more space between them than in liquids or solids. The particles move very fast, so they can flow freely past each other.

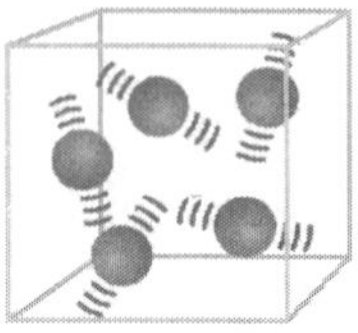

Particles in a gas

Changing States

The diagram below shows how the movement of particles changes when heated or cooled. When a solid heats up, the particles begin to move faster and slide around each other. This breaks some of the bonds between the particles, and the solid changes into a liquid. When a liquid heats up, the particles begin to move even faster. This breaks additional bonds between the particles, and the liquid changes into a gas.

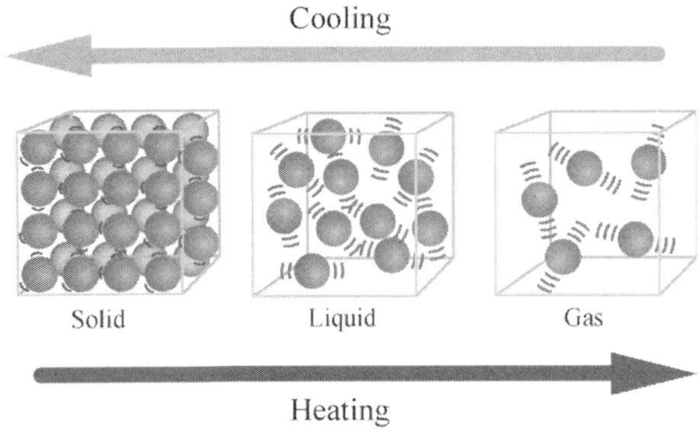

Cooling a gas causes the particles to slow down and take up less space. The gas becomes a liquid. Cooling a liquid causes the particles to slow down and take up less space. The liquid then becomes a solid.

7. Which of the following statements is **not** part of the particle theory?
   A. All matter is made up of particles.
   B. The particles in gases are close together.
   C. All the particles in a pure substance are identical.
   D. The temperature affects the speed at which the particles move.

Use the following information to answer the next question.

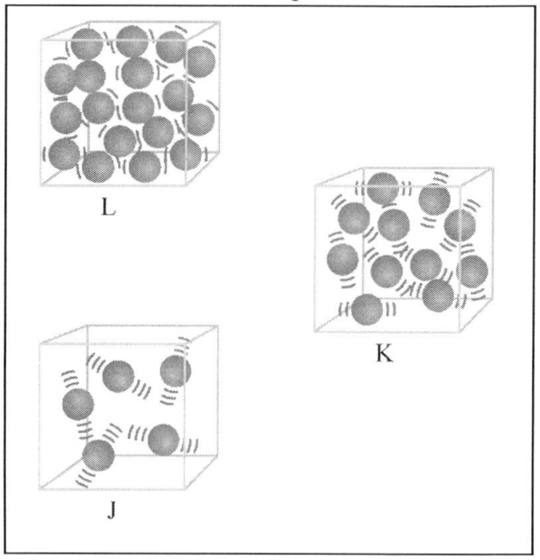

8. What is the order of the given diagrams representing the particles in matter if they are arranged according to their states of matter, in the order of solid, liquid, and gas?
   A. Diagram K, diagram J, diagram L
   B. Diagram L, diagram K, diagram J
   C. Diagram K, diagram L, diagram J
   D. Diagram L, diagram J, diagram K

9. Which of the following changes does **not** occur when a solid becomes a liquid?
   A. The particles gain energy
   B. The distance between the particles increases
   C. The bonds that hold the particles together become stronger
   D. The particles that make up the substance vibrate faster in the liquid

7ME3.3 use the particle theory to describe the difference between pure substances and mixtures

Applying the Particle Theory

A pure substance is made up of only one kind of particle. There are strong forces of attraction between the identical particles in a pure substance. Distilled water is a pure substance that is made up of only water particles.

The following diagrams show how the particles of distilled water might look. Distilled water is a pure substance whether it is a frozen solid, a warm liquid, or a boiling- hot gas.

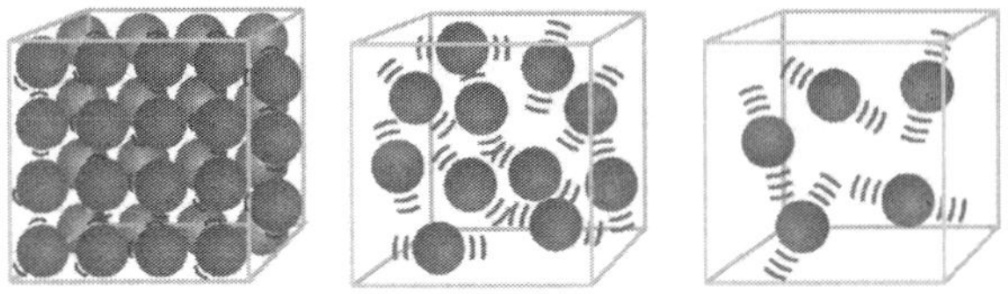

A mixture is made up of two or more different kinds of particles. Two different pure substances, such as water and salt, can mix together to create a mixture.

In a salt-water mixture, the salt particles will break apart and spread out in the water. The salt particles attract the water particles and cling to them. The mixture contains both salt particles and water particles.

The following diagram shows how the particles in a salt-water mixture might look. The water particles are shown in dark grey and the salt particles are shown in light grey.

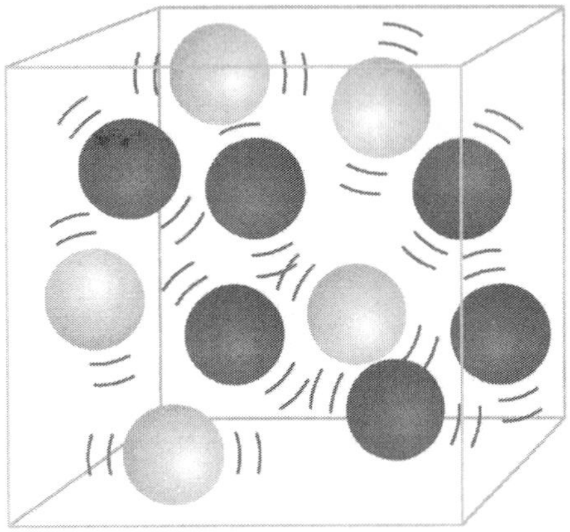

The particles in a solution.

Use the following information to answer the next question.

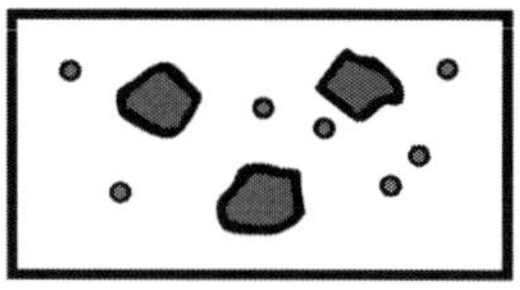

Diagram 1

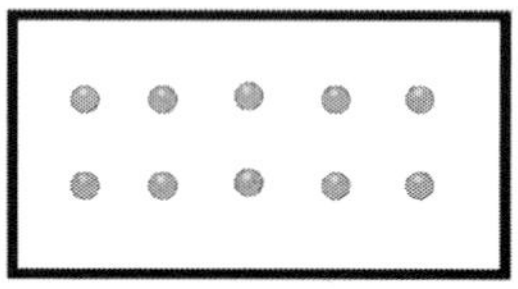

Diagram 2

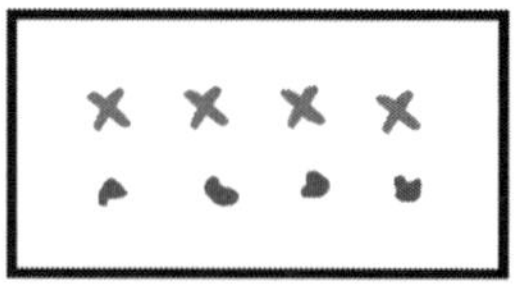

Diagram 3

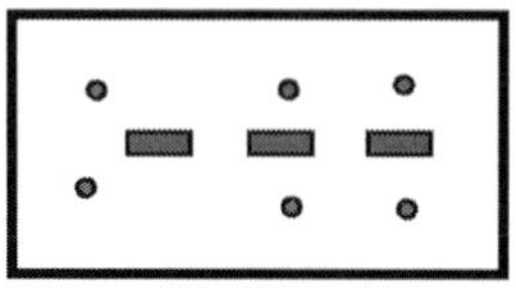

Diagram 4

Terri's teacher showed her diagrams of different materials.

10. Which of the diagrams represents a pure substance?

A. Diagram 1 **B.** Diagram 2

C. Diagram 3 **D.** Diagram 4

Use the following information to answer the next question.

Jacoby tried to explain the particle theory of matter to his friend. He told his friend the following four statements about matter:

I. All matter is made up of particles.
II. There are no spaces between particles in a solid.
III. Particles in a gas move more quickly than in a solid.
IV. Different substances are made up of the same types of particles.

11. Which two of Jacoby's statements about the particle theory of matter are **false**?

A. Statements I and II

B. Statements I and III

C. Statements II and III

D. Statements II and IV

7ME3.4 distinguish between solutions and mechanical mixtures

Types of Mixtures

A mixture is made up of two or more pure substances. There are two types of mixtures: **mechanical mixtures** and **solutions**.

Mechanical Mixtures

A mechanical mixture is any mixture in which the different parts of the mixture are visible. Gravel is an example of a mechanical mixture. Mechanical mixtures can be made of a combination of solids, liquids, and gases.

Solutions

A solution is a mixture in which the different parts mix thoroughly and completely with each other. The different parts cannot be seen. Salt mixed with water is a solution. Once mixed, you can no longer see the salt particles, even though they are still there. Solutions can also be a mixture of solids, liquids, and gases.

12. Which of the following pairs of food items are mechanical mixtures?

A. Mixed nuts and vinegar

B. Vinegar and apple juice

C. Apple juice and tossed salad

D. Tossed salad and mixed nuts

7ME3.5 describe the processes used to separate mixtures or solutions into their components, and identify some industrial applications of these processes

7ME2.3 investigate processes used for separating different mixtures

Separating Mixtures

There are times when it is useful to separate a mixture into its parts. The different substances in a mixture have different physical properties. These differences can be used to separate the substances from the mixture. Different methods of separation focus on different physical properties.

Evaporation

The process of evaporation separates a mixture made of a solid within a liquid. This process involves heating the solution until the liquid boils and evaporates, or turns into vapour, leaving only the solid material behind. Evaporation is used to make maple syrup. Maple syrup comes from the sap of a maple tree, which consists of water and sugar. Most of the water from the sap evaporates, leaving mostly sugar behind.

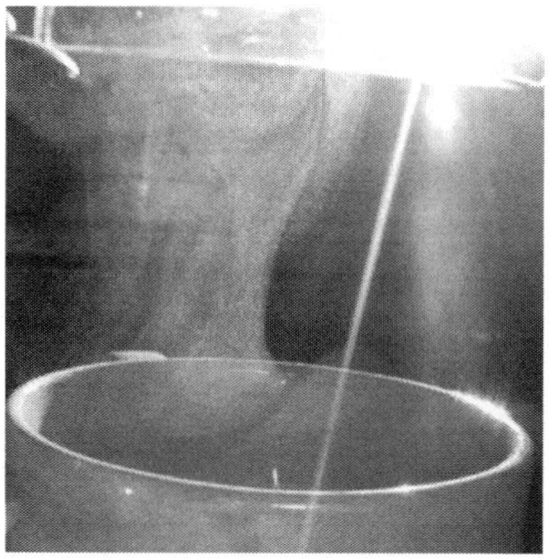

Maple syrup is made by evaporation

DISTILLATION

The process of distillation separates mixtures of two or more liquids, or solid-liquid mixtures. Distillation uses evaporation to remove one or more of the liquids, but the vapour is collected during distillation. Different liquids usually have different boiling temperatures. Therefore, in a solution of two or more liquids, one liquid will boil first. A condenser collects the vapour of this liquid. The vapour cools in the condenser and turns into a liquid again.

The petroleum industry uses this process to separate crude oil into different oils and gases. The crude oil is heated to a high temperature, and the refinery's condensers collect the different gases produced. One product of this process is gasoline.

An oil refinery uses distillation

SIFTING

Sifting is a process that separates a mechanical mixture that comprises two or more solids of different sizes. This process uses a mesh filter that only allows the smaller pieces of the mixture to pass through. The mixture pours through the mesh, which traps the particles of the larger solid in the mesh.

A sifting mesh

FILTRATION

Similar to sifting, filtration uses a filter to separate a mixture into its parts. However, filtration removes solids from a solid-liquid mixture. Many different materials can make up a filter, including paper and cotton. The process of making jams and jellies uses a cheesecloth filter to separate the skins and seeds from the fruit liquid.

A cheesecloth filter

MAGNETISM

If one component of a mechanical mixture is magnetic, then magnetism can be used to separate the mixture. Recycling depots use this process to separate metal tin cans from a mixture of glass, paper, and plastic.

INVESTIGATING SEPARATION PROCESSES

The properties of the substances within a mixture determine which separation process is most appropriate. The effectiveness of using one process over another can be investigated in a laboratory.

13. Gasoline is separated from crude oil by the process of

A. sifting　　**B.** filtration

C. distillation　　**D.** magnetism

Use the following information to answer the next question.

When hematite ore is mined, many impurities and unwanted things are collected along with it. Mining companies use a separation technique to separate these impurities and unwanted substances from the hematite ore.

14. The separation technique **most likely** used to separate hematite from the impurities and unwanted materials is

A. magnetic separation

B. hand separation

C. distillation

D. sifting

Use the following information to answer the next question.

Kendra's science teacher gives her four different mixtures and asks her to determine which of the mixtures can be separated using a magnet.

15. Which of the following mixtures can Kendra separate using a magnet?

A. Sand and rocks

B. Stones and marbles

C. Iron filings and sand

D. Nickel particles and iron filings

Use the following information to answer the next question.

Ruth sets up an apparatus for making salt water drinkable.

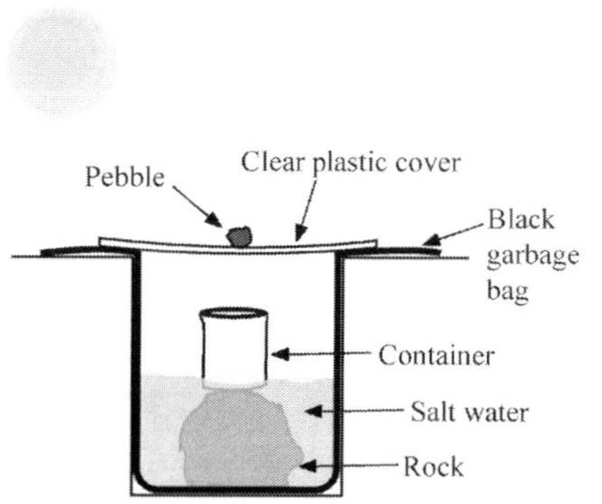

16. Which of the following processes will Ruth's water purification apparatus **not** perform?

A. Filtration **B.** Distillation

C. Evaporation **D.** Condensation

17. Which of the following statements **best** describes filtration?

A. A process by which two non-dissolving substances are mixed.

B. A process by which components of a mixture are separated.

C. A process by which metals are separated from other metals.

D. A process by which atoms are separated from molecules.

7ME3.6 identify the components of a solution

7ME2.2 use scientific inquiry/experimentation skills to investigate factors that affect the solubility of a substance and the rate at which substances dissolve

Components of a Solution

Solutions are made up of two parts:

Solvent– the substance in a solution that does the dissolving. It is also the substance that is present in the largest amount. For example, in seawater, water is the solvent.

Solute– the substance in a solution that is dissolved. It is a substance that is present in a smaller amount than the solvent. For example, in seawater, salt is a solute.

Solutions are often thought of as having solid solutes dissolved in liquid solvents. However, both the solutes and solvents can be solid, liquid, or gas.

Investigating Solubility

Many factors can affect the ability of one substance to dissolve into another or the rate at which the substance dissolves. Some of these factors include:

- temperature
- size of the particles
- type of solute and solvent
- stirring and motion of the substances

These factors can be studied in laboratory experiments. Recall that a good laboratory experiment:

- asks questions that arise from practical problems and issues
- builds fair-testing elements into the experimental design
- uses safe and appropriate tools and equipment to observe and measure results
- records and organizes data using standard measurements in tables, graphs, or charts
- identifies patterns in the data, summarizes the data, and suggests explanations for discrepancies
- evaluates the experimental design and suggests improvements
- communicates the results of the experiments clearly

18. Which of the following statements regarding solutions is **true**?

A. A solution can easily contain more than one solute.

B. A solute is the substance that is present only in the lowest quantity in a solution.

C. During the formation of a solution, the physical state of the solute always changes.

D. During the formation of a solution, the physical state of the solvent always changes.

Use the following information to answer the next question.

Dennis designed an experiment to find out whether sand or sugar dissolves faster in water?

19. After testing the two substances, Dennis **most likely** found that the

A. sand dissolved, but the sugar did not dissolve

B. sugar dissolved, but the sand did not dissolve

C. sand dissolved faster than the sugar dissolved

D. sugar dissolved faster than the sand dissolved

20. The sugar in a sugar cube dissolves in liquid more quickly if the cube is crushed than if it is left whole because the rate at which sugar dissolves is affected by the

A. temperature

B. exposed surface area

C. energy in the molecules

D. changing concentration of materials

Use the following information to answer the next question.

Jeremy did an experiment to determine the rate of dissolving 10 g of sugar in 100 mL of water under different conditions. The diagram shows the different conditions that Jeremy tested.

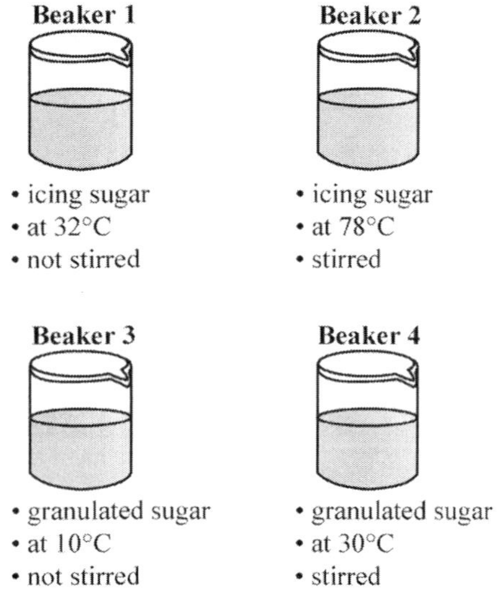

21. Which of the following charts identifies the beakers that dissolved the sugar the fastest and the slowest?

A.

Fastest	Slowest
Beaker 1	Beaker 3

B.

Fastest	Slowest
Beaker 1	Beaker 4

C.

Fastest	Slowest
Beaker 2	Beaker 3

D.

Fastest	Slowest
Beaker 2	Beaker 4

Use the following information to answer the next question.

Megan carried out a science experiment in which she dissolved sugar in one litre of water. She gradually increased the temperature of the solution and recorded the amount of sugar that dissolved at each temperature.

Temperature of Solution (°C)	Amount of Sugar Dissolved (g)
0	250
15	320
30	440
45	580
60	900

Open Response

22. Using the information in the table, draw and label a line graph to show the amount of sugar dissolved versus the temperature of the solution.

7ME3.7 identify solutes and solvents in various kinds of solutions

Identifying Solvents and Solutes in Everyday Solutions

People use different solutions everywhere. Water is probably used as the solvent in many of these solutions. However, other substances can also serve as the solvent in solutions.

An iodine solution

Many solutions have liquids as the solvent. For example, pharmacists make solutions of iodine by adding three drops of iodine to one litre of alcohol. In this case, alcohol is present in the largest amount in the solution. Therefore, alcohol is the solvent, and iodine is the solute. Liquid solvents are also used as cleaning supplies. For example, paint thinner is a solvent that dissolves paint (solute) from a paintbrush.

Many solids are also solutions. For example, bronze is a solution of copper with tin as the main additive. It is used to make bells, cymbals, and saxophones. A brass bell is a solution containing copper as the solvent and tin as a solute.

Brass Bell

Brass cymbals

Brass saxophone

Solutions can also contain or be made up of gases. For example, a soft drink is a solution composed of purified water with carbon dioxide gas dissolved in it. In this case, carbon dioxide is a solute. Gases can also serve as solvents. For example, air is a solution of gases with a gas as the solvent. The greatest amount of gas in air is nitrogen, the solvent, which is mixed with other gases, such as oxygen.

A soft drink contains a gas solute

23. Which of the following solutions contains both a solute and a solvent in liquid states?

A. Iodine solution

B. Saltwater solution

C. Maple syrup solution

D. Bronze-metal solution

7ME3.8 describe the concentration of a solution in qualitative terms and in quantitative terms

Describing Solutions: Concentration

While a solution is a mixture of a solvent and at least one solute, a solution can contain several solutes. The amount of solute dissolved within a solution is the **concentration** of the solution. The concentration can be described both qualitatively and quantitatively.

Qualitative Descriptions

A qualitative description of concentration compares the concentration of one solution with that of another. If the solutions do not have the same concentration, then one solution will be more concentrated, and the other will be more dilute. These are relative terms that describe the difference between the amount of solute in a solution compared with the amount of solvent.

- Dilute— the solution has few solute particles compared to the number of solvent particles.
- Concentrated— the solution has many solute particles compared to the number solvent particles.

Quantitative Descriptions

A quantitative description of concentration involves measuring the exact amount of solute compared with the exact amount of solvent. This results in the formula to calculate concentration, which is given below:

$$\text{Concentration} = \frac{\text{amount of solute}}{\text{amount of solvent}}$$

Example

If one sugar cube, with a mass of 1.2 g, dissolves in a 250 mL cup of tea, what is the concentration of sugar in the tea?

In this case, the sugar is the solute and the tea is the solvent. The amount of solute is 1.2 g, and the amount of solvent is 250 mL. This is written into the formula for concentration as:

$$\text{Concentration} = \frac{1.2\text{ g}}{250\text{ mL}}$$
$$= 0.0048\text{ g/mL}$$

The concentration of sugar in the tea is 0.0048 g/mL. Note that the units for concentration will change depending how the solute and solvent are measured.

Use the following information to answer the next question.

Jamie's teacher told the class that more particle collisions will occur in a chemical reaction if they use a highly concentrated solution rather than a diluted solution.

24. The particles in the concentrated solution **probably** collide more frequently because

A. they move faster

B. there are more of them

C. they become larger in size

D. there is more exposed surface area

Use the following information to answer the next question.

Jillian made a saltwater solution by dissolving 10 g of salt in 100 mL of water. Then she heated the solution so that half of the water evaporated.

25. Which of the following statements about Jillian's solution is **true**?

A. The concentration of the saltwater solution decreases as the solution heats up.

B. As the solution heats up, the amount of solvent in the saltwater solution increases.

C. The concentration of the saltwater solution remains the same as the solution heats up.

D. As the solution heats up, the amount of solute in the saltwater solution remains the same.

7ME2.4 use scientific inquiry/experimentation skills to investigate the properties of mixtures and solutions

7ME3.9 describe the difference between saturated and unsaturated solutions

Solutions

A solution consists of a solute dissolved into a solvent. However, there is a maximum amount of solute that can be dissolved in the solvent. Once the maximum amount of solute dissolves, the solvent will not dissolve any more solute. The solution has reached the point of saturation; it is **saturated**.

For example, when juice crystals are added to water, there is a point when the crystals will no longer dissolve because the water will not hold any more of the crystals. This is the point of saturation, and the juice is described as saturated.

- A **saturated** solution is a solution in which the solvent cannot dissolve any more solute.
- An **unsaturated** solution is a solution in which the solvent could still dissolve more solute. An unsaturated solution has not reached the saturation point.

The ability of a solute to dissolve in a solvent is a physical property of the solute called solubility. Whether or not a solute is **soluble** depends on three factors:

- Temperature
- Type of solute
- Type of solvent

If a solute cannot dissolve at all in a solvent, the solute is called **insoluble**. Oil, for example, is insoluble in water. This is seen in salad dressing, where oil sits on top of the water and does not dissolve.

26. At room temperature, Melissa dissolves 10 g of potassium nitrate into 50 g of water to get a saturated solution. To dissolve 20 g of the same solute in the same solvent, Melissa needs to

A. heat the solution

B. cool the solution

C. alternately cool and heat the solution

D. add extra solute and continuously stir the solution

Use the following information to answer the next question.

Markus makes some iced tea from a powder. He puts several heaping teaspoons of the powder into a glass, adds water, and stirs the mixture. No matter how much he stirs the mixture, some of the powder does not dissolve.

27. The **most likely** reason that some of the powder does not dissolve is that

A. Markus should let the powder dissolve on its own

B. the iced tea powder needs sugar to help it dissolve

C. Markus added more iced tea powder than the water could dissolve

D. even though Markus stirs for a long time, he does not stir it fast enough

28. Emily makes a saturated solution of table salt and water. She **cannot** add more solute to the solution by increasing the temperature of the solution because

A. table salt reacts with water at high temperatures

B. table salt becomes insoluble in water at high temperatures

C. the solubility of table salt in water decreases with an increase in temperature

D. the solubility of table salt in water changes very slightly with a rise in temperature

Use the following information to answer the next question.

Dave needs to carry out an experiment at home for homework. In his experiment, he needs 100 g of sugar to make a saturated solution in 1 000 mL of water.

29. If Dave uses only half the amount of water in his experiment, then how much sugar does he need to use in order to make a saturated solution?

A. Half as much

B. Twice as much

C. The same amount

D. Three-quarters of the amount

7ME3.10 explain why water is referred to as the universal solvent

Water: The Universal Solvent

Water is a very common and important substance on Earth. Water particles have special properties that allow them to dissolve the particles of many different solutes. As a result, water is the most common solvent in nature.

Water dissolves many different salts to make salt water. Rainwater dissolves nutrients in the soil to be absorbed by plants. A rushing mountain stream erodes rocks and carries away dissolved minerals from the rocks. Water also dissolves and transfers nutrients that are vital for animals and plants. In fact, the human body is 65–80% composed of water acting as a solvent. Because water can dissolve so many different solutes, it is considered the universal solvent.

Water can dissolve parts of rock

30. Water is often called the "universal solvent" because it

A. is dissolved into most mixtures

B. dissolves many different solutes

C. is the most common substance in the universe

D. makes up the largest component of the human body

7ME2.5 use appropriate science and technology vocabulary, including mechanical mixture, solution, solute, insoluble, saturated, unsaturated, and dilute, in oral and written communication

Communicating in Science

It might seem that science has its own language. In a way, it does. When you speak and write about science, you need to use the proper terminology. The important terms for this unit are on the following list found below. It is important that you understand these terms and that you can use them properly. If you need help understanding these terms, refer to the other lessons in this unit or use the glossary in the back of this *Key*.

Important Terms in Matter and Energy

- dilute
- solute
- solvent
- solution
- insoluble
- saturated
- mechanical mixture

31. A saturated solution can change into an unsaturated solution by

A. stirring the solution vigorously

B. adding more solvent to the solution

C. lowering the temperature of the solution

D. increasing the amount of solute in the solution

Use the following information to answer the next question.

Shayna's teacher showed her class a table that places different mixtures into different categories. When Shayna copied the table into her notebook, she forgot to write down the labels for each column. She looked at each of the mixtures listed in the chart and tried to come up with a label for each column.

Different Types of Mixtures

I	*II*	*III*
Sand and pebbles	Milk and oil	Water and flour
Dry cement and gravel	Oil and vinegar	Flour and milk
Salt and baking powder	Molasses and corn syrup	Baking soda and water

32. Which of the following tables identifies the **best** label for each column?

A.

I	*II*	*III*
Liquid Mixtures	Solid Mixtures	Solid with Liquid Mixtures

B.

I	*II*	*III*
Solid Mixtures	Liquid Mixtures	Solid with Liquid Mixtures

C.

I	*II*	*III*
Liquid Mixtures	Solid with Liquid Mixtures	Solid Mixtures

D.

I	*II*	*III*
Solid with Liquid Mixtures	Solid Mixtures	Liquid Mixtures

ANSWERS AND SOLUTIONS
MATTER AND ENERGY: PURE SUBSTANCES AND MIXTURES

1. D	8. B	15. C	22. OR	29. A
2. D	9. C	16. A	23. A	30. B
3. A	10. B	17. B	24. B	31. B
4. B	11. D	18. A	25. D	32. B
5. D	12. D	19. B	26. A	
6. D	13. C	20. B	27. C	
7. B	14. A	21. C	28. D	

1. D

Each of the pieces of garbage is an example of a mixture. Human-made mixtures, such as the milk carton, plastic cup, and pop can, degrade, or change, much slower than organic mixtures, such as the apple. The correct answer is D.

2. D

Although nuclear energy has some benefits, its waste is radioactive and does not easily decompose. As a result, nuclear waste is difficult to dispose of. The correct answer is D.

Wind, tidal, and solar energy do not produce waste.

3. A

The gases sulfur oxide and nitrogen oxide both cause acid rain when they are released into the atmosphere. Sulfur dioxide, for example, reacts with oxygen and water vapour to form sulfurous acid and sulfuric acid. As a result, before refineries and power plants release the waste gases they produce into the air, they must remove as much sulfur and nitrogen oxide gases as possible. The correct answer is A.

Sulfur oxide can have an unpleasant odour, but this is not its greatest environmental impact. Wind and water cause topsoil erosion, not sulfur or nitrogen oxide gases. Since sulfur and nitrogen oxide create acid rain, they will not cause excessive moss growth.

4. B

Marc's experiment involves using a strong acid. He wears rubber gloves and a lab coat to protect his skin from the acid. The glasses he wears are not safety glasses, so they do not protect his eyes properly in case some of the chemical splashes onto his face. He should wear safety goggles over top of his regular glasses to better protect his eyes. The correct answer is B.

5. D

A copper pipe contains only a single substance, so it belongs in the pure substances column. Mixtures, like oatmeal raisin cookies, fruit salad, and paint, contain several different substances combined together. The correct answer is D.

6. D

Salt is a pure substance. It is made up of only one type of particle. The correct answer is D.

Chocolate chip cookies, salad dressing, and gravel are all mixtures.

7. B

The particles in liquids and solids are close together and have strong forces of attraction between them. The particles in gases have larger spaces between them, so they are not close together. The correct answer is B.

8. B

The particle theory of matter provides models for the behaviour of particles in solids, liquids, and gases. The spacing of the particles goes from being close together in a solid to being widely spaced in a gas. The relative motion of the particles goes from being very slow to being very fast and random. The order of the given diagrams is then given as:
Diagram L, diagram K, diagram J

The correct answer is B.

9. C

When a solid changes into a liquid, the bonds that hold the particles together weaken and break. This allows the particles to move farther away and even past one another, which allows the substance to flow. The correct answer is C.

The process of changing a solid into a liquid requires energy. As energy is applied to the particles in a substance, the particles gain this energy and begin to vibrate faster. As the particles vibrate faster, their bonds weaken and break. The particles then move apart from one another, which means that the distance between the particles increases.

10. B

A pure substance contains only one kind of matter. Diagram 2 shows only one kind of matter.

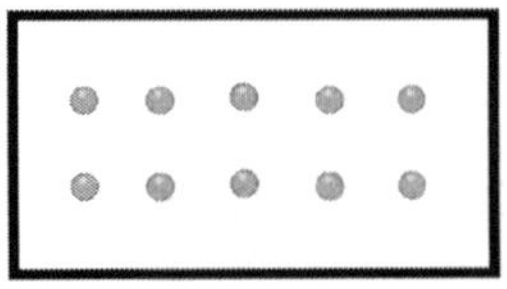

11. D

Even though the particles in a solid are close together, there are spaces between them. Therefore, statement II is incorrect. Different substances are made up of different types of particles, so statement IV is also incorrect. The correct answer is D.

12. D

A mechanical mixture is a combination of different substances in which the different parts can be seen, such as a tossed salad and mixed nuts. The correct answer is D.

A mixture in which the different parts cannot be distinguished, such as apple juice and vinegar, is called a solution.

13. C

Gasoline is a liquid fuel that is also a component of crude oil. It is separated from crude oil by the process of distillation. The correct answer is C.

14. A

Hematite is an iron ore, and iron is a magnetic substance. Therefore, magnetic separation can be used to separate hematite from non-magnetic impurities and unwanted substances. The correct answer is A.

Hand separation is not used to separate hematite from unwanted substances, as the process would take a very long time and be very inefficient. Distillation can only be used for separating a liquid from a mixture. Hematite and its unwanted substances are both solids, so distillation cannot separate hematite from unwanted substances. For sifting, the particle sizes of the substances must be very different. This is not the case with mined materials, so sifting cannot separate hematite from unwanted substances.

15. C

Mixtures of magnetic and non-magnetic materials can be separated with a magnet. The mixture of iron filings and sand can be separated using a magnet because iron filings are magnetic and sand is non-magnetic. A magnet cannot separate mixtures of non-magnetic materials, like a sand and rock mixture or a stone and marble mixture, or mixtures that are made of only magnetic materials, like a nickel and iron mixture.

16. A

There is no filter in the apparatus; therefore the apparatus will not carry out filtration. The correct answer is A.

In this apparatus, the sun will cause the water to evaporate. The water vapour will condense on the plastic cover. The condensation will be collected in the small container. The combined processes of evaporation and condensation is called distillation.

17. B

A mixture of two components can be separated through the process of filtration. For example, a mixture of sand and water can be separated by filtration. The water passes through a filter paper, while the sand is held back. The process of filtration works by allowing smaller particles to pass through the filter, while larger particles are held behind by the filter. The correct answer is B.

18. A

A solution is a mixture of two or more substances. This means that a solution can easily contain more than one solute. The correct answer is A.

When a solution is made of three or more substances, the substance present in the greatest amount is the solvent. The substances that are present in amounts less than the solvent are the solutes.

The physical state of a solute does not always change. It will change only when it is in a state different from that of the solvent. For example, when honey is added to water to make a solution, the physical state of honey does not change, since honey remains a liquid.

19. B

Water can break sugar particle bonds; therefore sugar can dissolve in water. Water cannot break sand particle bonds; therefore sand does not dissolve in water. Dennis most likely found that the sugar dissolved but that the sand did not. The correct answer is B.

20. B

Small solute particles dissolve more quickly than large particles because there is more exposed surface area on which the solvent particles can act. The correct answer is B.

21. C

Icing sugar particles are smaller than granulated sugar particles, so icing sugar will dissolve faster because there is more surface area. As well, increasing the temperature increases the dissolving rate because it makes the particles move faster, which results in the solvent particles bumping into solute particles faster. Stirring also increases the dissolving rate because it causes the solvent particles to move and bump into solute particles.

In beaker 2, the sugar is icing sugar, the water is warmer than any of the other beakers, and the solution is stirred, so the sugar in beaker 2 will dissolve the fastest. Since beaker 3 has the larger granulated sugar particles, the lowest temperature, and it is not stirred, the sugar in beaker 2 will dissolve the slowest. The correct answer is C.

22. OR

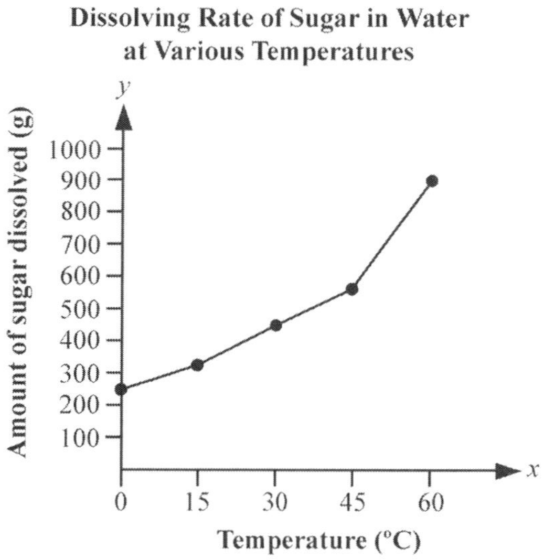

23. A

An iodine solution contains alcohol as the solvent and iodine as the solute, and both are in liquid state. The correct answer is A.

A saltwater solution contains salt as the solute, which is in a solid state, and liquid water as the solvent. A maple syrup solution contains sugar as the solute, which is in a solid state, and liquid water as the solvent. Bronze metal contains tin as a solute, which is in a solid state, and copper as the solvent, which is also in a solid state.

24. B

The concentration of a solution refers to the number of solute and solvent particles, not the speed or size of particles. The more concentrated a solution is, the more solute particles there are in the solution. When there are more solute particles in a solution, they will collide more frequently. The correct answer is B.

25. D

In the saltwater solution, the solute is the salt, and the solvent is the water. As the water evaporates, the amount of salt in the solution remains the same; therefore the amount of solute remains the same. The correct answer is D.

As the water evaporates, the amount of solvent in the solution decreases. As the amount of water in the solution decreases, there is more salt in the solution compared to the amount of water, so the concentration of the solution increases.

26. A

The solubility of potassium nitrate in water rapidly increases with temperature. Therefore, if the solution is heated, the capacity of the solvent to hold more solute increases. Melissa can dissolve 20 g of potassium nitrate in the water by heating the solution. The correct answer is A.

27. C

The iced tea powder does not completely dissolve because the iced tea solution is saturated. A solution is saturated when the solvent particles cannot dissolve any more added solute particles.
The correct answer is C.

28. D

The solubility of table salt, or sodium chloride, in water remains almost the same when the temperature rises. Therefore, increasing the temperature of the solution will not make it possible to dissolve more solute in an already saturated solution of sodium chloride. The correct answer is D.

29. A

The solubility of a compound is directly related to the amount of the solvent used. If the amount of water is reduced by half, then the amount of sugar needed to make a saturated solution is also reduced by half. The correct answer is A.

30. B

Water is called the universal solvent because it can dissolve many different substances. The correct answer is B.

31. B

A saturated solution is one where the solvent particles cannot dissolve any more added solute particles. By adding more solvent to the solution, it can dissolve more added solute particles and change into an unsaturated solution. The correct answer is B.

32. B

Column *I* contains mixtures that are made from two solids. Column *II* is made up of mixtures that are made from two liquids, and column *III* is made up of mixtures that are made from both liquids and solids together. Therefore, the table that identifies the correct column labels is as follows.

I	***II***	***III***
Solid Mixtures	Liquid Mixtures	Solid with Liquid Mixtures

UNIT TEST — MATTER AND ENERGY: PURE SUBSTANCES AND MIXTURES

1. The **best** disposal method for a pure copper substance, such as a copper pipe, is to

A. separate the harmful components

B. bury it in sealed drums

C. dispose it in a landfill

D. recycle it

Use the following information to answer the next question.

> Oil refineries use distillation to refine crude oil into parts. The refining process has many negative effects on society and the environment.

2. Which of the following effects of an oil refinery is **not** a negative effect?

A. Oil refineries produce noise and odours.

B. Oil refineries are large and sprawling complexes.

C. There is a risk of fire and explosion at oil refineries.

D. There is a risk of oil spills at oil refineries during crude oil extraction.

Use the following information to answer the next question.

> Melad tries to dissolve sugar in water. After some time, he cannot dissolve any more sugar. However, Melad wants to dissolve more sugar and still have a clear solution.

3. What can Melad do in order to dissolve more sugar and still have a clear solution?

A. Heat up the solution

B. Cool down the solution

C. Put the solution in the light

D. Keep the solution in the dark

Use the following information to answer the next question.

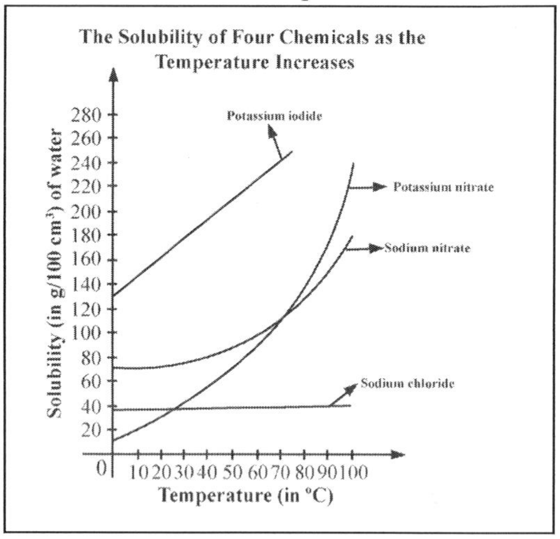

4. Which of the following chemicals shows the **least** increase in solubility with an increase in temperature?

A. Sodium nitrate

B. Sodium chloride

C. Potassium iodide

D. Potassium nitrate

Use the following information to answer the next question.

In class, Maria learns that distilled water is the purest form of water. She intends to purify her tap water at home by distillation.

5. Which of the following devices shows the **best** way for Maria to purify her tap water?

A.

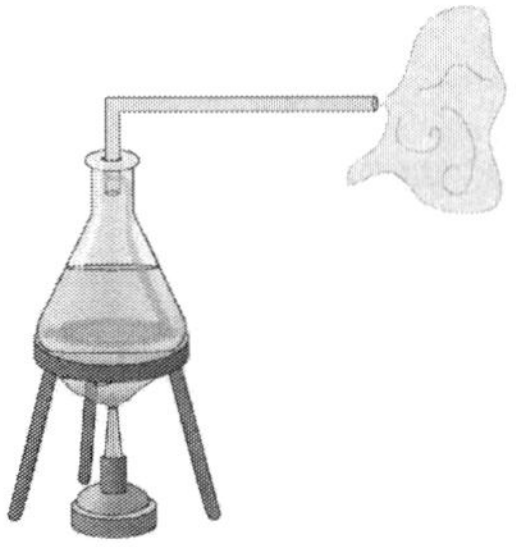

B.

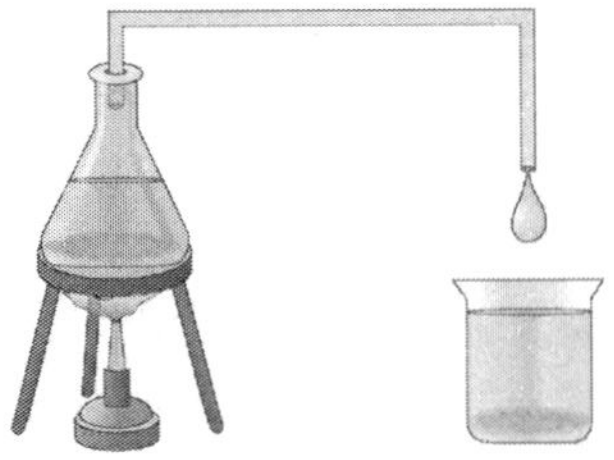

C.

D.

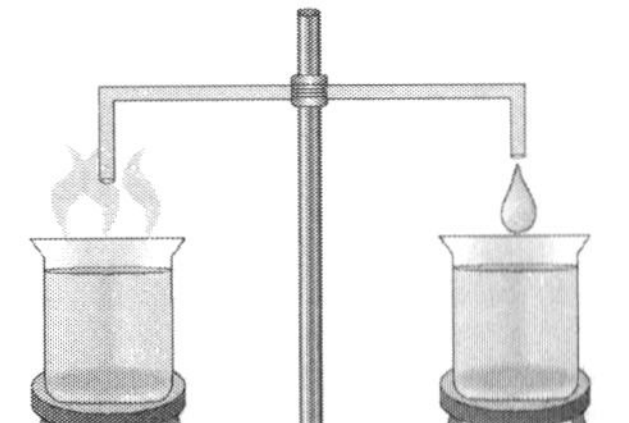

6. When more solute is added to a solution, the concentration of the solution increases. This shows that the solution was
   A. saturated
   B. unsaturated
   C. supersaturated
   D. partly saturated

7. Which of the following combinations of liquids and solids is **not** a mixture?
   A. Salt and water
   B. Milk and cereal
   C. Soda pop and ice
   D. Baking soda and vinegar

Use the following information to answer the next question.

Dani's science teacher gave her two unknown liquids. She pours them together, but neither liquid dissolves.

8. The liquids are best described as
   A. soluble **B.** insoluble
   C. unsaturated **D.** supersaturated

9. If a material cannot be physically separated into different components, it is
   A. a mixture
   B. a solution
   C. a pure substance
   D. an impure substance

10. Which of the following scenarios **best** represents a gaseous state of matter?
    A. Two teams playing floor hockey
    B. An assembly where everyone is seated
    C. A store about to close with few people spread out in it
    D. A science fair where some people are walking and others are seated

Use the following information to answer the next question.

When Phong heats a beaker of wax pieces using a hot plate on a low setting, he notices that the wax changes state.

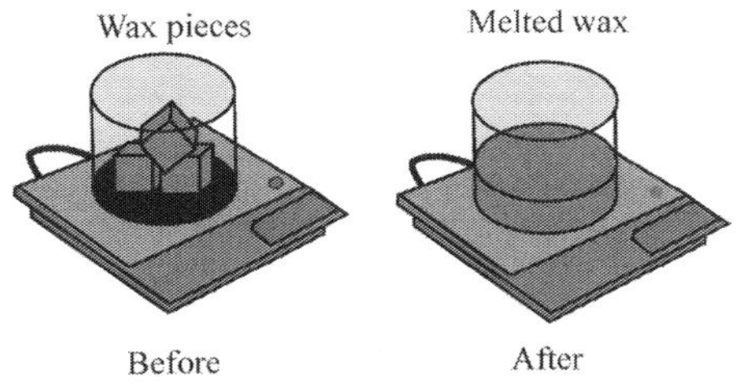

11. Which of the following statements **best** describes this change in state?

A. The wax particles increased in size.

B. The wax particles decreased in size.

C. The spaces between the wax particles increased.

D. The spaces between the wax particles decreased.

Use the following information to answer the next question.

Andreas uses the particle theory to describe different types of matter. He explains that ___*i*___ are made up of identical particles, and ___*ii*___ are made up of different particles.

12. Which of the following tables **best** completes these statements?

A.

i	*ii*
mechanical mixtures	solutions

B.

i	*ii*
solutions	pure substances

C.

i	*ii*
pure substances	mixtures

D.

i	*ii*
solutions	mixtures

Use the following information to answer the next question.

Fertilizers and pesticides that run off from farm soil can pollute the water in lakes, rivers, and oceans. Industrial and municipal wastes can also pollute water.

13. Which of the following methods would **best** separate pure water from these contaminants?

A. Sifting **B.** Filtration

C. Distillation **D.** Evaporation

Use the following information to answer the next question.

Sewage is usually treated before the water is returned to waterways. The first step of sewage treatment has the sewage pass through a steel sieve that removes solid matter.

14. Which separation technique is used in this first stage of sewage treatment?

A. Evaporation **B.** Magnetism

C. Distillation **D.** Filtration

Use the following information to answer the next question.

A substance dissolves in a liquid.
The substance that is dissolved is the *i* and the liquid that does the dissolving is the *ii*. Together, the *i* and the *ii* make a *iii*.

15. Which of the following tables completes the given statement?

A.

i	*ii*
solute	solvent

B.

i	*ii*
solute	solution

C.

i	*ii*
solvent	solution

D.

i	*ii*
solvent	solute

16. Bronze is a metal solution that is made of copper, with tin as the main additive. In bronze, the solute is

A. copper B. bronze
C. steel D. tin

17. If 3 g of a solute dissolves in 100 mL of water, what is the concentration of the solution?

A. 0.03 g B. 0.03 g/mL
C. 3 g D. 3 g/mL

Use the following information to answer the next question.

Nadia's mom makes a gelatin dessert. When her mom leaves the kitchen, Nadia decides to make the dessert sweeter by adding extra sugar into the warm water. She dumps an extra cup of sugar into the bowl and stirs it, but it does not dissolve.

18. The sugar will not dissolve because the gelatin solution is

A. unsaturated B. dissoluble
C. saturated D. insoluble

19. Which of the following statements **best** explains the reason that water is often referred to as a universal solvent?

A. Water dissolves more substances than other solvents.
B. Water is a very good cleaning agent.
C. No substance can dissolve in water.
D. Water cannot dissolve oil.

ANSWERS AND SOLUTIONS — UNIT TEST

1. D	6. B	11. C	16. D
2. D	7. D	12. C	17. B
3. A	8. B	13. C	18. C
4. B	9. C	14. D	19. A
5. B	10. C	15. A	

1. D

Pure copper, such as the copper in a pipe, does not contain harmful components. Copper can be easily melted down and reused. Therefore, the best method for disposing of a used pure substance is to recycle it. The correct answer is D.

2. D

Oil refineries use distillation to separate crude oil into more useful products. The extraction of crude oil does not occur at the the oil refinery. The risk of an oil spill as a result of extraction is not a negative effect of an oil refinery. The correct answer is D.

Oil refineries are large, sprawling complexes that produce a lot of noise and air pollution. They are also at risk for fire and explosion as a result of the processes that occur to distill the oil.

3. A

A solvent can only hold a certain amount of solute. Once it is holding as much solute as it can, the solution is saturated. However, if you heat the solvent, it can hold more solute before it becomes saturated. The warmer the solvent, the more solute it can hold. Therefore, when a mixture of sugar and water is heated, more sugar can be dissolved in the solution.

4. B

The line that shows the solubility of sodium chloride is horizontal. This means that the solubility does not increase. The correct answer is B.

The lines for sodium nitrate, potassium iodide, and potassium nitrate all show increases.

5. B

In order to distill the water, the setup needs to prevent the heated water from escaping as vapour.
This means that the water should be heated in a flask, which will limit the amount of vapour that can escape. The vapour then needs to be collected and condensed, which will turn the vapour back into water. The condensed water needs to be captured in a second container. The only device that does this is shown in setup B

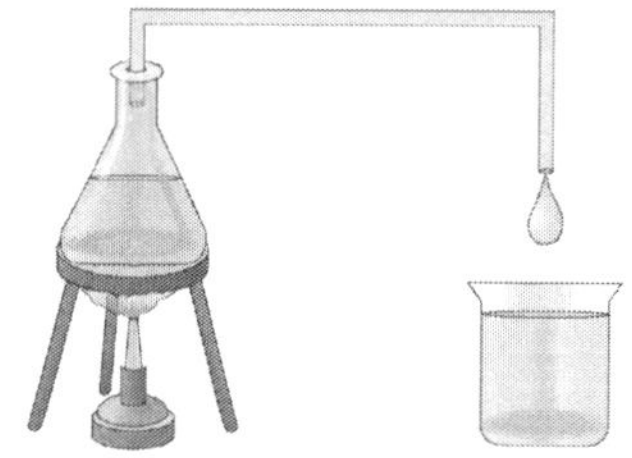

The correct answer is B.

In setup A the impure water is heated in the beaker. The water evaporates, leaving behind impurities. Pure water is not obtained from this setup.

In setup C the impure water is heated in the first beaker and cooled in the second beaker by ice. Simply changing the temperature of the water does not purify it.

In setup D the impure water is heated in the beaker. The water vapours condense in the glass tube and then collects in the beaker beside it. This is not an efficient method because most of the vapours will escape from the open beaker in which the impure water is heated.

6. B

The concentration of the solution increases because the added solute dissolves in the solution. A solution in which more solute can dissolve at a particular temperature is an unsaturated solution. The correct answer is B.

7. D

A mixture is made up of different kinds of particles. A mixture does not form a new substance, and it can usually be separated easily. Baking soda and vinegar do not form a mixture because when they are mixed together, a new substance is formed. This new substance, carbon dioxide gas, cannot be separated into vinegar and baking soda. Therefore, baking soda and vinegar is not a mixture. The correct answer is D.

Salt and water, milk and cereal, and soda pop and ice are all mixtures.

8. B

The liquids are best described as insoluble.
A substance that will not dissolve in another substance is called insoluble. The correct answer is B.

9. C

A pure substance cannot be further broken down by physical means. The correct answer is C.

Mixtures, solutions, and impure substances can all be separated into their components by physical means.

10. C

Compared with the particles in a solid or liquid, a gas has particles that move faster and with more space between the particles. A store about to close with few people in it represents a gas because the people move about the store faster than those at an assembly or a science fair. They are also spread out so there is more space between them compared with the players in a floor hockey game. The correct answer is C.

11. C

Increasing the temperature causes the particles in the wax to vibrate faster, which causes the bonds between the particles break. The particles can move past each other and the space between the particles increases. These changes result in a phase change from a solid to a liquid. The size of the particles does not change during this process. The correct answer is C.

12. C

Mixtures, mechanical mixtures, and solutions are composed of different types of particles. Pure substances are composed of identical particles. Therefore, term *i* is pure substances, and term *ii* is mixtures. The correct answer is C.

13. C

Distillation would be the best method to purify water because it separates and collects pure water vapour, which cools down and becomes liquid again.
The correct answer is C.

Filtration only separates solids from the polluted water, not the dissolved pollutants. Evaporation separates pure water from the pollutants, however, it does not collect the water vapour. Sifting separates solids from other solids and could not be used to purify water.

14. D

Filtration uses a filter or sieve to remove solid particles from the mixture based on particle size. The water particles are small enough to fit through the sieve, but the large particles cannot, so they are removed from the sewage. The correct answer is D.

The process of evaporation separates one part of the mixture by turning that part into vapour. Distillation also involves turning one of the components into vapour. Magnetism uses magnets to separate metals from mixtures.

15. A

A solute is the substance that dissolves in another substance. The substance that dissolves the solute is called the solvent. A solution is formed when a solute is dissolved in a solvent. The correct answer is A.

16. D

Bronze is the solution, so it is not the solute.
The solute is the material that dissolves within the substance that is present in the larger quantity.
In bronze, copper occurs in the largest amount, so it is the solvent. Therefore, the solute is tin.
The correct answer is D.

17. B

The concentration of the solution is found using the given formula:

$$\text{concentration} = \frac{\text{weight of the solute}}{\text{weight of the solvent}}$$

$$= \frac{3\text{ g}}{100\text{ mL}}$$

$$0 = 0.03\text{ g/mL}$$

The correct answer is B.

18. C

The extra sugar will not dissolve because the solution is saturated, meaning the water cannot hold any more sugar. The correct answer is C.

19. A

Water is considered the universal solvent because it can dissolve many substances. No other substance can dissolve as many substances as water can. The correct answer is A.

NOTES

Earth and Space Systems: Heat in the Environment

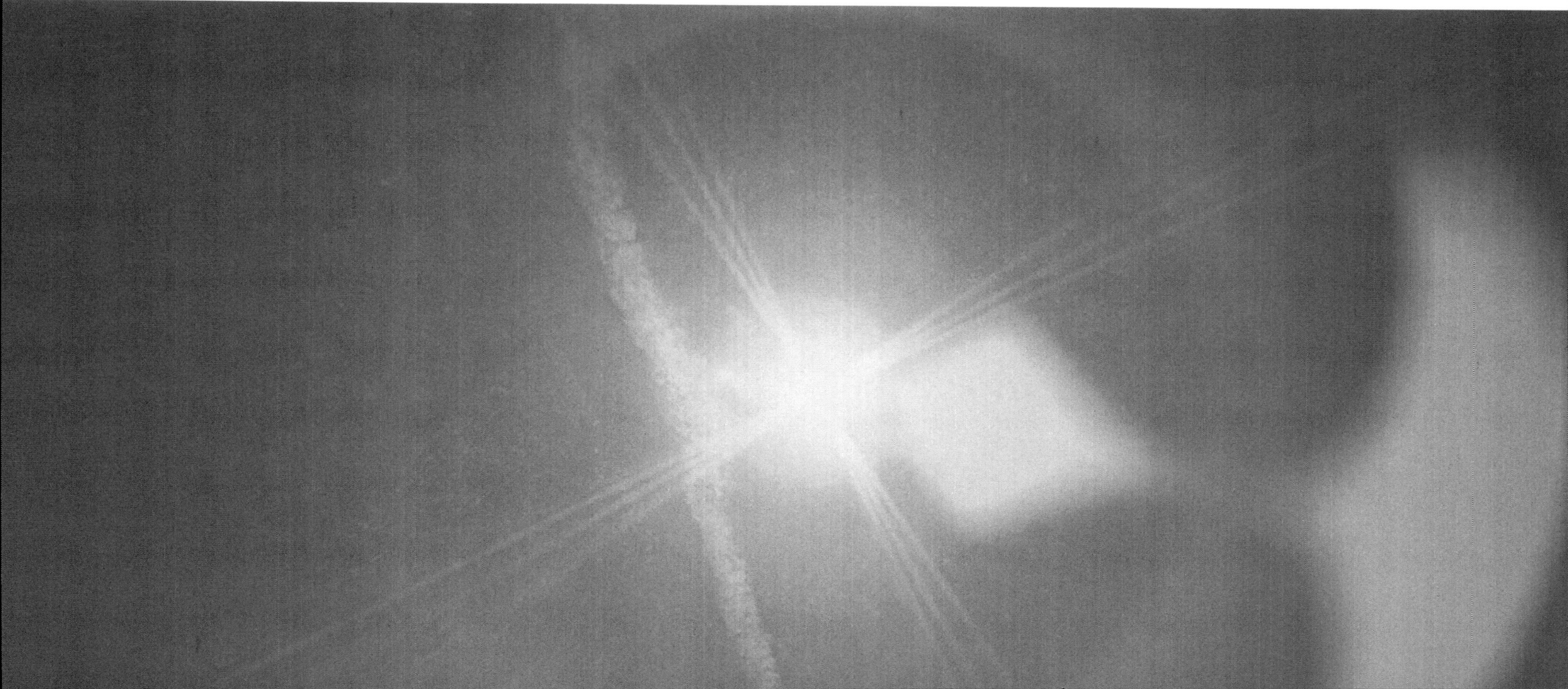

EARTH AND SPACE SYSTEMS: HEAT IN THE ENVIRONMENT

Table of Correlations

Specific Expectation		Practice Questions	Unit Test Questions	Practice Test 1	Practice Test 2
7ESS1:STSE	Assess the costs and benefits of technologies that reduce heat loss or heat-related impacts on the environment;				
7ESS1.1	*assess the social and environmental benefits of technologies that reduce heat loss or transfer*	1	1	1	
7ESS1.2	*assess the environmental and economic impacts of using conventional and alternative forms of energy*	5	2		1
7ESS2:Skills	Investigate ways in which heat changes substances, and describe how heat is transferred;				
7ESS2.1	*follow established safety procedures for using heating appliances and handling hot materials*	6			
7ESS2.2	*investigate the effects of heating and cooling on the volume of a solid, a liquid, and a gas*	7, 8	3, 4	2	2
7ESS2.3	*use technological problem-solving skills to identify ways to minimize heat loss*	2, 3, 4	5	3	3
7ESS2.4	*use scientific inquiry/experimentation skills to investigate heat transfer through conduction, convection, and radiation*	14, 15, 16	6, 7	4	4
7ESS2.5	*use appropriate science and technology vocabulary, including heat, temperature, conduction, convection, and radiation, in oral and written communication*	31, 32	8	5	5
7ESS2.6	*use a variety of forms to communicate with different audiences and for a variety of purposes*				
7ESS3:Concepts	Demonstrate an understanding of heat as a form of energy that is associated with the movement of particles and is essential to many processes within the earth's systems.				
7ESS3.1	*use the particle theory to compare how heat affects the motion of particles in a solid, a liquid, and a gas*	9, 10	9	6	6
7ESS3.2	*identify ways in which heat is produced*	23, 24	10		7
7ESS3.3	*use the particle theory to explain the effects of heat on volume in solids, liquids, and gases*	11, 12, 13	11, 12	7	8
7ESS3.4	*explain how heat is transmitted through conduction, and describe natural processes that are affected by conduction*	17, 18	13	8	9
7ESS3.5	*explain how heat is transmitted through convection, and describe natural processes that depend on convection*	19, 20	14, 15	9	10
7ESS3.6	*explain how heat is transmitted through radiation, and describe the effects of radiation from the sun on different kinds of surfaces*	21, 22	16	10	11
7ESS3.7	*describe the role of radiation in heating and cooling the earth, and explain how greenhouse gases affect the transmission of radiated heat through the atmosphere*	25, 26, 27	17, 18	11	12
7ESS3.8	*identify common sources of greenhouse gases, and describe ways of reducing emissions of these gases*	28, 29, 30	19	12	13

7ESS1.1 assess the social and environmental benefits of technologies that reduce heat loss or transfer

7ESS2.3 use technological problem-solving skills to identify ways to minimize heat loss

Minimizing Heat Loss With Technology

The climate in Canada, particularly its cold winters, makes heat conservation an important factor for engineers to consider. Technology has made great advances in reducing heat loss and heat transfer. Materials that prevent heat loss **insulate** the heat source. Therefore, technologies designed to limit heat loss involve materials that have insulative properties.

Grass can serve as an insulating material on the roofs and sides of buildings.

Engineers continue to investigate better methods and materials to prevent heat loss and transfer to increase the energy-efficiency of the devices and structures they design. Some examples of items that have been designed to reduce heat loss are insulated clothing, building insulation, green roofs, and energy-efficient buildings. These technologies have both social and environmental benefits:

- Social— insulated clothing allows Canadians to work outdoors and enjoy many outdoor recreation activies during the cold winter season. Areas that previously could not support year-round settlement can now be settled and developed.
- Environmental— reducing heat loss means less heat needs to be generated. In Canada, generating heat usually involves the burning of fossil fuels, non-renewable resources that create pollution problems when burned.

Every technology will have its own costs and benefits and should be assessed for efficiency and potential trouble spots.

1. Which of the following materials would be a **poor** insulating material for a building?

A. Fibreglass

B. Foam panels

C. Metal sheeting

D. Reflective panels

2. Which of the following devices does **not** minimize heat loss?

A. Insulated food bag

B. Thermos flask

C. Coffee mug

D. Frying pan

Use the following information to answer the next question.

An energy audit of a house shows that the windows lose a significant amount of heat.

3. Which of the following solutions would be **most effective** for reducing this heat loss?

A. Adding storm windows to the existing windows

B. Covering the windows with heavy curtains

C. Adding weather-stripping around the windows

D. Installing triple-glazed windows

Use the following information to answer the next question.

Items such as winter jackets are designed to minimize heat loss. Designers of cold-weather clothing need to understand heat and heat transfer.

Open Response

4. List one feature of a winter jacket that minimizes heat loss, and explain how it reduces heat transfer.

____

____

7ESS1.2 assess the environmental and economic impacts of using conventional and alternative forms of energy

The Impact of Energy Sources

In Canada, **heat** and electricity come from a variety of energy sources. These different energy sources can be divided into two categories: conventional and alternative. Both categories have different environmental and economic impacts.

Conventional Energy Sources

The energy sources that industrial countries have used for much of the last century are called conventional energy sources. Conventional energy sources include nuclear power and fossil fuels, such as coal, oil, and natural gas. In general, these sources have negative environmental impacts because they pollute the air, water, and soil. However, many people still use these energy sources because they are more affordable and the materials needed to use these sources already exist.

Alternative Energy Sources

Sources of energy that are not widely used but can supply the energy needed are called alternative energy sources. Geothermal, solar, wind, water, and biofuels are all considered alternative energy sources. Usually, these sources cause less harm to the environment than conventional sources, but they can still have negative impacts. Often these sources require a lot of space or a change to the physical structure of Earth's surface. As well, changing the energy supply system to accomodate these alternative sources will require a lot of money and construction to replace the existing supply system.

5. Which of the following types of energy creates a waste disposal problem?

A. Wind
B. Solar
C. Nuclear
D. Geothermal

7ESS2.1 follow established safety procedures for using heating appliances and handling hot materials

Working With Heat

Many experiments in the science lab involve the use of heat. Since heat can be dangerous in the laboratory, follow these safety procedures to avoid hurting yourself or others in the lab:

- Never leave a lit Bunsen burner unattended
- Tie long hair back and do not wear baggy clothes
- Only use heat-safe glassware like Pyrex or Kimax
- Obtain instructions for properly using the heating equipment
- Use heat-resistant gloves or tongs when handling heated equipment
- Keep the open flame away from any flammable materials, such as alcohol
- Know the location of the fire extinguisher in your lab, and know how to use it
- Point open test tubes and beakers away from yourself and others when heating

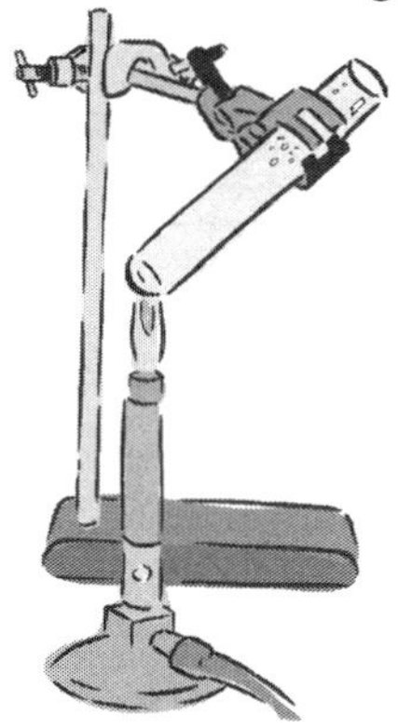

Use the following information to answer the next question.

Amanda and Joseph both conduct the same scientific experiment.

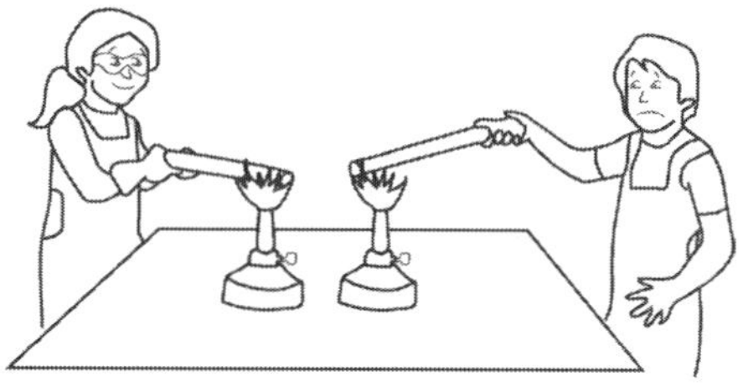

6. Which of the following safety precautions should Joseph have used in the experiment?

A. Wear gloves and safety goggles

B. Wear safety goggles and an apron

C. Stand back farther and wear gloves

D. Stand back farther and wear safety goggles

7ESS2.2 investigate the effects of heating and cooling on the volume of a solid, a liquid, and a gas

7ESS3.1 use the particle theory to compare how heat affects the motion of particles in a solid, a liquid, and a gas

7ESS3.3 use the particle theory to explain the effects of heat on volume in solids, liquids, and gases

Particle Motion and Heat

The particle theory of matter states that all matter is composed of extremely small particles, and that these particles move constantly. The more heat energy these particles possess, the faster they move. The particle theory explains how the addition of heat affects the movement of particles in each of the three states of matter: solids, liquids, and gases.

Compared with the particles in liquids and gases, those in solids do not have a lot of heat energy. The particles in a solid are packed very close together and cannot move freely. As a result of heat energy, they move by vibrating back and forth. Adding more heat energy to the particles will cause their **temperature** to increase, so the particles will vibrate faster. Eventually, the solid will gain enough energy that it will become a liquid.

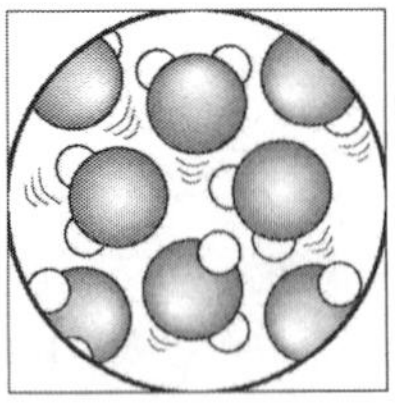

Particles in a solid

The particles in liquids have more heat energy than the particles in solids, and they are free to move around. This creates spaces between particles that allows them to move past each other. Adding more heat will cause the particles to move faster until the liquid becomes a gas.

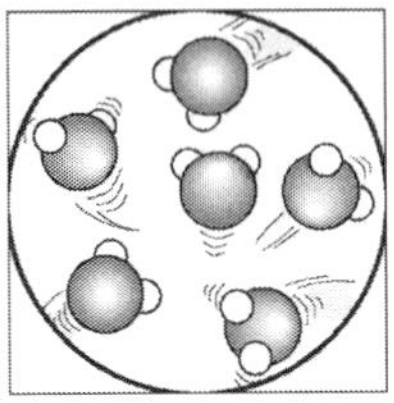

Particles in a liquid

In gases, the particles have more energy than the particles in liquids. As a result, the particles move around more quickly than they do in liquids. This creates larger spaces between the particles that allows even more freedom for the particles to move past one another.

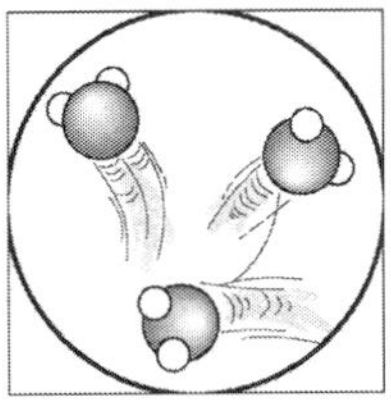

Particles in a gas

For example, adding heat energy causes solid ice to change into liquid water. Adding more heat causes liquid water to change into water vapour, a gas. The water vapour particles move much faster than the particles in the ice. Adding heat energy to the particles increases their motion.

Since the space between particles increases as they increase in speed, the matter will occupy more space. This can be seen in matter of all three states: solids, liquids, and gases.

You can investigate these effects on matter in a laboratory, by developing experiments to observe the changes. The following chart gives examples of how each of the three types of matter expand as they heat up.

State of Matter	Examples of Expansion when Heated
Solid	paved sidewalks, roads, and bridge decks all expand in hot weather
	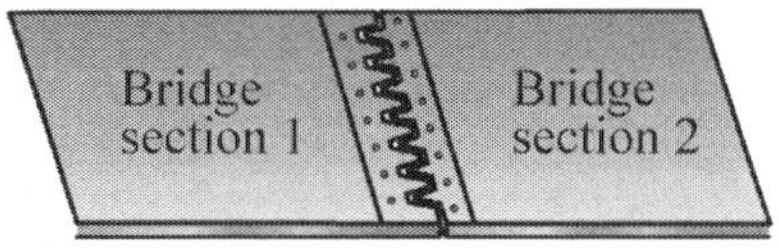
Liquid	sea level rises as global warming makes the oceans warmer, and the water in the oceans expands
	mercury expands and rises in a thermometer as the temperature increases
	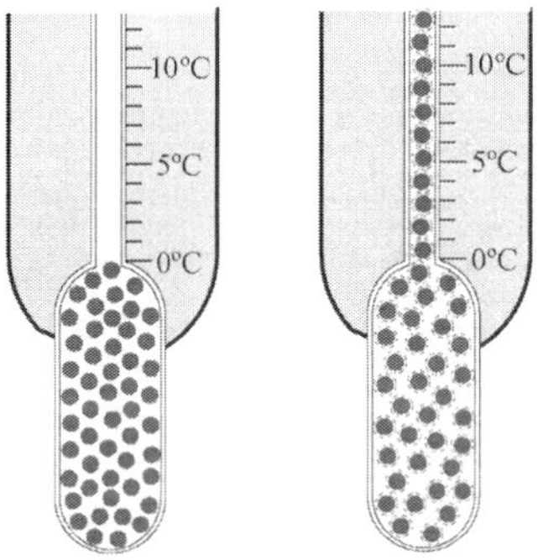 Thermometer 1 Thermometer 2
Gas	air in car tires expands on hot pavement
	a full balloon shrinks when placed in a freezer and re-expands when returned to room temperature
	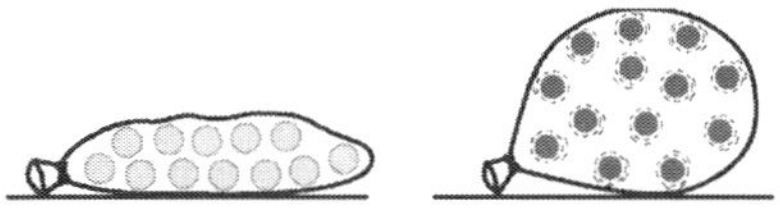 Balloon in a freezer Temperature: −10°C; Balloon on a countertop Temperature: 20°C

Use the following information to answer the next question.

The given diagram shows the change that ice undergoes when heated and transformed into water.

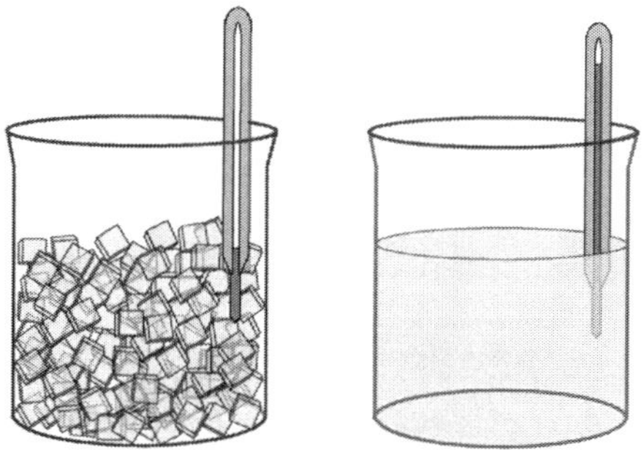

7. Which of the following physical properties of water does **not** change during this transformation?

A. Mass **B.** Density

C. Volume **D.** Temperature

Use the following information to answer the next question.

Natalie observed four different changes in volume during an experiment.
She concluded that each of the following changes occurred as a result of a change in temperature.

I. hot air balloon rising
II. water boiling in a kettle
III. popcorn popping in a pan
IV. a soft drink fizzing in an open bottle

8. Which of Natalie's observation does **not** occur because of a change in temperature?

A. I **B.** II

C. III **D.** IV

Use the following information to answer the next question.

Jonas set up a metal spit for roasting food over a campfire.

9. Which of the following tables shows what will happen to both the kinetic energy and particle movement in the metal spit?

A.

Kinetic Energy	Particle Movement
decreases	decreases

B.

Kinetic Energy	Particle Movement
increases	decreases

C.

Kinetic Energy	Particle Movement
decreases	increases

D.

Kinetic Energy	Particle Movement
increases	increases

10. Which of the following scenarios **best** represents the motion of particles in the solid state of matter?

A. A science fair where some people are walking and others are seated

B. An assembly where everyone is seated

C. Two teams playing floor hockey

D. A fire drill at a school

Use the following information to answer the next question.

The diagram shows the spacing of particles in a substance at room temperature.

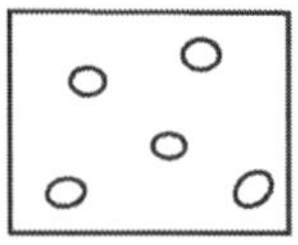

11. Which of the following diagrams shows the spacing of the particles if the substance were cooled almost to its freezing point?

A. 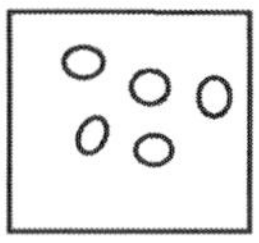

B. 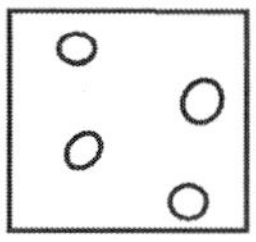

C. 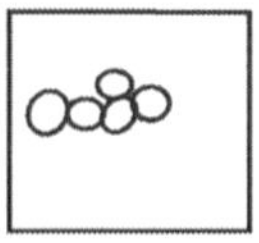

D. 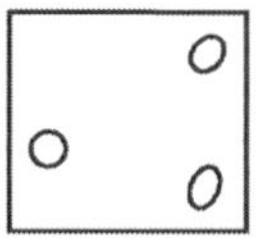

Use the following information to answer the next question.

While riding her bicycle across a concrete bridge, Tina noticed a gap between each of the sections of the bridge.

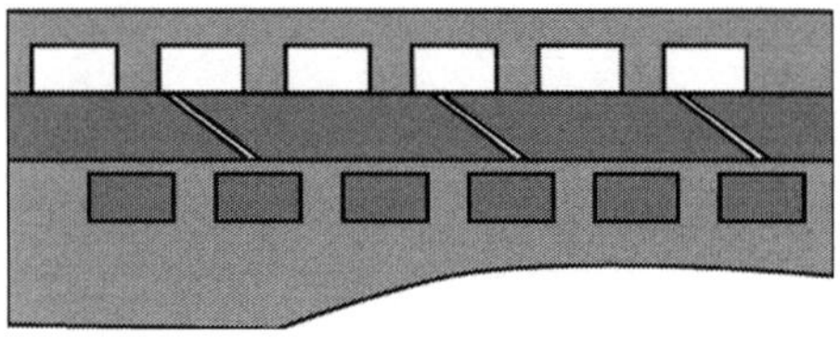

12. The reason that there is a gap between the sections in a bridge deck is to

A. make the bridge aesthetically appealing

B. permit water to run off the bridge deck surface

C. make the bridge structurally stronger in sections

D. permit expansion and contraction of the sections

Use the following information to answer the next question.

Erin conducted an experiment in which she changed a substance. During the experiment, she observed the following characteristics of the substance:

I. The particles have some kinetic energy to move about.
II. The particles of the substance are held together by weak forces.
III. The volume of the substance increases during the experiment.

13. The substance that Erin observed during her experiment was a

A. liquid being heated

B. liquid being cooled

C. solid being heated

D. solid being cooled

7ESS2.4 use scientific inquiry/experimentation skills to investigate heat transfer through conduction, convection, and radiation

7ESS3.4 explain how heat is transmitted through conduction, and describe natural processes that are affected by conduction

7ESS3.5 explain how heat is transmitted through convection, and describe natural processes that depend on convection

7ESS3.6 explain how heat is transmitted through radiation, and describe the effects of radiation from the sun on different kinds of surfaces

Heat Transfer

Heat can transfer between the particles of materials by three methods: radiation, conduction, and convection. You can see these processes in nature, and you can investigate them in the laboratory. These experiments will require you to use a heat source; it is important to follow established safety guidelines when using heat in the lab.

Conduction

Heat can transfer by the particles within a solid colliding with each other. This form of heat transfer is called **conduction**. A pot placed on a burner, for example, will heat up because the particles in the pot near the hot burner gain energy and begin to vibrate more quickly. They collide with other particles and cause them to vibrate, transferring the heat energy from one particle to the next in a chain reaction. Eventually, the heat transfers to the handle. For that reason, the handle of the pot gets hot even though it does not make contact with the hot burner.

Heat transfers from the pot to the handle.

All solids conduct heat. Some solids, such as metal, are good conductors of heat. Wood, glass, and plastics are poor conductors of heat. Poor conductors are often used as insulators to prevent heat loss or transfer.

Conduction occurs in nature as well. All rocks start out either as igneous, sedimentary, or metamorphic rocks. The intense heat from within Earth's surface can change the appearance of surrounding rocks. As well, during a volcanic eruption, the heat that surrounding rocks absorb by conduction causes then to become new igneous and metamorphic rocks.

CONVECTION

The particles in liquids and gases have spaces between them. This allows them to transfer heat by the process of **convection**. This process transfers heat by moving one part of a fluid (liquid or gas) to another part in a circular motion. This transfer of heat occurs when the particles closest to the heat source heat up first. The particles gain energy and move away from the heat source. Cooler particles move in and take the place of hotter particles, and as the cooler particles gain energy, they also move away. This cycle repeats itself.

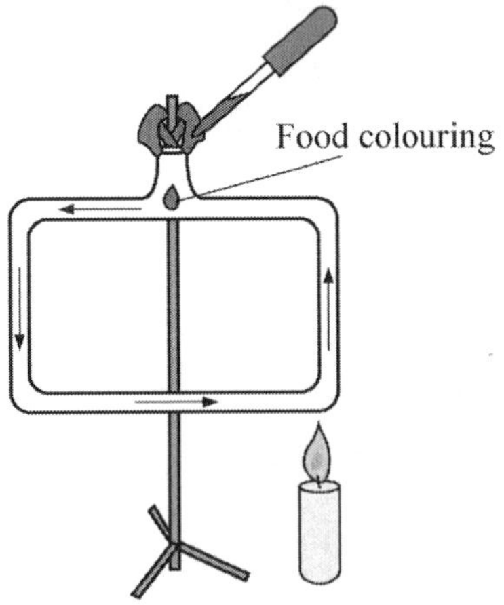

The food colouring will move by convection.

The water in a pot on the stove heats up by convection. Many other examples of convection also occur in nature. Ocean currents are convection currents that occur when cold Arctic water moves to replace the rising warm water in tropical areas.

Sea and land breezes are also examples of convection. A sea breeze forms when the sun heats up the air above the land, causing it to rise up in the atmosphere. The cool air above the sea moves in to take the place of the land air that rises, creating a pattern where air moves from above the sea to above the land.

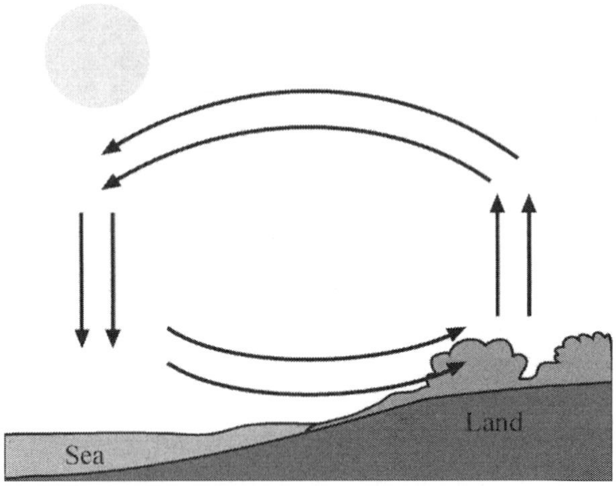

The pattern of a sea breeze

RADIATION

The transfer of heat by conduction and convection depends on the movement of particles. The transfer of heat by **radiation** does not require particles. Radiated energy travels as waves, so it can travel through space where very few particles exist. Light is a form of radiated energy that moves in waves as it travels through space from the sun to Earth.

When heat radiation strikes a surface, three things happen to the heat:

- Some reflects, or bounces, off the matter
- Some is absorbed, or taken in, by the matter
- Some passes through the matter without absorption or reflection

The type of matter that the radiation strikes affects the amount of radiation reflected or absorbed. For example, more sunlight reflects when it hits an ice-covered lake than when it strikes a black asphalt road.

Use the following information to answer the next question.

Brayden was disappointed to find out that the snowman he had built in late February started to melt one sunny day in March.

14. Brayden indicated that the melting snowman was the result of heat transfer to the snowman by the process of

A. transmission **B.** conduction

C. convection **D.** radiation

15. Heat transfer in fluids occurs by

A. conduction and convection

B. convection and radiation

C. conduction only

D. radiation only

Use the following information to answer the next question.

Marius completes an experiment that involves testing the boiling point of different liquids. He places the same amount of each liquid into different beakers and heats them on hot plates. He then measures the temperatures of each of the liquids when they start to boil.

16. The temperature of the all of the water in the beaker increases because of

A. combustion **B.** conduction

C. convection **D.** radiation

Use the following information to answer the next question.

In a car engine, a water pump circulates a liquid coolant (antifreeze) into the radiator. The copper tubing in the radiator absorbs heat from the coolant. The heat then passes into the air that surrounds the copper tubing. This keeps the engine from overheating when it is in use.

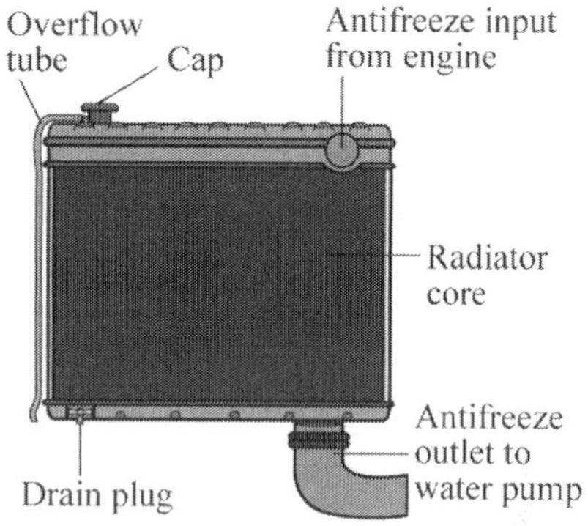

17. Which type of heat transfer takes place when the heat from the liquid coolant transfers to the copper metal in the radiator?

A. Conduction **B.** Convection

C. Radiation **D.** Induction

Use the following information to answer the next question.

Jackson inserts four rods of different materials into a hot-water bath. After five minutes, he measures and records the temperatures of the outer ends of the rods.

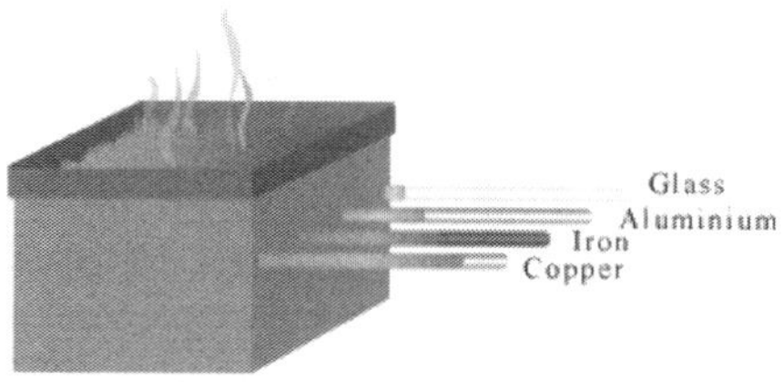

18. What method of heat transfer occurs in the metal rods?

A. Induction **B.** Radiation

C. Convection **D.** Conduction

Use the following information to answer the next question.

During his trip to the mountains, Justin spots a hang glider rising sharply over a meadow.

19. The method of heat transfer that creates the hang glider's lift is known as

A. transmission **B.** conduction

C. convection **D.** radiation

Use the following information to answer the next question.

Most homes use electricity or natural gas to heat water in a specially designed hot-water tank.

20. Which of the following diagrams shows the **most efficient** method of heating cold water in a hot-water tank?

A.

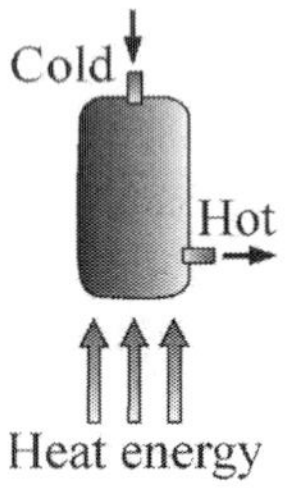

B.

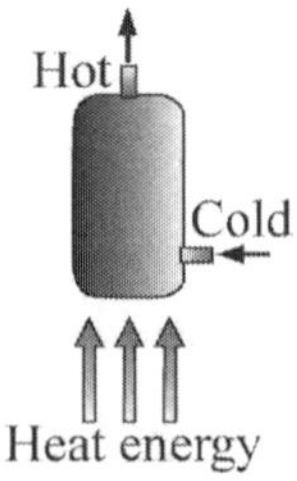

C.

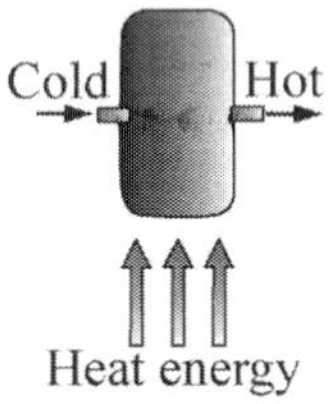

D.

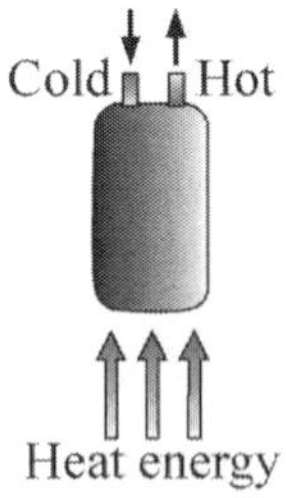

21. The heat from the sun is felt on Earth because of the method of energy transfer called

A. conduction **B.** convection

C. induction **D.** radiation

Use the following information to answer the next question.

Eve and Grace set up an experiment to determine which surface colour absorbs the most radiant heat. They place four differently coloured boxes in direct sunlight for 30 minutes.

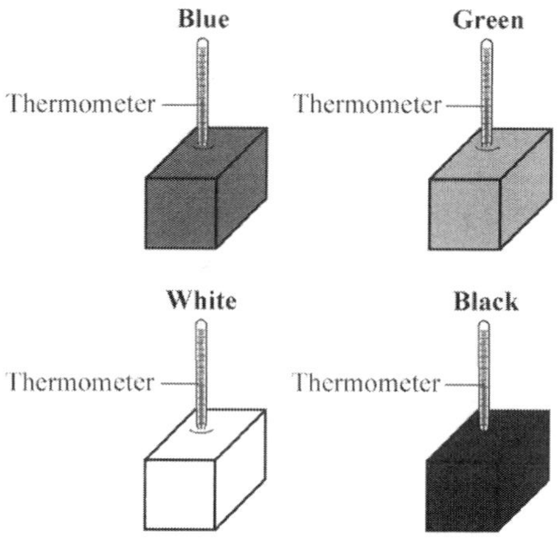

22. Which of the coloured boxes will have the highest thermometer reading after 30 minutes?

A. Blue box **B.** Black box

C. White box **D.** Green box

7ESS3.2 identify ways in which heat is produced

Generating Heat

The sun is the most important source of heat energy. Since the sun is an inconsistent and unreliable source of heat energy, especially during the night, other sources are used to produce heat energy. Heat can be generated by mechanical, electrical, and chemical means. Examples of each are provided in the following table:

Source of Heat	Example
Mechanical	A metal coat hanger gets hot at the joint when it is bent back and forth. The heat comes from distortion of the metal.
	The wheels on a car get hot after the car comes to a skidding stop. The heat comes from friction between the wheel and the road.
	Air is compressed in a bicycle tire. The heat comes from compression of the gases.
Electrical	A stove burner slows down the electricity flowing through it, and the electrical resistance creates heat. The heat comes from electrical resistance.
	The filament at the top of a light bulb resists electrical flow and glows white hot.
Chemical	Fossil fuels are burned.
	The human body heats up as it exercises because its cells are using stored chemical energy.

23. Vigorously rubbing two dry sticks together can start a fire. The heat energy that produces the fire comes from

A. mechanical energy

B. chemical energy

C. electrical energy

D. solar energy

Use the following information to answer the next question.

Each of the following four diagrams shows heat produced by a different energy source.

Diagram W

Diagram X

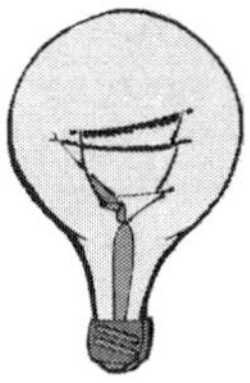

Diagram Y

Diagram Z

24. Which diagram **best** illustrates heat energy produced by resistance?

A. Diagram W **B.** Diagram X

C. Diagram Y **D.** Diagram Z

7ESS3.7 describe the role of radiation in heating and cooling the earth, and explain how greenhouse gases affect the transmission of radiated heat through the atmosphere

Heating Earth's Atmosphere

Most of the sun's energy that strikes Earth passes through the atmosphere and is absorbed by Earth's surface, warming the surface. However, the clouds and gases in the atmosphere reflect some of the energy back into space. As well, some of the energy that strikes Earth's surface reflects off the surface and returns to space. However, some of the reflected energy is trapped by the gases in the atmosphere, such as carbon dioxide, methane, and nitrous oxide. This process is similar to how a greenhouse stays warm. As a result, this process is called the greenhouse effect, and the gases that cause it are called **greenhouse gases**.

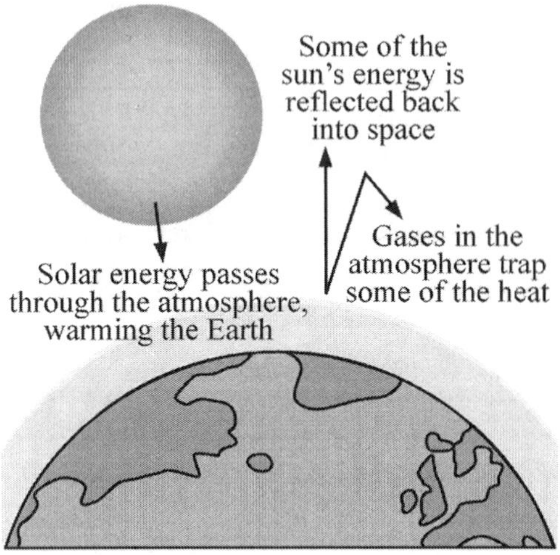

The greenhouse effect keeps Earth's atmosphere warm enough for plants and animals to live within it. However, when the amount of greenhouse gases in the atmosphere increases, they keep more heat in, making Earth's atmosphere warmer than it naturally should be. Many human activities increase the amount of greenhouse gases in the environment. This traps more heat in the atmosphere and leads to the problem known as climate change.

Use the following information to answer the next question.

Stephen noticed that the air cools off more quickly after the sun sets if the sky is clear than it does if the sky is cloudy.
This observation puzzled Stephen, and he asked his teacher for an explanation.

25. Stephen's teacher explained that the air temperature remains warmer on a cloudy evening because the clouds

A. produce lightning, which heats up Earth

B. trap the heat radiation given off by Earth's surface

C. produce heat energy and release it during the evening

D. absorb the sun's heat during the day and release it during the evening

Use the following information to answer the next question.

Each day the sun provides Earth with a huge amount of energy. The illustration shows what happens to the sun's energy that reaches Earth's surface.

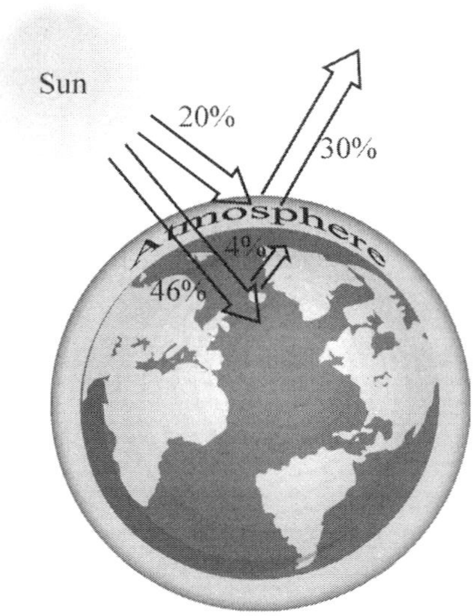

26. What percentage of the sun's energy is reflected back into space by Earth's surface and atmosphere?

A. 4% **B.** 30%

C. 34% **D.** 50%

Use the following information to answer the next question.

The heat energy produced by the sun passes through the atmosphere and strikes Earth's surface. Most of the heat is absorbed by Earth, but some of it is reflected back into the atmosphere and space. Certain gases in the atmosphere are able to trap the reflected heat and prevent it from escaping back into space.

27. Which of the following sources does **not** produce a gas that prevents heat from escaping into space?

A. Cattle grazing

B. Cars running on gas

C. Rice growing in paddies

D. Plants photosynthesizing

7ESS3.8 identify common sources of greenhouse gases, and describe ways of reducing emissions of these gases

Greenhouse Gas Emissions

There are three main gases that contribute to the greenhouse effect:

- carbon dioxide
- nitrous oxide
- methane

Other gases contribute in small amounts, including ozone and CFCs, which are the chemicals produced by aerosol products.

Carbon Dioxide

Combustion, or the burning of materials like fossil fuels, produces carbon dioxide. It is estimated that nearly 75% of the carbon dioxide released into the air comes from energy-related industries. For example, both the oil refineries that produce gasoline and the power plants that burn fossil fuels to generate electricity produce large amounts of carbon dioxide. Other large contributors of carbon dioxide are gasoline and diesel-burning vehicles, which release carbon dioxide as their exhaust.

There are also natural sources of carbon dioxide, such as decaying organic matter, respiration of living animals, fermentation, volcanoes, hot springs, and forest fires.

Nitrous Oxide

Burning fossil fuels also produces nitrous oxide. As well, a large portion of the nitrous oxide released into the atmosphere comes from the use of nitrogen fertilizers in agriculture.

Methane

Certain bacteria that decay organic material release methane gas into the atmosphere. These bacteria are found in landfill sites, rice paddies, and the digestive system of many grass eating animals, such as cows and sheep.

Methane gas naturally occurs in coal seams and large layers of ice. When these coal seams are opened up, or the layers of ice melt, the methane escapes into the atmosphere.

Reducing Greenhouse Gas Emissions

In light of the negative effects of the presence of too many greenhouse gases in the atmosphere, such as climate change, humans are looking for ways to reduce their emissions of these gases. Individuals can reduce their contribution to the greenhouse effect by conserving electricity and reducing their use of fuel-burning vehicles. Governments around the world also have a role to play in reducing greenhouse gas emissions.

Use the following information to answer the next question.

Environmental scientists tested the air quality near a coal-fired power plant. They determined that the smoke stacks emitted several different gases into the atmosphere.

28. Which of the following gases detected by the scientists is not a greenhouse gas?

A. Methane

B. Nitrous oxide

C. Sulfur dioxide

D. Carbon monoxide

29. The logging industry contributes to the greenhouse effect because the cutting down trees

A. increases the level of nitrous oxide in the atmosphere

B. decreases the level of nitrous oxide in the atmosphere

C. increases the level of carbon dioxide in the atmosphere

D. decreases the level of carbon dioxide in the atmosphere

Use the following information to answer the next question.

The process of cogeneration uses one energy source to produce two or more forms of energy. A wastewater treatment facility near the city of Springbox produces a large quantity of methane gas in its digesters. The facility uses cogeneration to heat the buildings and to produce electricity to run their motors.

30. The wastewater treatment facility **mainly** uses cogeneration to

A. reduce their total energy needs

B. prevent the emission of methane gas

C. remove the methane gas from their facility

D. eliminate their emission of greenhouse gases

7ESS2.5 use appropriate science and technology vocabulary, including heat, temperature, conduction, convection, and radiation, in oral and written communication

Communicating in Science

It might seem that science has its own language. In a way, it does. When you speak and write about science, you need to use the proper terminology. The important terms for this unit are on the following list. It is important that you understand these terms and that you can use them properly. If you need help understanding these terms, refer to the other lessons in this unit, or use the glossary in the back of this *Key*.

Important Terms in Earth and Space Systems

- heat
- radiation
- convection
- conduction
- temperature

Use the following information to answer the next question.

Celina heats a large pot of water on a burner on her kitchen stove. Celina wants to be sure that she describes the terms related to the hot water correctly.

31. Which of the following terms should Celina use to describe the measure of the average motion of the particles in the water?

A. Heat

B. Vibration

C. Temperature

D. Thermal energy

Use the following information to answer the next question.

Mr. Brown wrote three definitions related to the transfer of energy on the whiteboard at school.

I. Flow of heat energy that involves moving liquid and gas particles

II. Flow of energy between particles that are in contact

III. Flow of energy in the form of waves

Mr. Brown asked his class to identify each of the terms from these definitions.

32. Definitions I, II, and III, respectively, define the terms

A. conduction, convection, and radiation

B. convection, radiation, and conduction

C. convection, conduction, and radiation

D. conduction, radiation, and convection

ANSWERS AND SOLUTIONS
EARTH AND SPACE SYSTEMS: HEAT IN THE ENVIRONMENT

1. C	8. D	15. A	22. B	29. C
2. D	9. D	16. C	23. A	30. B
3. D	10. B	17. A	24. C	31. C
4. OR	11. A	18. D	25. B	32. C
5. C	12. D	19. C	26. C	
6. A	13. A	20. B	27. D	
7. A	14. D	21. D	28. D	

1. C

Metals are good conductors. Heat energy easily moves through metals. Therefore, metal sheeting would be a poor insulating material for a building. The correct answer is C.

Fibreglass, foam, and reflective panels are poor conductors; heat energy does not easily pass through them. Therefore, they are good insulating materials for a building.

2. D

A frying pan cooks food items by passing heat from the stove top to the food in the pan. Since the pan does not retain the heat in a closed and insulated structure, it is not minimizing heat loss. The correct answer is D.

An insulated food bag keeps stored food insulated. It minimizes heat loss by preventing heat from escaping from the bag. A thermos flask stores liquids, and it keeps its contents hot for long periods of time. A vacuum separates the walls of the thermos flask to minimize heat loss. A coffee mug minimizes heat loss because of its round shape and its composing material, which does not allow heat to escape through it.

3. D

In the average house, 10% of the heat lost occurs through its windows. Glazed windows reduce heat transfer by conduction, convection, and radiation because they have three panes of glass with layers of gas sealed between them that provide insulation. The correct answer is D.

Storm windows have a single layer of insulating air and two panes of glass to prevent heat loss by conduction, convection, and radiation, so it is less effective than triple-glazed windows.
Weather stripping prevents air from leaking around the sides of the existing windows, but it will not prevent heat loss through the glass. Heavy curtains will prevent heat loss by radiation, but will do little to prevent loss by conduction.

4. OR

Either of:

1. The outer shell of a winter jacket stops wind from entering the clothing. This reduces heat transfer due to convection.
2. The insulation layer of a winter jacket traps warm air within its fibers. This reduces heat transfer due to conduction.

5. C

Although nuclear energy has many benefits, its byproducts are difficult to dispose of because they are radioactive and do not easily break down.
The correct answer is C.

Solar, geothermal, and wind energy do not produce waste materials that need disposal.

6. A

Amanda and Joseph both heat an object above a flame. Joseph should wear safety goggles and gloves to protect his eyes and his hands. The correct answer is A.

Joesph is already wearing an apron. Standing back farther from the flame will not help Joseph with his experiment. He needs to stand close enough to carry out the experiment.

7. A

Water is neither removed from nor added to the beaker. Therefore, as the ice converts into water, the mass of the water remains the same.

The density of water depends upon its volume. Since the volume of water changes during this transformation, its density also changes. As the ice melts and becomes water, its volume decreases. Once the water reaches 4°C, its volume increases as it is heated. The temperature of a substance increases when it is heated. The thermometer in the diagram indicates an increase in temperature.

8. D

The soft drink in an open bottle fizzes because the carbon dioxide gas in the liquid forms bubbles and escapes. Therefore, the volume of the soft drink changes because it loses matter, not because of a change in temperature. The correct answer is D.

A hot air balloon rises because the change in temperature causes the gas to expand, which allows the balloon to rise. Water boils as heat transfers to the water particles by convection. Popcorn pops in a pan because the heat causes a chemical change in the kernels as they explode.

9. D

The particles in the metal spit will gain heat energy. This cause the particles to vibrate more than before. Therefore, both the kinetic energy and particle movement increase. The correct answer is D.

10. B

The particles in a solid are close to each other. Adding heat causes the particles to vibrate back and forth. The particles do not move about freely. Therefore, the best analogy for the particles in a solid is an assembly where everybody is seated.
The correct answer is B.

11. A

As a substance cools, its particles have less energy to use to move around. They move more slowly, and the spaces between the particles decrease.
The correct answer is A.

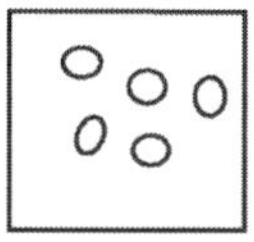

When a substance cools almost to its freezing point, the substance does not become a solid; it remains in a liquid state. Diagram C is incorrect because its particles have almost no space between them, as they would be if the substance had reached its freezing point and became a solid.

Diagrams B and D show an increase in the space between the particles, and some of the particles have even disappeared. These diagrams show an increase in the temperature of the particles.

12. D

Objects generally expand when heated and contract when cooled. The gaps allow room for expansion during the hot summer days. The room for expansion prevents structural damage to the bridge. The correct answer is D.

13. A

Since the particles have weak forces between them and have some kinetic energy to move around, the substance is a liquid. Since the volume increases during the experiment, the liquid gains energy, meaning that it is heated. The correct answer is A.

14. D

The snowman melted because the sun radiates heat energy. Radiation is the transfer of heat energy in the form of radiant energy waves. The correct answer is D.

15. A

In fluids, heat can transfer both by convection and conduction. In convection, moving particles transfer heat. Since the particles in fluids move freely, they can undergo convection. However, the particles in fluids can also vibrate in their positions, so they can conduct heat to the neighbouring particles.
The correct answer is A.

16. C

Convection is the flow of heat energy that involves moving liquid and gas particles. Convection is responsible for the increase in temperature of the water. The correct answer is C.

Combustion is the process of burning. Conduction only occurs between the hotplate and the beaker, and the beaker and the water because it only involves the flow of energy between particles that are in contact. Radiation is the flow of energy in the form of waves.

17. A

The heat passes from the liquid coolant to the copper metal, and then from the copper metal of the radiator to the surrounding air. When heat transfers from one particle, or substance, to another with which it is in contact, it transfers by conduction. Thus, the heat passes from the liquid coolant to the copper tubing, and then from the copper tubing into the air, by conduction. The correct answer is A.

18. D

Conduction is the process by which heat transfers between particles that are in contact with each other. Heat transfers as the particles vibrate. Conduction occurs between particles that are in contact.
The correct answer is D.

19. C

Convection air currents occur on a hot day when the sun heats up the air near the ground, which rises up in the atmosphere. The rising air lifts up the hang glider as the glider passes through the warm air. This is similar to what eagles and hawks do when they appear to be gliding effortlessly in the sky. They ride the air currents.

20. B

The most efficient design for heating water in a hot-water tank should have the cold water enter the tank at the bottom near the heat source. As the cold water heats up, it rises to the top of the tank by convection. This results in even heating of water in the tank. The correct answer is B.

21. D

The space between Earth and the sun is mostly a vacuum. Because heat cannot pass from particle to particle in space, it travels to Earth by radiation in the form of waves. The correct answer is D.

22. B

The radiation from the sun provides both light and heat on Earth. The darker the colour of an object, the greater the amount of heat the object absorbs. Of the four boxes, the black coloured box will absorb the greatest amount of radiation, so it will have the highest thermometer reading.

23. A

The fire begins when the surfaces of the moving sticks heat up until they catch fire. The surfaces of the sticks heat up because of friction, which occurs when two objects move against one another.
Since this heat energy is produced by movement, it is a form of mechanical energy. The correct answer is A.

24. C

The wire in an ordinary incandescent light bulb prevents electricity from passing from one end to the other. Since the wire resists the flow of electricity, the electricity causes the wire to heat up and glow. About 95% of the electrical energy in a light bulb converts into heat, and 5% converts into light.
The correct answer is C.

25. B

During the day, Earth's surface gains heat from the sun, and then radiates the heat during the night when the atmosphere cools down. Clouds in the atmosphere act like blankets, trapping some of the heat radiated from Earth's surface. This keeps the atmosphere warm. On a clear evening, the atmosphere does not trap the heat in, so it escapes into space. The correct answer is B.

26. C

According to the information in the illustration, Earth's land mass and water reflect 4% of the sun's energy back into space. The atmosphere reflects an additional 30% of the energy. That means that a total of 34% of the sun's energy is reflected back into space. The correct answer is C.

27. D

Photosynthesis produces oxygen. This process actually lowers the amount of carbon dioxide in the atmosphere. The correct answer is D.

Both cattle grazing and rice paddies produce methane gas, which is a greenhouse gas that prevents heat from returning to space. Cars that run on gas produce carbon dioxide, which is also a greenhouse gas.

28. D

Burning coal releases a significant portion of carbon dioxide, methane, nitrous oxide, and sulphur dioxide gases into the atmosphere. Methane, nitrous oxide, and sulfur dioxide are all greenhouse gases. Carbon monoxide is released in small quantities, and it is not a greenhouse gas. The correct answer is D.

29. C

Trees consume carbon dioxide during the process of photosynthesis to produce oxygen. When trees are cut down, less trees remain to consume the carbon dioxide that is present in the atmosphere. As a result, more carbon dioxide remains in the atmosphere, contributing to the greenhouse effect. The correct answer is C.

30. B

In the case of the wastewater treatment facility, cogeneration involves the burning of methane gas as fuel to heat the buildings and to generate electricity. This limits the amount of methane gas released into the atmosphere. The correct answer is B.

Using methane gas to produce electricity and heat does not reduce the energy needs of the facility, but it does allow the facility to meet their energy needs without drawing energy from conventional energy suppliers. As well, while burning the methane gas does remove the gas from the facility, they could also remove the gas simply by releasing it without the process of cogeneration. Cogeneration removes the methane gas while preventing it from doing environmental harm. Lastly, while cogeneration prevents the emission of methane gas, it does produce carbon dioxide during the burning of the gas. This is also a greenhouse gas, and it is released into the atmosphere as waste. Thus, it does not eliminate the emission of all greenhouse gases.

31. C

Temperature is a measure of how fast the average particles move. The correct answer is C.

Thermal energy is the total amount of energy that a substance has because of the motion of its particles. Vibration describes a type of particle movement. Heat refers to the amount of energy that transfers from a warmer object to a cooler one.

32. C

Particles in both liquids and gases have the freedom to move about. They can both transfer heat energy by convection. Conduction occurs only in solids. The particles that are in contact with each other transfer the energy that they gain to the particles with which they are in contact. Heat that transfers by radiation does not require any particles because it moves in the form of waves.

Therefore, the correct order for the definitions is convection, conduction, and radiation. The correct answer is C.

UNIT TEST — EARTH AND SPACE SYSTEMS: HEAT IN THE ENVIRONMENT

Use the following information to answer the next question.

Doug and Corrine built their house facing south with a veranda on the front, as shown in the drawing.

1. How does the veranda help with the passive solar heating of the house?

A. In the winter, the sun is high in the sky and the veranda's roof reflects most of the sun's rays, keeping the house warm.

B. In the summer, the sun is high in the sky and the veranda's roof reflects most of the sun's rays, keeping the house warm.

C. In the winter, the sun is low on the horizon and the veranda's roof does not reflect the sun's rays, allowing the sun's heat to enter through the windows to heat the house.

D. In the summer, the sun is low on the horizon and the veranda's roof does not reflect the sun's rays, allowing the sun's heat to enter through the windows to heat the house.

2. Which of the following natural resources is used in a geothermal plant to carry energy from within Earth to the surface?

A. Sun **B.** Wind

C. Water **D.** Gasoline

Use the following information to answer the next question.

Judd heats up four different materials at a constant pressure.

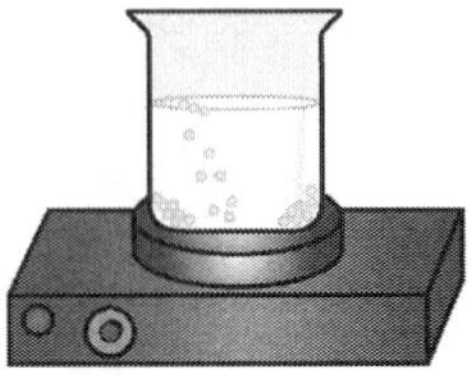

Milk

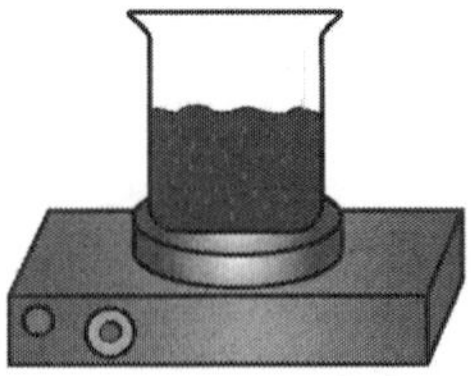

Jam

Wood

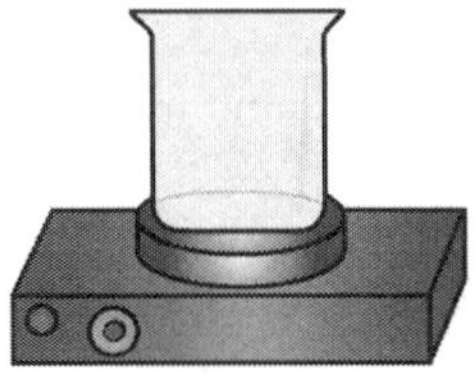

Oxygen

3. Which of the given materials will expand the **most** while Judd heats them up?

A. Jam **B.** Milk

C. Wood **D.** Oxygen

Use the following information to answer the next question.

Tanner's grandmother told him that he could open a glass jar of pickles more easily by pouring hot water on the metal lid first.

4. The hot water helps open the jar of pickles because the glass expands
   A. at the same rate as metal
   B. while metal contracts
   C. more than the metal
   D. less than the metal

Use the following information to answer the next question.

An energy audit of Mr. Green's house indicates that a heat loss occurs through the roof.

5. Mr. Green could reduce this heat loss **most significantly** by
   A. painting the ceiling a different colour
   B. increasing the amount of insulation in the attic
   C. replacing the wooden trusses with aluminum trusses
   D. replacing the roof shingles with a better grade shingles

Use the following information to answer the next question.

6. Chimneys are usually at the top of a house to take advantage of
   A. conduction **B.** convection
   C. induction **D.** radiation

7. Which of the following terms describes the transfer of energy that occurs through the collision of particles?
   A. Radiation **B.** Transition
   C. Convection **D.** Conduction

Use the following information to answer the next question.

Bowden tried to explain heat to his friend Ryan when they were studying. He made the following four statements about heat:

I. Heat is a form of radiation.
II. Temperature is a form of heat.
III. Convection is a form of radiation.
IV. Conduction is a form of heat transfer.

8. Which of Bowden's statements is **true**?
   A. I **B.** II
   C. III **D.** IV

Use the following information to answer the next question.

Geromar boils some water in a stainless steel pot on a stovetop. She understands that the heat from the burner on the stove transfers to the metal pot and the surrounding air, and that some of the heat in the metal pot transfers to the water in the pot.
Geromar draws the following illustration to show the spacing of the particles in each of the substances as they gain heat.

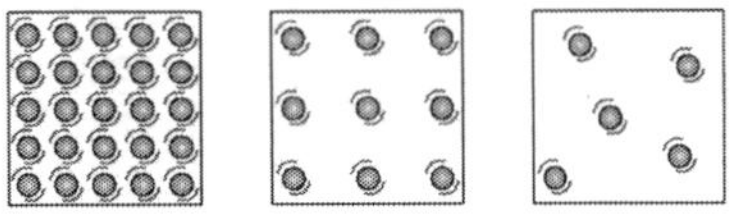

I *II* *III*

9. Which of the following charts identifies the materials represented by each of the particle diagrams?

A.

I	II	III
Water	Metal pot	Air

B.

I	II	III
Air	Metal pot	Water

C.

I	II	III
Air	Water	Metal pot

D.

I	II	III
Metal pot	Water	Air

Use the following information to answer the next question.

Ali knows that heat can be produced by several different mechanical methods, such as friction, distortion, compression, and percussion.

10. Which of the following situations is an example of heat produced by the method of distortion?

A. Using a hand pump to inflate a bicycle tire

B. Rubbing the palms of your hands together

C. Driving a nail into a block of wood with a hammer

D. Bending a metal coat hanger back and forth rapidly

Use the following information to answer the next question.

Brayden's teacher explained that electrical transmission lines provide power to farmers in rural areas. These electrical lines are long metal wires through which electricity can pass. Brayden observed that the electrical lines that his bus passes every day hang down lower at the end of the school year than they do during the winter time.

11. The electrical lines hang higher in the winter than in the summer because the

A. cold air in the winter causes the volume of the metal wires to decrease

B. warm air in the summer causes the volume of the metal wires to decrease

C. ground beneath the electrical lines contracts in the winter, increasing the distance between the ground and wires

D. ground beneath the electrical lines expands in the summer, decreasing the distance between the ground and wires

Use the following information to answer the next question.

Mrs. Clarke inverted and opened two paper penny-candy bags and attached one upside down to each end of a drinking straw. She then balanced the bags by placing a pin through the centre of the drinking straw into the bulletin board. Mrs. Clarke carefully placed differently sized light bulbs under each bag.

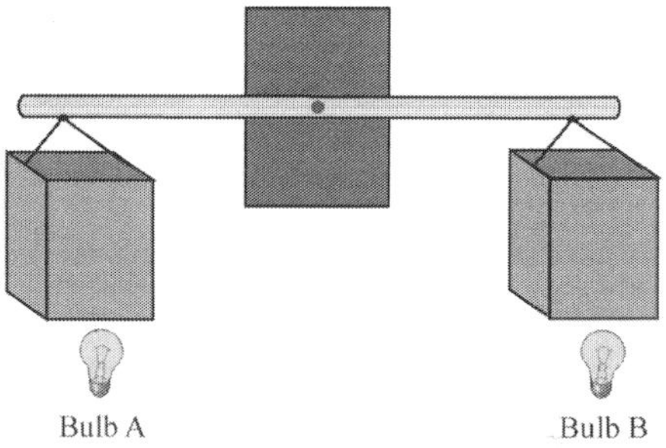

Mrs. Clarke used the following combinations of light bulbs for her demonstration.

	Bulb A	Bulb B
Trial 1	60 W	40 W
Trial 2	100 W	150 W
Trial 3	40W	100 W
Trial 4	150 W	60 W

12. Which two trials will cause the Bulb A side of the apparatus to swing in an upward direction?

A. Trials 1 and 3 **B.** Trials 1 and 4

C. Trials 2 and 3 **D.** Trials 2 and 4

Use the following information to answer the next question.

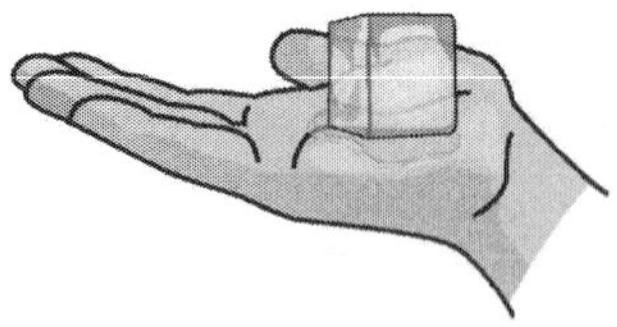

13. Renee placed an ice cube in her hand and noticed that it started to melt.
She predicted that heat transferred from her hand to the ice cube through the process of

A. radiation **B.** convection

C. conduction **D.** subduction

Use the following information to answer the next question.

Janet has a cottage near the ocean.
She notices that the wind blows in one direction during the day and reverses its direction in the evening.

14. Which of the following factors causes the change in the wind's direction in the evening?

A. Uneven heating and cooling of the atmosphere

B. Reverse movement of the ocean currents

C. Gravitational attraction by the moon

D. Changing tidal patterns

Use the following information to answer the next question.

A small container filled with 70° water is kept inside a larger container filled with water at 20°.

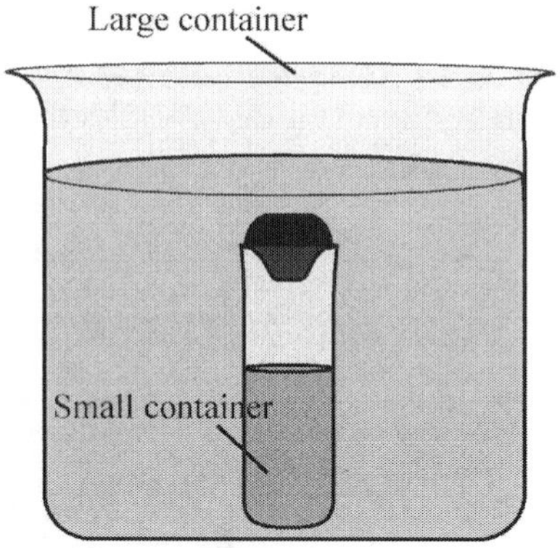

15. After some time, the temperature of the water in the large container increased to 23°C. The temperature in the large container increased because heat transferred from the water in the small container to the water in the large container by

A. radiation through the glass and convection in the water

B. conduction through the glass and convection in the water

C. convection through the glass and conduction in the water

D. conduction through the glass and radiation in the water

Use the following information to answer the next question.

Reid was disappointed to find out that his snowman was almost completely melted.

16. Which type of heat transfer is responsible for the first step in the melting of Reid's snowman?

A. Induction **B.** Radiation

C. Convection **D.** Conduction

Use the following information to answer the next question.

Andrea attended a conference concerning the greenhouse effect. At the conference, she learned that the average temperature of Earth is 20-30°C warmer than it would be without the greenhouse effect. She also learned that various modes of transportation have lead to an increase in the greenhouse effect.

17. Which of the following modes of transportation has the **greatest** impact on the greenhouse effect?

A. Bicycle **B.** Airplane

C. Horse cart **D.** Electric train

Use the following information to answer the next question.

Alicia did a science presentation on the greenhouse effect for her class. She used a large diagram to indicate the region, in which the greenhouse effect occurs.

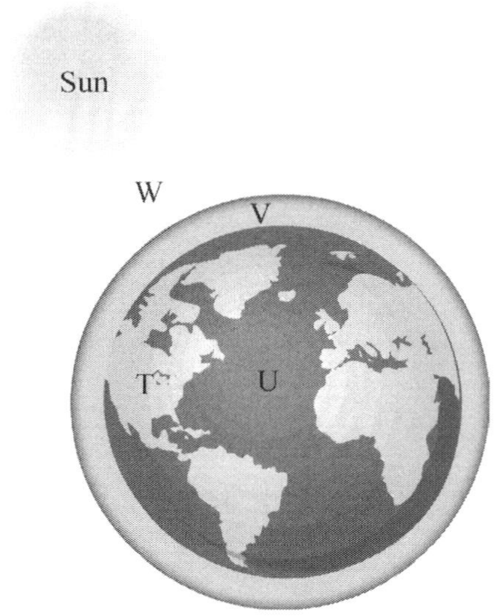

18. The greenhouse effect **most likely** occurs when gases become trapped in

A. Region T **B.** Region U

C. Region V **D.** Region W

Use the following information to answer the next question.

A feedlot operation has a capacity for 30 000 cattle. Environmental scientists constantly monitor the air quality in the area around the feedlot.

19. Which greenhouse gas is **most likely** detected in high levels near the feedlot?

A. carbon dioxide **B.** nitrous oxide

C. methane **D.** ozone

ANSWERS AND SOLUTIONS — UNIT TEST

1. C	**6. B**	**11. A**	**16. B**
2. C	**7. D**	**12. B**	**17. B**
3. D	**8. D**	**13. C**	**18. C**
4. D	**9. D**	**14. A**	**19. C**
5. B	**10. D**	**15. B**	

1. C

During the summer, the sun is high in the sky, and the sun's rays are more direct. As a result, the veranda will block the sun's rays, keeping the house cool, not warm. During the cooler winter months, the sun is lower in the sky. Therefore, the sun will shine in through the windows to help warm up the air inside the house. The correct answer is C.

2. C

Geothermal energy is the heat energy produced within Earth's surface. A geothermal plant sends water deep under Earth's surface. This water changes into steam, which drives the turbines of a generator to generate electricity. Therefore, water is the natural resource that carries the geothermal energy from within Earth to the surface. The correct answer is C.

The sun produces solar energy, which changes into electrical energy in solar cells. It does not bring energy out from Earth's surface. The wind is the moving air currents above Earth's surface. It cannot be used to carry energy from within Earth's surface. Gasoline is a fossil fuel found within Earth's surface. However, it is not used in geothermal plants.

3. D

The particles in gases are further apart than they are in solids or liquids. When they are heated, these particles spread further apart. As a result, the volume of the oxygen, which is a gas, will expand more than the other materials.The correct answer is D.

(**Note:** heating oxygen is very dangerous. Compressed oxygen may explode and should not be done without proper supervision and safety procedures.)

Jam is a mixture of solid and liquid materials. Its volume may expand when heated, but not very much. Milk is a liquid, so it might expand when heated, but not as much as oxygen. Wood is a solid, it will not expand noticeably when heated.

4. D

The hot water heats both the glass and metal of the pickle jar. The heat causes both objects to expand, but the heat causes the metal to expand more than the glass. This loosens the seal of the metal lid, making it easier to open the jar. The correct answer is D.

5. B

Insulation materials are any materials that limit heat transfer by being poor conductors of heat. The best way to reduce the heat loss through the roof is to add more insulation to the attic. The correct answer is B.

6. B

Convection is the process in which heat transfers from one place to another by the movement of the particles in the medium. Chimneys are at the top of houses to provide an outlet for warm air, while cooler fresh air enters in through doors and windows. The correct answer is B.

7. D

Conduction is the transfer of heat by direct contact with the heat source. The particles in the material that are in contact with the heat source transfer the heat energy to the particles they are in contact with, increasing their temperature. The correct answer is D.

8. D

Bowden's only true Statement is IV: conduction is a form of heat transfer. The correct answer is D.

Radiation is a form of heat transfer; heat is not a form of radiation. Temperature is not a form of heat; temperature measures heat. Convection is a form of heat transfer. It is not a form of radiation.

9. D

As the metal pot gains heat, the particles vibrate back and forth, but they remain very close to each other. When the heat transfers to the water, the particles are farther apart and have more freedom of movement. When heat transfers to the surrounding air, the particles move quickly and with the most energy. Their spaces are the greatest.

Therefore, image I represents the particles in the metal pot, image II represents the particles in water, and image III represents the particles in air.
The correct answer is D.

10. D

When a wire hanger bends back and forth, it becomes very hot at the location of the bend. This is an example of heat produced by distortion. The correct answer is D.

Using a hand pump compresses the air inside to produce heat. Rubbing your hands together produces heat because of friction. Driving a nail into wood with a hammer produces heat by friction.

11. A

The summer heat causes the metal particles to move apart. As a result, the metal electrical lines expand, causing them to sag. During the winter, the cold air causes the particles in the metal move more slowly, so the volume of the metal wires decreases. As a result, the power lines become tighter and the lines hang higher in the winter. The correct answer is A.

12. B

A high-wattage bulb produces more heat than a low-wattage bulb. The heat expands the air in the bag above the light bulb, causing the lunch bag to rise upward. Therefore, a bulb with a higher wattage on side A will cause the apparatus on that side to swing upward. This situation occurs in trials 1 and 4. The correct answer is B.

13. C

Heat transfers between solids by conduction. In this case, heat transfers from the solid hand to the solid ice cube. The correct answer is C.

14. A

Water and land heat up and cool off at different rates. This occurs because the land reflects more of the sun's radiant energy, while the ocean absorbs more of the energy.

As a result, the air above the land is exposed to more heat energy during the day, so it warms up. The air above the ocean is not exposed to as much reflected heat energy, so it remains cooler. The warm air above the land rises in the atmosphere, and it needs to be replaced. The air from above the ocean blows in to replace the rising air, creating a wind from the ocean to the land.

However, after the sun sets in the evening, the land cools off quickly because it does not absorb much heat energy, while the ocean remains warm because of the heat it absorbs during the day. The ocean then radiates this energy into the air above it, causing the air above the ocean to be warmer than the air above the land. Thus, the air rises and is replaced by the air from above the land, creating a wind from the land to the ocean.

The correct answer is A.

15. B

Recall that heat transfers by three different methods: conduction, convection, and radiation.

Conduction occurs when heat transfers by the contact of two different materials. In this case, heat transfers through the glass by conduction.

Convection occurs when heat transfers within a fluid by the movement of the fluid's particles. Heat transfers throughout the water by convection.

Radiation occurs when heat passes through a material without heating the particles in the material. The transfer of heat by radiation does not directly apply to this example.

The correct answer is B.

16. B

The initial source of heat energy came from the sun. The heat travelled by waves through empty space. This heat energy transferred to the snowman by radiation. The correct answer is B.

17. B

The emission of greenhouse gases causes an increase in the greenhouse effect. Greenhouse gases include water vapour, carbon dioxide, methane, nitrous oxide, and ozone. Among the given modes of transportation, airplanes emit the greatest amount of gases into the atmosphere. Thus, airplanes have the greatest impact on the greenhouse effect.
The correct answer is B.

A bicycle does not emit any greenhouse gases, but its rider does emit carbon dioxide with each breath. A horse cart releases a small amount of carbon dioxide with each breath of the horse. An electric train does not directly emit any gases into the atmosphere. However, it does impact the greenhouse effect if the electricity used to power the train comes from power plants that use fossil fuels to generate electricity.

18. C

The greenhouse effect occurs when radiant heat is trapped around Earth by gases in the atmosphere. These gases prevent the reflected radiant heat from Earth's surface from escaping back into space. The region in Alicia's diagram that represents the atmosphere is Region V. The correct answer is C.

19. C

When cattle digest food, they create methane gas as a byproduct. The gas passes through the digestive system and into the air. The manure created by the cattle also produces methane gas as it decomposes. The air quality test near the farmer's feedlot would probably indicate higher levels of methane gas. The correct answer is C.

Key Strategies for Success on Tests

KEY STRATEGIES FOR SUCCESS ON TESTS

THINGS TO CONSIDER WHEN TAKING A TEST

It is normal to feel anxious before you write a test. You can manage this anxiety by using the following strategies:

- Think positive thoughts. Imagine yourself doing well on the test.
- Make a conscious effort to relax by taking several slow, deep, controlled breaths. Concentrate on the air going in and out of your body.
- Before you begin the test, ask questions if you are unsure of anything.
- Jot down key words or phrases from any instructions your teacher gives you.
- Look over the entire test to find out the number and kinds of questions on the test.
- Read each question closely, and reread if necessary.
- Pay close attention to key vocabulary words. Sometimes, these words are **bolded** or *italicized*, and they are usually important words in the question.
- If you are putting your answers on an answer sheet, mark your answers carefully. Always print clearly. If you wish to change an answer, erase the mark completely, and ensure that your final answer is darker than the one you have erased.
- Use highlighting to note directions, key words, and vocabulary that you find confusing or that are important to answering the question.
- Double-check to make sure you have answered everything before handing in your test.
- When taking tests, students often overlook the easy words. Failure to pay close attention to these words can result in an incorrect answer. One way to avoid this is to be aware of these words and to underline, circle, or highlight them while you are taking the test.
- Even though some words are easy to understand, they can change the meaning of the entire question, so it is important that you pay attention to them. Here are some examples.

all	always	most likely	probably	best	not
difference	usually	except	most	unlikely	likely

Example

1. Which of the following expressions is **incorrect**?

A. $3 + 2 \geq 5$

B. $4 - 3 < 2$

C. $5 \times 4 < 15$

D. $6 \times 3 \geq 18$

TEST PREPARATION AND TEST-TAKING SKILLS

HELPFUL STRATEGIES FOR ANSWERING MULTIPLE-CHOICE QUESTIONS

A multiple-choice question gives you some information and then asks you to select an answer from four choices. Each question has one correct answer. The other choices are distractors, which are incorrect.

The following strategies can help you when answering multiple-choice questions:

- Quickly skim through the entire test. Find out how many questions there are, and plan your time accordingly.
- Read and reread questions carefully. Underline key words, and try to think of an answer before looking at the choices.
- If there is a graphic, look at the graphic, read the question, and go back to the graphic. Then, you may want to underline the important information from the question.
- Carefully read the choices. Read the question first and then each choice that goes with it.
- When choosing an answer, try to eliminate those choices that are clearly wrong or do not make sense.
- Some questions may ask you to select the best answer. These questions will always include words like *best*, *most appropriate*, or *most likely*. All of the choices will be correct to some degree, but one of the choices will be better than the others in some way. Carefully read all four choices before choosing the answer you think is the best.
- If you do not know the answer, or if the question does not make sense to you, it is better to guess than to leave it blank.
- Do not spend too much time on any one question. Make a mark (*) beside a difficult question, and come back to it later. If you are leaving a question to come back to later, make sure you also leave the space on the answer sheet, if you are using one.

- Remember to go back to the difficult questions at the end of the test; sometimes, clues are given throughout the test that will provide you with answers.
- Note any negative words like *no* or *not*, and be sure your answer fits the question.
- Before changing an answer, be sure you have a very good reason to do so.
- Do not look for patterns on your answer sheet, if you are using one.

HELPFUL STRATEGIES FOR ANSWERING WRITTEN-RESPONSE QUESTIONS

A written response requires you to respond to a question or directive indicated by words such as explain, predict, list, describe, show your work, solve, or calculate. The following strategies can help you when answering written-response questions:

- Read and reread the question carefully.
- Recognize and pay close attention to directing words such as *explain*, *show your work*, and *describe*.
- Underline key words and phrases that indicate what is required in your answer, such as *explain*, *estimate*, *answer*, *calculate*, or *show your work*.
- Write down rough, point-form notes regarding the information you want to include in your answer.
- Think about what you want to say, and organize information and ideas in a coherent and concise manner within the time limit you have for the question.
- Be sure to answer every part of the question that is asked.
- Include as much information as you can when you are asked to explain your thinking.
- Include a picture or diagram if it will help to explain your thinking.
- Try to put your final answer to a problem in a complete sentence to be sure it is reasonable.
- Reread your response to ensure you have answered the question.
- Ask yourself if your answer makes sense.
- Ask yourself if your answer sounds right.
- Use appropriate subject vocabulary and terms in your response.

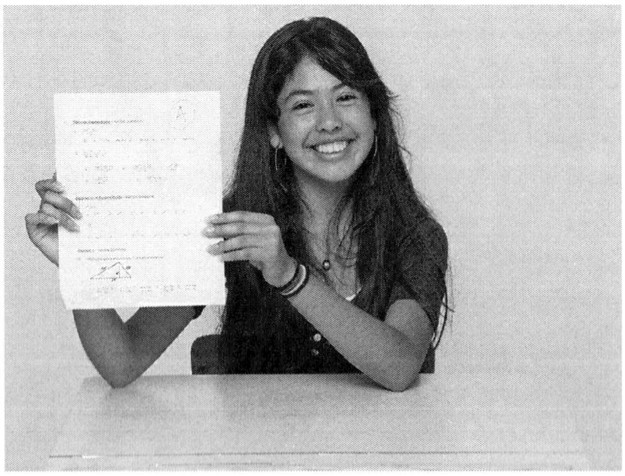

What You Need to Know about Science Tests

To do well on a science test, you need to understand and apply your knowledge of scientific concepts. Reading skills can also make a difference in how well you perform. Reading skills can help you follow instructions and find key words, as well as read graphs, diagrams, and tables.

Science tests usually have two types of questions: knowledge questions and skill questions. Knowledge questions test for your understanding of science ideas. Skill questions test how you would use your science knowledge.

How You Can Prepare for Science Tests

The following strategies are particular to preparing for and writing science tests:

- Note taking is a good way to review and study important information from your class notes and textbook.
- Sketch a picture of the process or idea being described in a question. Drawing is helpful for learning and remembering concepts.
- Check your answer to practice questions the require formulas by working backward to the beginning. You can find the beginning by going step by step in reverse order.
- Use the following steps when answering questions with graphics (pictures, diagrams, tables, or graphs):
  1. Read the title of the graphic and any key words.
  2. Read the test question carefully to figure out what information you need to find in the graphic.
  3. Go back to the graphic to find the information you need.
- Always pay close attention when pressing the keys on your calculator. Repeat the procedure a second time to be sure you pressed the correct keys.

Test Preparation Countdown

If you develop a plan for studying and test preparation, you will perform well on tests.

Here is a general plan to follow seven days before you write a test.

Countdown: 7 Days before the Test

1. Use "Finding Out about the Test" to help you make your own personal test preparation plan.
2. Review the following information:
   - Areas to be included on the test
   - Types of test items
   - General and specific test tips
3. Start preparing for the test at least seven days before the test. Develop your test preparation plan, and set time aside to prepare and study.

Countdown: 6, 5, 4, 3, 2 Days before the Test

1. Review old homework assignments, quizzes, and tests.
2. Rework problems on quizzes and tests to make sure you still know how to solve them.
3. Correct any errors made on quizzes and tests.
4. Review key concepts, processes, formulas, and vocabulary.
5. Create practice test questions for yourself, and answer them. Work out many sample problems.

Countdown: The Night before the Test

1. Use the night before the test for final preparation, which includes reviewing and gathering materials needed for the test before going to bed.
2. Most importantly, get a good night's rest, and know you have done everything possible to do well on the test.

Test Day

1. Eat a healthy and nutritious breakfast.
2. Ensure you have all the necessary materials.
3. Think positive thoughts, such as "I can do this," "I am ready," and "I know I can do well."
4. Arrive at your school early, so you are not rushing, which can cause you anxiety and stress.

SUMMARY OF HOW TO BE SUCCESSFUL DURING A TEST

You may find some of the following strategies useful for writing a test:

- Take two or three deep breaths to help you relax.
- Read the directions carefully, and underline, circle, or highlight any important words.
- Look over the entire test to understand what you will need to do.
- Budget your time.
- Begin with an easy question or a question you know you can answer correctly rather than follow the numerical question order of the test.
- If you cannot remember how to answer a question, try repeating the deep breathing and physical relaxation activities. Then, move on to visualization and positive self-talk to get yourself going.
- When answering questions with graphics (pictures, diagrams, tables, or graphs), look at the question carefully, and use the following steps:
    1. Read the title of the graphic and any key words.
    2. Read the test question carefully to figure out what information you need to find in the graphic.
    3. Go back to the graphic to find the information you need.
- Write down anything you remember about the subject on the reverse side of your test paper. This activity sometimes helps to remind you that you do know something and are capable of writing the test.
- Look over your test when you have finished, and double-check your answers to be sure you did not forget anything.

NOTES

Practice Tests

PRACTICE TEST 1

1. People wear heavy woollen clothes in the winter because these clothes
   A. allow moisture in
   B. keep the skin cool
   C. keep the body from getting wet
   D. prevent body heat from escaping

Use the following information to answer the next question.

In an experiment, Michelle used the heat from one candle to melt ice blocks of different sizes. In the given table, she recorded the amount of time that it took each ice block to melt.

Volume of the ice	Time to melt
10 mL	1 min
50 mL	4 min
90 mL	8 min
130 mL	12 min

2. It can be inferred from Michelle's data that the amount of heat required to melt an ice block is directly proportional to the ice block's
   A. mass
   B. density
   C. volume
   D. temperature

Use the following information to answer the next question.

The thermos flask, invented by Scottish scientist Sir James Dewar in the 1890s, was first used to store liquid gases at very low temperatures. A thermos can also be used to carry and insulate hot liquids. A thermos, however, is not able to maintain liquids at a constant temperature indefinitely.

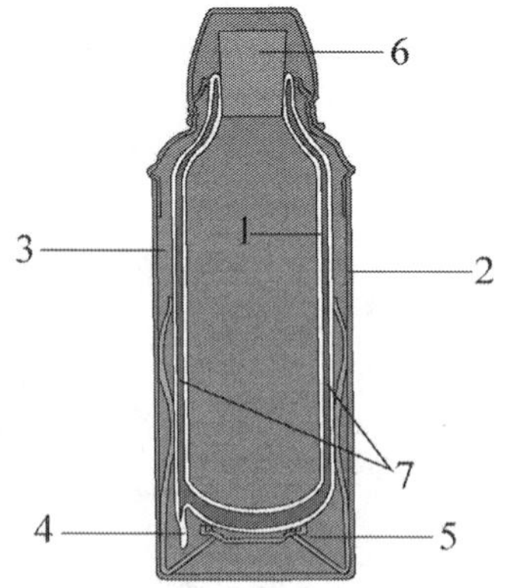

The structure of most thermos flasks is very simple. The flask has a double-walled glass vessel (1 and 2) sealed at the neck with a plastic cap (6). A vacuum (3) exists between the two glass walls. This vacuum prevents the flow of heat into and out of the flask. As well, reflective material inside the container reduces heat loss by radiation.

3. The flask should be kept upright so that no fluid comes in contact with the plastic cap because
   A. the liquid can escape from the flask through the neck
   B. heat loss through the sides of the flask is greater than through the lid
   C. too much pressure on the lid will cause the glass walls in the thermos to break
   D. no vacuum exists at the neck of the flask, so the loss of heat would be greatly accelerated

4. In solids, heat transfer occurs by
   A. conduction and radiation
   B. convection and radiation
   C. conduction only
   D. convection only

Use the following information to answer the next question.

Jacob gave an oral presentation to his class about heat. He made the following four statements about heat:

1. Heat is measured in degrees Celsius
2. Heat travels from a cold object to a hot object.
3. Heat transfer has an effect on weather patterns.
4. Heat transfer by convection helps large birds glide for hours.

5. Which two of Jacob's statements about heat are **false**?
   A. Statements 1 and 2
   B. Statements 2 and 3
   C. Statements 1 and 4
   D. Statements 3 and 4

Use the following information to answer the next question.

Joanne draws a diagram to represent the particles in a beaker of water. She also wants to draw a diagram of the same beaker of water after it is heated to a temperature that is less than 100°C.

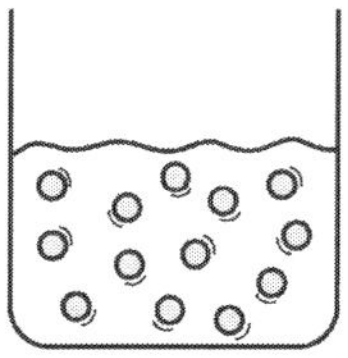

6. Which of the following diagrams **best** shows what happens to the particles in the water as it is heated?

A.
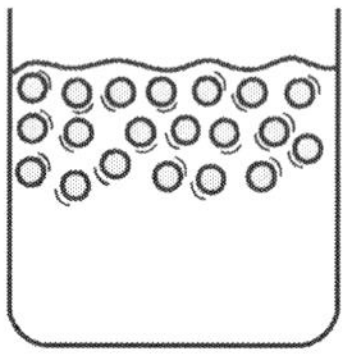

B.
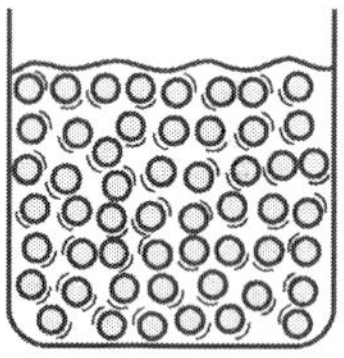

C.
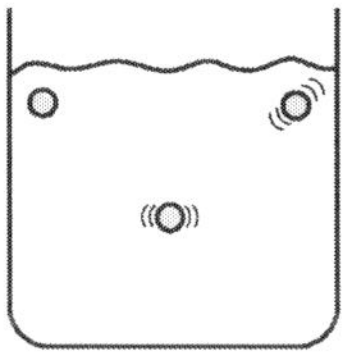

D.
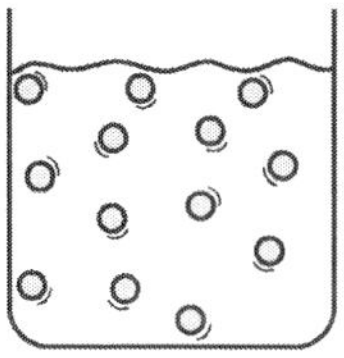

Use the following information to answer the next question.

Jamie filled four balloons to the same level with different matter. The following chart shows the different matter that he used.

Balloon 1	salt
Balloon 2	sand
Balloon 3	water
Balloon 4	helium

Jamie then placed all four balloons in the freezer.

7. Which balloon would have the **smallest** volume after five hours in the freezer?
   A. Balloon 1 **B.** Balloon 2
   C. Balloon 3 **D.** Balloon 4

Use the following information to answer the next question.

Kim set up an experiment to determine the heat conductivity of four different materials.

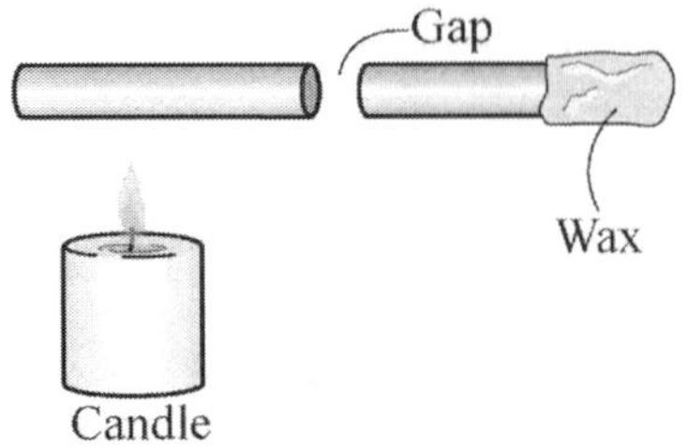

8. When placed in the gap, which of the following materials will cause the wax to melt the fastest?

A. Brick **B.** Wood

C. Copper **D.** Plastic

Use the following information to answer the next question.

Simon used a convection box model to demonstrate the movement of air currents for his science fair project.

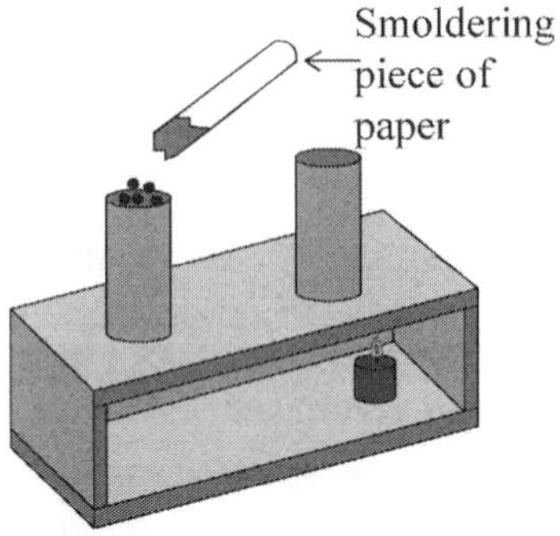

9. Which of the following diagrams shows the direction that the smoke-filled air currents will travel in Simon's apparatus?

A.
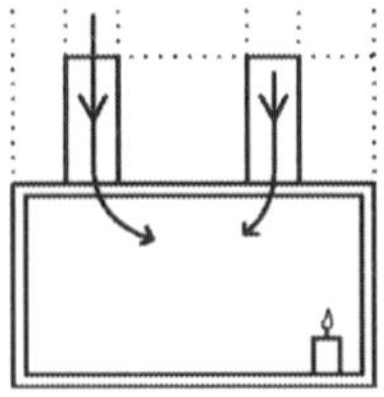

B.
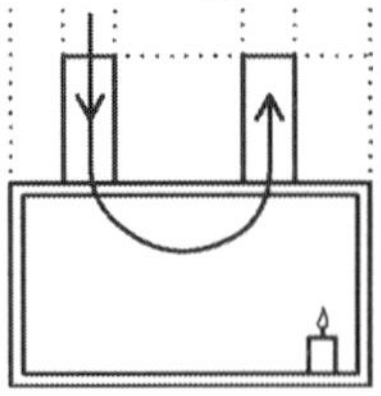

C.
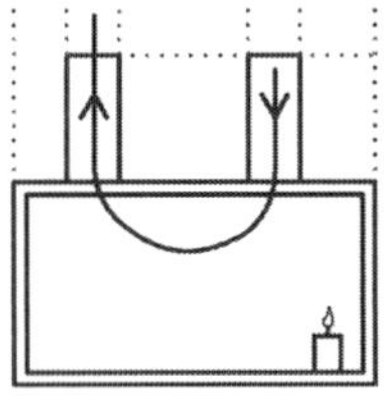

D.
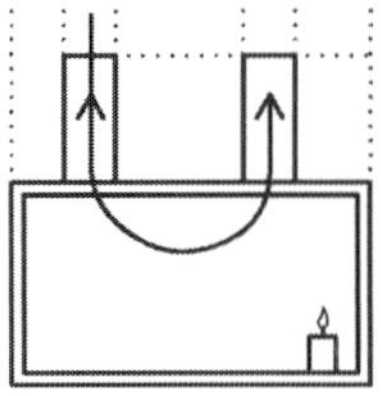

Use the following information to answer the next question.

Stephen uses two identical cans in an experiment. He paints one of the cans black and the other white. Then he fills both cans with the same amount of water and places a thermometer into the water in each. Simon places both of the cans in the sunlight. After 30 minutes, he records the temperature of the water in each can. Stephen notices that the temperature of the water in the black can is higher than the temperature of the water in the white can.

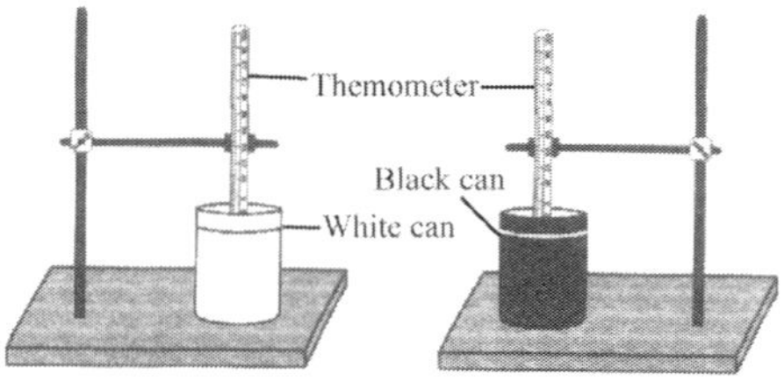

10. The temperature of the water in the black can is higher because the black paint

A. absorbs more radiant heat

B. reflects more radiant heat

C. prevents more heat loss

D. produces more heat

Use the following information to answer the next question.

The graph shows the average yearly surface temperature in a particular country from 1845 to 2005.

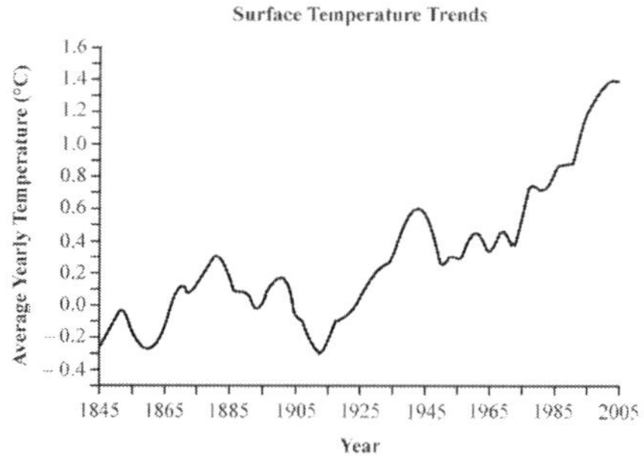

11. The sharp rise in the average yearly temperature from 1985 to 2005 was **most likely** caused by

A. a change in the sun's activity

B. a decrease in the amount of cloud cover

C. an increase in volcanic activity around the world

D. an increase in the amount of greenhouse gases in the atmosphere

12. A carbon tax is an environmental tax that certain provinces use to reduce greenhouse emissions. Which industry will be **most** affected by a carbon tax?

A. Fishing industry

B. Steel industry

C. Dairy industry

D. Oil industry

13. A sports company designing a new pair of hockey skates experiments with different synthetic materials. The **most important** factor to consider when choosing this material is its

A. brittleness **B.** hardness

C. plasticity **D.** ductility

Use the following information to answer the next question.

Taylor tries to lift a big box with the help of a pulley and a rope that does not stretch, as shown in the figure.

14. Which type of force acts on the rope because of the weight of the box?

A. Shear **B.** Torsion

C. Tension **D.** Compression

15. The magnitude of a load caused by an earthquake does **not** depend on the

A. mass of the structure

B. height of the structure

C. stiffness of the structure

D. building materials of the structure

Use the following information to answer the next question.

Abby built the following four model bridges out of Popsicle sticks.

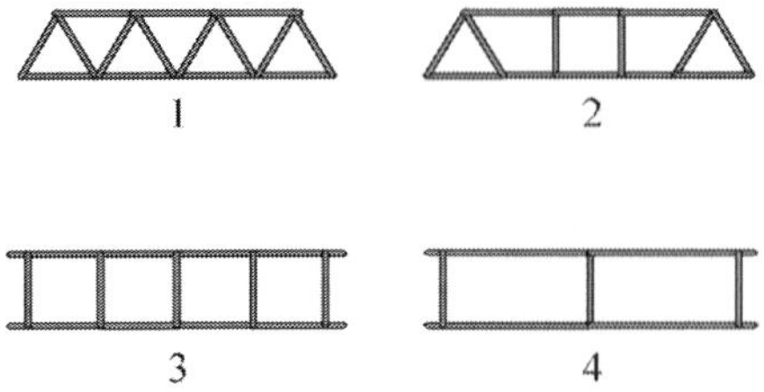

16. Which of Abby's model bridges will **most likely** hold the heaviest weight?

A. Bridge 1 **B.** Bridge 2

C. Bridge 3 **D.** Bridge 4

17. Many people in coastal regions build their houses with light-weight wood because this wood

A. protects the house from severe damage during earthquakes

B. is more environmentally friendly and prevents pollution

C. costs less than other materials

D. resists water damage

Use the following information to answer the next question.

Jaya plays with a ball of plasticine. He flattens the ball of plasticine into a pancake shape.

18. What type of force did Jaya apply to the ball of plasticine in order to change its shape?

A. Shear **B.** Torsion

C. Tension **D.** Compression

Use the following information to answer the next question.

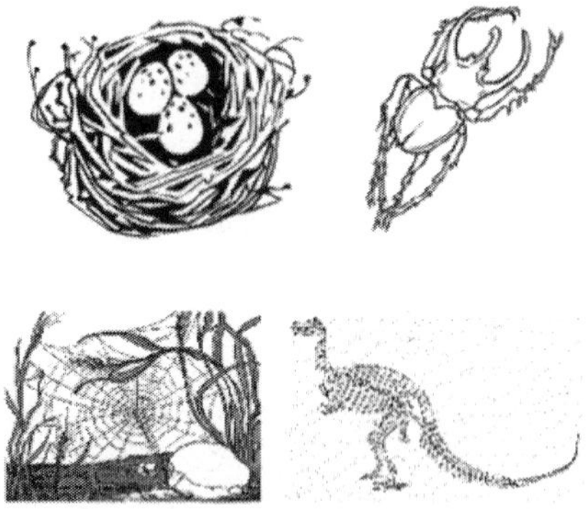

Four Structures

19. Which two of the given structures are examples of shell structures?

A. Bird's eggs and exoskeleton

B. Skeleton and spiders web

C. Skeleton and exoskeleton

D. Bird's eggs and skeleton

20. The centre of gravity for a symmetrical structure is located at the structure's

A. geometrical centre

B. highest point

C. lowest point

D. entire mass

Use the following information to answer the next question.

Kenny built a model sailboat. He set it in a long tank and placed a fan at the end of the tank to act as the wind. When he turned on the fan, however, Kenny found that his boat did not sail to the other end of the tank. Instead it tipped into the water.

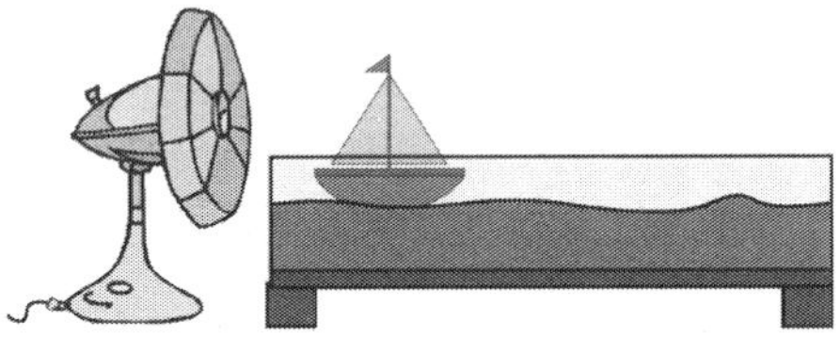

21. To make his boat sail straight across the tank of water, Kenny should change the

A. direction of the fan to create a wind force from the other side of the tank

B. angle of the sail to capture the wind force at the proper angle

C. size of the sail to capture a stronger wind force

D. size of the fan to create a stronger wind force

22. Which of the following forces is an external force?

A. Shear **B.** Gravity

C. Torsion **D.** Compression

23. Which of the following factors will have a negative effect on the structural stability of a building?

A. Using pre-approved materials

B. Distributing the load evenly

C. Decreasing the symmetry

D. Reinforcing the base

24. The Tacoma Narrows Bridge in Washington was built with girders that were only 2.4 metres deep. As a result, wind could easily move the bridge, which eventually caused the bridge to collapse. This is an example of

A. an extraordinary load

B. a foundation failure

C. a faulty construction

D. a poor design

Use the following information to answer the next question.

The disposal of mixtures can have negative environmental impacts. Mixtures may be composed of both harmful and non-harmful components. If the harmful component can be easily separated from the mixture, it can be disposed carefully while the non-harmful component can be reused.

25. An example of a mixture where the harmful component can be easily separated and disposed of is

A. sewage **B.** uranium

C. lead paint **D.** latex paint

Use the following information to answer the next question.

Hazardous product symbols are framed to indicate the substance's degree of danger.

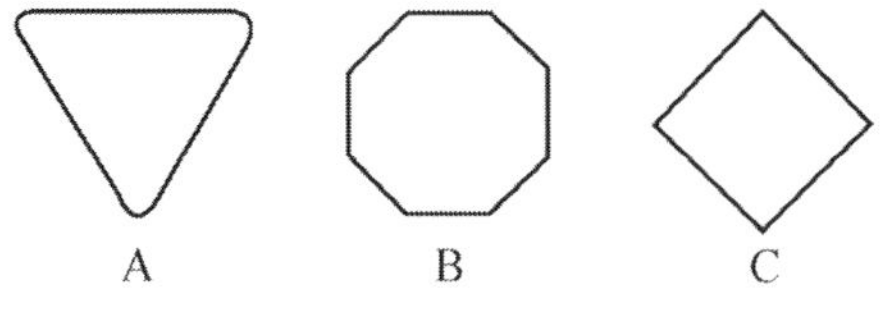

26. The product symbol frames A, B, and C refer to, respectively,

A. caution, warning, and danger

B. warning, danger, and caution

C. caution, danger, and warning

D. warning, caution, and danger

Use the following information to answer the next question.

Megan carried out a science experiment in which she dissolved salt in diluted hydrochloric acid. She gradually increased the temperature of the solution and recorded the amount of salt that dissolved at each temperature.

Temperature of Solution (°C)	Amount of Salt Dissolved (g)
0	125
15	160
30	220
45	290
60	450

27. According to Megan's data, which of the following statements is **true**?

A. Less salt dissolved in the acid as the temperature increased.

B. More salt dissolved in the acid as the temperature increased.

C. The difference in the amount of salt dissolved in the acid when the temperature increased from 0°C to 15°C is greater than the difference in the amount of salt dissolved when the temperature increased from 15°C to 30°C.

D. The difference in the amount of salt dissolved in the acid when the temperature increased from 45°C to 60°C is less than the difference in the amount of salt dissolved when the temperature increased from 30°C to 45°C.

28. If Mischa wants to separate paper clips from a mixture of sand, salt, and marbles, the separation method Mischa should use is

A. filtration **B.** distillation

C. magnetism **D.** evaporation

Use the following information to answer the next question.

Todd heated a solution to 100°C.
He added a solute to the heated solution until it was saturated. Then, he cooled the solution to room temperature.

29. When the solution reaches room temperature, the solution will be

A. saturated

B. unsaturated

C. supersaturated

D. mildly saturated

30. A solution is made by adding salt crystals to water. The salt crystals within the solution are the

A. solute **B.** solvent

C. sediment **D.** suspension

Use the following information to answer the next question.

Chloe classified some materials into three different groups.

Pure Substances	Solutions	Mechanical Mixtures
salt	gravy	cement
gold	juice crystals in water	topsoil
diamond	coffee with cream and sugar	rainwater

31. Which of the following items did Chloe place into the wrong group?

A. Salt **B.** Topsoil

C. Cement **D.** Rainwater

Use the following information to answer the next question.

The particles that make up gaseous substances are spaced *i* and have *ii*.

32. Which of the following tables completes the given statement?

A.

i	*ii*
far apart	free movement

B.

i	*ii*
far apart	limited movement

C.

i	*ii*
close together	free movement

D.

i	*ii*
close together	limited movement

Use the following information to answer the next question.

Jasmine used the following chart to describe the particles of four different liquids.

Type of Liquid	Description of Particles
Distilled water	Identical particles
Cheese sauce	Different particles
Orange juice	Different particles
Apple juice	Identical particles

33. Which of the liquids did Jasmine describe **incorrectly**?

A. Distilled water

B. Cheese sauce

C. Orange juice

D. Apple juice

Use the following information to answer the next question.

Crude oil is a complex mixture of organic liquids. It occurs naturally beneath Earth's surface and was formed over millions of years. Crude oil is vapourized and undergoes fractional distillation in which the liquid components are separated.

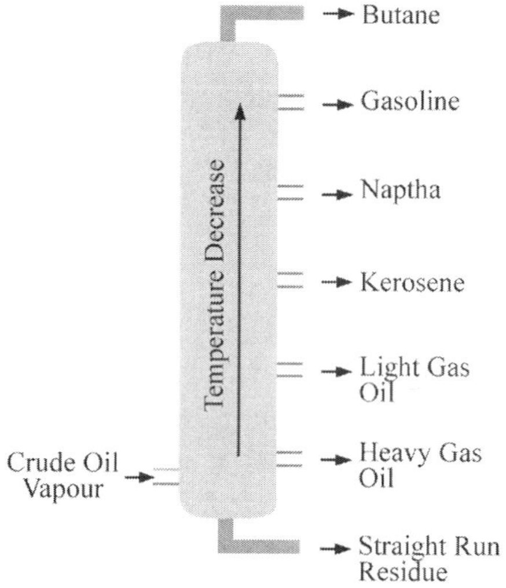

34. The liquids that are present in crude oil are separated in a distillation chamber because they have different

A. densities **B.** viscosities

C. boiling points **D.** melting points

Use the following information to answer the next question.

A solution is created by mixing 10 mL of water, 60 mL of liquid bluing, 40 mL of salt, and 35 mL of ammonia.

35. Which of the liquids acts as the solvent in the created solution?

A. Milk **B.** Water

C. Honey **D.** Sugar syrup

36. Which of the following units is **not** used to describe concentration?

A. mL **B.** g/L

C. ppm **D.** mg/L

37. Which of the following terms expresses the amount of solvent required to dissolve and saturate a specific amount of solute at a given temperature?

A. Solubility **B.** Malleability

C. Conductivity **D.** Melting point

38. Computers are much smaller today than they used to be. Which of the following statements **best** explains why the amount of natural resources used to make computers has not also decreased?

A. Smaller computers require a lot of electricity.

B. Old computers can now be recycled at eco-stations.

C. Computers are quickly outdated and are replaced frequently.

D. The manufacturing processes for computers have not changed.

Use the following information to answer the next question.

Julia wants to study the effects of different fertilizers on geranium plants.
She performs her experiments in a greenhouse.

39. The main advantage of using the same greenhouse for each trial in the experiment is that it sticks to fair testing principles because

A. the temperature, humidity, and sunlight will be the same for each trial

B. it is cheaper to use one greenhouse than several greenhouses

C. Julia will be able to check all her plants at the same time

D. the geraniums are protected from the wind and rain

Use the following information to answer the next question.

Recent droughts in Ontario, brought on by higher than normal temperatures, have negative impacts on the environment. It is believed that these droughts may be directly linked to human-caused climate change.

40. Which of the following scenarios is **not** an environmental concern associated with droughts?

A. Increased fire risk

B. Hot and humid weather

C. Soil erosion and dust storms

D. Increased pressure on fish habitats

Use the following information to answer the next question.

Linda planted her flower garden in May.

41. In order for Linda to properly describe the different flowers and insects in her garden, she should use the term

A. biotic **B.** non-living

C. producers **D.** population

42. The two basic components that make up all ecosystems are

A. permanent and temporary

B. terrestrial and aquatic

C. natural and artificial

D. biotic and abiotic

43. In a community, energy passes though a sequence of different species that is usually called the

A. energy pyramid **B.** nutrient cycle

C. water cycle **D.** food chain

44. The phytoplankton in a pond ecosystem act as

A. producers

B. decomposers

C. primary consumers

D. secondary consumers

Use the following information to answer the next question.

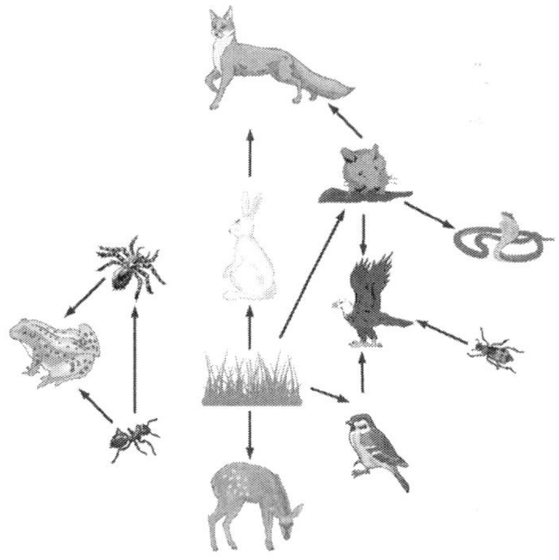

A Food Web

45. An increase in the spider population in this food web will lead to an increase in the population of

A. coyotes **B.** frogs

C. deer **D.** ants

Use the following information to answer the next question.

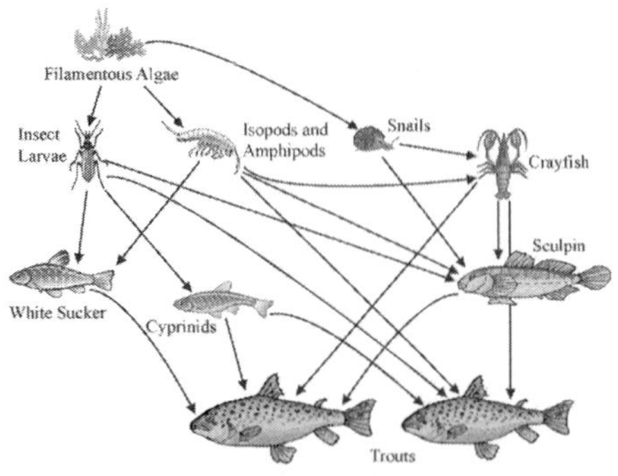

An aquatic food web for a particular region

46. If humans entered into the given food web and began to trap the snails, which organism would be the **most** affected by the decline of the snail population?

A. Trout **B.** Crayfish

C. Cyprinid **D.** White sucker

Use the following information to answer the next question.

The Water Cycle

47. Water vapour forms water droplets at position *Y*. This process is called

A. evaporation **B.** precipitation

C. transpiration **D.** condensation

48. On which of the following landforms will primary succession occur?

A. Deforested land

B. Agricultural fields

C. Water-logged soil

D. Newly emerged land

Use the following information to answer the next question.

A herd of 1 000 white-tailed deer lives in a woodland area near Lake Superior. The following resources are available in the woodland area:

- Food for 10 000 white-tailed deer
- Water for 20 000 white-tailed deer
- Shelter for 2 500 white-tailed deer
- Space for 5 000 white-tailed deer

49. How many **more** white-tailed deer could live in this woodland area?

A. 1 500 **B.** 4 000

C. 9 000 **D.** 19 000

Use the following information to answer the next question.

Humans often alter the natural balances and interactions in an ecosystem. Sometimes this is done intentionally. For example, in the early 1990s, the Yukon government introduced a plan to reduce the wolf population in the Yukon by killing and sterilizing large numbers of wolves.

50. Which of the following statements **best** explains the government decision to reduce the wolf population?

A. Fewer wolves would help stop the decline in caribou and moose populations.

B. Wolves were beginning to threaten humans in the towns and cities.

C. Fewer wolves would increase tourism in the area.

D. Wolves were killing too many livestock animals.

PRACTICE TEST 2

Use the following information to answer the next question.

The following diagrams all depict alternate methods for producing electricity.

X

Y

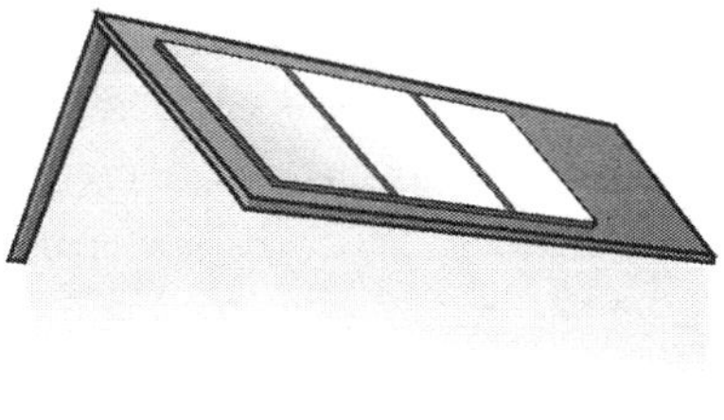

Z

1. Which of the following charts identifies each of the energy sources depicted in the given diagrams?

A.

X	Y	Z
Solar energy	Hydroelec-tric energy	Geothermal energy

B.

X	Y	Z
Wind energy	Geothermal energy	Nuclear energy

C.

X	Y	Z
Nuclear energy	Geothermal energy	Solar energy

D.

X	Y	Z
Wind energy	Hydroelectric energy	Solar energy

2. When a solid substance converts into a liquid, the
   A. temperature of the substance decreases
   B. volume of the substance increases
   C. mass of the substance decreases
   D. mass of the substance increases

Use the following information to answer the next question.

Luc wants to improve the energy efficiency of his room. He needs a device that will show him where heat escapes from his room.

3. Which of the following devices will be **most helpful** for determining where heat loss occurs in Luc's room?
   A. Thermographic camera
   B. Digital video camera
   C. Thermometer
   D. Thermostat

4. An electric space heater heats a room through the combined processes of
   A. conduction and evaporation
   B. conduction and convection
   C. radiation and convection
   D. radiation and conduction

5. Which of the following concept maps shows the relationship between the terms heat, radiation, conduction, and convection?

A.

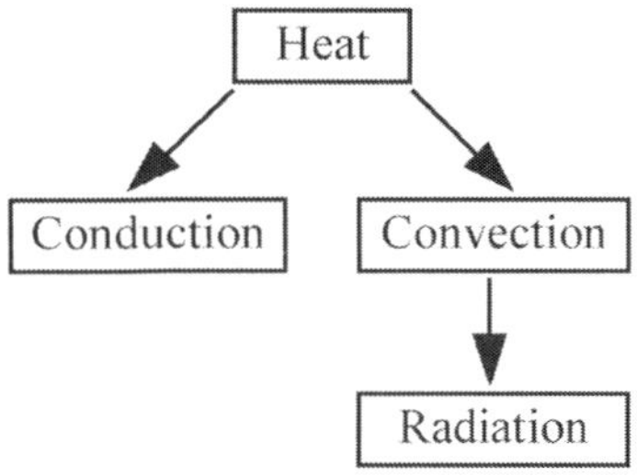

B.

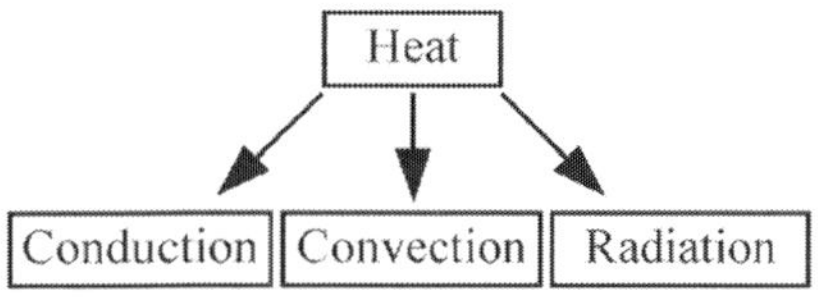

C.

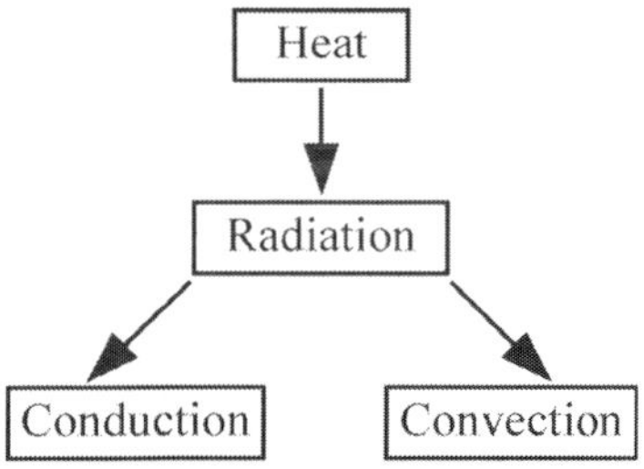

D.

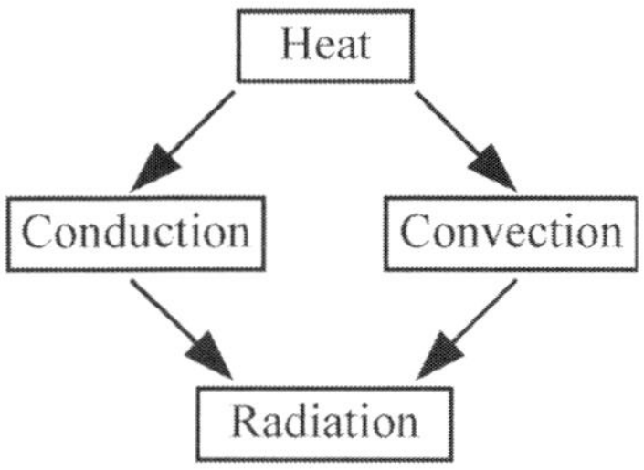

Use the following information to answer the next question.

> Sasha tried to explain to her friend how the particles in matter move. She made the following four statements about the movement of particles in the different states of matter:
>
> I. The particles in gases move faster than the particles in solids.
> II. The particles in solids move faster than the particles in liquids.
> III. The particles in gases are more spread apart than the particles in solids.
> IV. The particles in liquids are more spread apart than the particles in gases.

6. Which two of Sasha's statements about the movement of particles in matter are **true**?
   A. Statements I and III
   B. Statements II and IV
   C. Statements III and IV
   D. Statements II and III

Use the following information to answer the next question.

> Patrick made the following list of examples of renewable and non-renewable sources of heat energy for his class presentation.
>
> I. Collecting sunlight to warm a barrel of water
> II. Burning coal to produce electrical power
> III. Using geothermal energy to heat homes
> IV. Burning gasoline to run an engine

7. The two renewable sources of heat energy are given in examples
   A. I and II **B.** I and III
   C. II and III **D.** III and IV

Use the following information to answer the next question.

Sabrina constructed two diagrams to show the relationship between the heat gained or lost by matter and the volume of that matter.

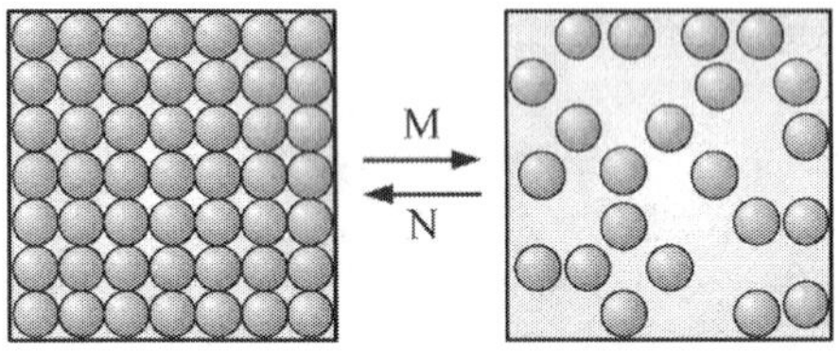

Diagram one

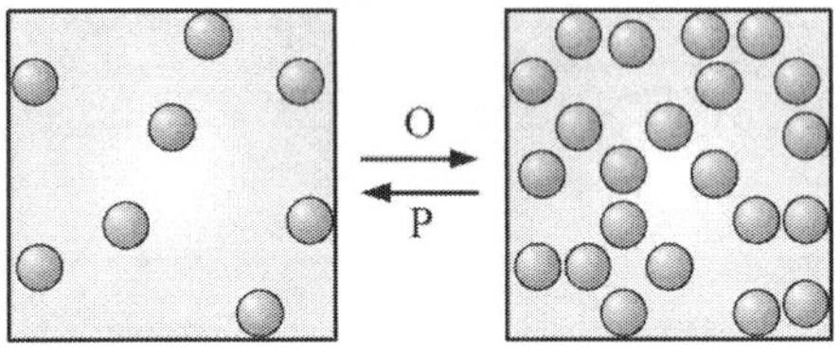

Diagram two

8. Which two arrows show the effect that cooling a substance has on the spacing of its particles?

A. Arrows M and O
B. Arrows N and P
C. Arrows O and N
D. Arrows P and M

Use the following information to answer the next question.

Three pins are attached to a metallic rod by wax. When the rod is heated at one end, each of the pins separates and falls from the rod.

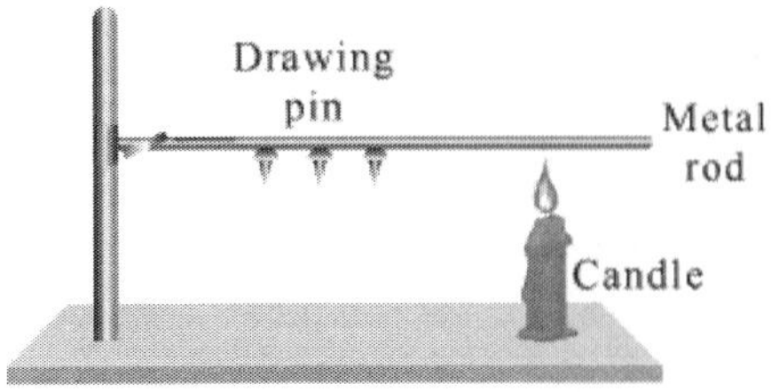

9. The heat transfers from the warm rod to the wax and pins by

A. radiation
B. induction
C. convection
D. conduction

10. Which of the following processes does **not** involve the transfer of heat by convection?

A. Formation of mineral crystals
B. Creation of ocean currents
C. Occurrence of sea breezes
D. Development of thermals

Use the following information to answer the next question.

Consider the following characteristics that relate to methods of heat transfer:

I. Travels from particle to particle
II. Takes place in a vacuum
III. Moves in waves
IV. Occurs in a gas

11. Which two of the given characteristics relate only to the transfer of heat by radiation?

A. I and III
B. I and IV
C. III and IV
D. II and III

Use the following information to answer the next question.

Tia knows that many objects on Earth give off radiant heat. She also knows that the atmosphere traps more of this heat than it used to, and that more heat in the atmosphere results in rising temperatures.

12. Which of the following factors is **least likely** to be affected by the trapped heat energy?

A. Rising sea levels
B. Increased daylight
C. Retreating glaciers
D. Severe drought conditions

Use the following information to answer the next question.

Clear-cutting and burning large areas of the Amazon rainforest has contributed greatly to the greenhouse effect and global warming.

13. The destruction of large areas of rainforest has
- **A.** increased the oxygen level and decreased the carbon dioxide level
- **B.** decreased the oxygen level and increased the carbon dioxide level
- **C.** decreased both the oxygen and carbon dioxide levels
- **D.** increased both the oxygen and carbon dioxide levels

14. It is important that tools, equipment, and furniture are ergonomically designed in order to
- **A.** make products more affordable
- **B.** make products environmentally friendly
- **C.** increase the safety of products for human use
- **D.** increase the maximum load that a product can bear

Use the following information to answer the next question.

Wilbur's little sister is fascinated with a jack-in-the-box toy that she received for her birthday. She wants to know what causes it to burst out of the box every time the lid opens.

15. Wilbur tells his little sister that the toy contains a spring that is
- **A.** cooled
- **B.** heated
- **C.** stretched
- **D.** compressed

16. The weight of a structure is also called its
- **A.** static load
- **B.** natural load
- **C.** dynamic load
- **D.** permanent load

17. Which of the following strategies will **not** help increase the stability of a beam bridge?
- **A.** Reinforcing the beam
- **B.** Building an arch under the beam
- **C.** Increasing the thickness of the beam
- **D.** Using a stronger material for the beam

Use the following information to answer the next question.

A structural engineer designs an apartment building with balconies. The engineer has determined that on average there will be an external load between 1 000–1 500 kg on each balcony.

18. To ensure structural safety, the balconies should be designed to support a maximum load of
- **A.** 1 000 kg
- **B.** 1 500 kg
- **C.** 1 550 kg
- **D.** 4 500 kg

Use the following information to answer the next question.

A truss is a frame built to support ceilings, walls, or beams. Tara built the four given trusses out of craft sticks and milk cartons. She tests each of the trusses by placing math textbooks on each one until it collapses.

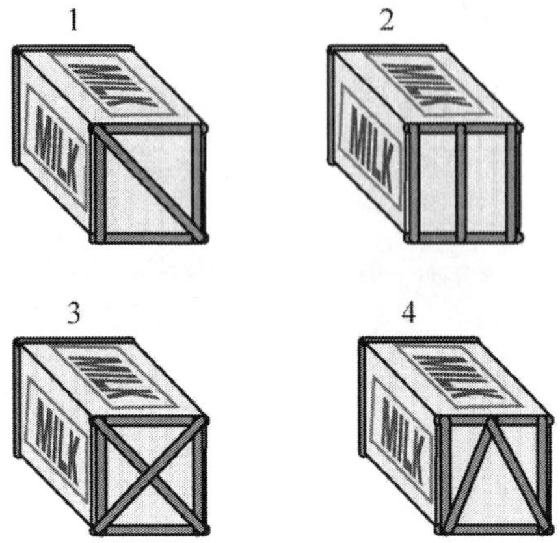

19. Which of Tara's trusses will hold the **greatest** number of math textbooks?

A. Truss 1 **B.** Truss 2

C. Truss 3 **D.** Truss 4

Use the following information to answer the next question.

Living Structure	Non-Living Structure
Skeleton	Domed roof
Chicken egg	Brick wall
Tree trunk	Bicycle

20. Which of the following pairs of living and non-living structures is an example of a frame structure?

A. Skeleton and bicycle

B. Tree trunk and brick wall

C. Skeleton and domed roof

D. Chicken egg and domed roof

21. The centre of gravity in an airplane is located in the

A. tail of the airplane

B. top of the airplane

C. wings of the airplane

D. middle of the airplane

Use the following information to answer the next question.

Simon holds a tea bag on a string, as shown in the figure.

22. Which of the following pairs of forces acts on the tea bag while Simon holds it in his hand?

A. Shear and torsion forces

B. Torsion and compression forces

C. Gravitational and tension forces

D. Compression and gravitational forces

23. Which of the following units describes the magnitude of a force applied to a structure?

A. Metres per second

B. Degrees

C. Newtons

D. Joules

24. When a truck crosses a bridge on a windy day, the static load experienced by the bridge is the

A. force of the expanding metal on the bridge deck

B. weight of the moving truck on the bridge deck

C. force of the wind acting on the bridge deck

D. weight of the bridge deck

25. Which of the following building concerns is **not** affected by symmetry?

A. Centre of gravity

B. Aesthetic appeal

C. Structural stability

D. Structural strength

26. Which of the following soil foundations would provide the **most stable** support for a large highrise building?

A. Sand **B.** Rock

C. Clay **D.** Silt

Use the following information to answer the next question.

During the production of maple syrup, the water component of the sap is evaporated. Evaporating most of the water leaves a thick sugar and water mixture that is called maple syrup.

27. A negative environmental impact of maple syrup production is that the evaporation process

A. produces water pollution

B. uses up too many trees

C. produces air pollution

D. uses a lot of energy

Use the following information to answer the next question.

Jacinta needs to set up an experiment where she dissolves sugar in water. She makes a list of the factors that will affect the rate of solubility of sugar in water.

1. stirring the water
2. using a smaller sugar cube
3. increasing the temperature of the water
4. breaking up the sugar cube

28. Which of the following procedures will **not** affect the solubility rate of the sugar cube in water?

A. Stirring the water

B. Using a smaller sugar cube

C. Breaking up the sugar cube

D. Increasing the temperature of the water

29. A spoonful of sand is mixed with a bucket of water. If the mixture is boiled indefinitely, the result will be that the

A. water will evaporate and the sand will remain

B. water will remain and the sand will evaporate

C. neither the sand nor the water will evaporate

D. both the sand and water will evaporate

30. Which of the following substances **cannot** be classified as a mixture?

A. Air **B.** Mercury

C. Concrete **D.** Salt water

Use the following information to answer the next question.

Stephanie and Brent make tea for themselves. Stephanie puts two tea bags into one cup of water. Brent puts a single tea bag into the same amount of water. Therefore, Brent's tea is more ____*i*____ than Stephanie's tea.

31. Which of the following terms completes the given statement?

A. Concentrated **B.** Saturated

C. Potent **D.** Dilute

32. Which of the following metals is an example of a mixture?

A. Bronze **B.** Zinc

C. Iron **D.** Tin

Use the following information to answer the next question.

A dance teacher asks her students to move with the speed of the music. Jolene, one of the students, points out that this exercise could illustrate the processes that occur when matter changes state.

33. Which process is **best** illustrated when the students move to extremely fast music that slows down but does not stop?

A. Condensation **B.** Solidification

C. Sublimation **D.** Evaporation

Use the following information to answer the next question.

Some Mixtures

I	II	III	IV
Sand and dry cement	Lime juice and water	Water and corn starch	Pancake mix and milk
Sugar and gelatin powder	Soda pop and water	Milk and cocoa powder	Flour and water
Flour and baking powder	Syrup and lemon-ade	Ginger ale and juice	Baking powder and oil

34. Which of the columns in the given chart should be labelled "Solutions"?

A. Column I **B.** Column II

C. Column III **D.** Column IV

Use the following information to answer the next question.

Anish needs to separate each of the following mixtures.

1. Salt and Pepper
2. Sand and Water
3. Sugar and Water
4. Iron filings and Sand

35. Which of the following charts shows the **best** method Anish should use to separate each mixture?

A.

Mixture	Method of Separation
1	Filtration
2	Attraction by static electricity
3	Magnetism
4	Evaporation

B.

Mixture	Method of Separation
1	Magnetism
2	Attraction by static electricity
3	Filtration
4	Evaporation

C.

Mixture	Method of Separation
1	Attraction by static electricity
2	Evaporation
3	Filtration
4	Magnetism

D.

Mixture	Method of Separation
1	Attraction by static electricity
2	Filtration
3	Evaporation
4	Magnetism

36. Which of the following solutions contains a solute that is in a gas state and a solvent that is in a liquid state?

A. Air **B.** Perfume

C. Soft drink **D.** Salt water

37. Jenna made a sugar solution by adding 50 g of sugar to 500 mL of water. The concentration of her solution, per 100 mL of solvent, is

A. 1 g/100 mL **B.** 10 g/100 mL

C. 50 g/100 mL **D.** 500 g/100 mL

38. Water is referred to as the universal solvent. One of the problems that results from this property of water is that

A. it is difficult to dissolve solutes in water

B. water can dissolve all substances

C. water can be easily polluted

D. oil easily mixes with water

Use the following information to answer the next question.

A farmer is told that he can wipe out an infestation of grasshoppers in his wheat crops by spraying his fields with large amounts of pesticide. The farmer is familiar with the principles of Integrated Pest Management (IPM), and disagrees with the recommendation.

39. Which of the following statements does **not** explain the farmer's position?

A. Too much pesticide might harm other insect species.

B. Large pesticide amounts could seep into water systems.

C. Multiple applications of the pesticide would be preferable.

D. Eliminating all the insects would require a large amount of money.

Use the following information to answer the next question.

Zebra mussels are an invasive species in the Great Lakes. New mussels settle on hard surfaces, including rocks, boats, wood, and even on top of native mussel species. Then, they feed on phytoplankton.

40. The zebra mussel is considered a dangerous invasive species in the Great Lakes because they

A. out-compete native species for valuable food resources

B. clog up the channels and get stuck in boat propellers

C. out-compete native species for mates

D. are parasites of the native fish species

41. When Michele and Diane discuss the ability of the ecosystem in their local lake to continue to thrive over time, they are discussing the ecosystem's

A. sustainability **B.** integrity

C. viability **D.** strength

Use the following information to answer the next question.

Painted turtles basking in the sun on logs in Ontario's Algonquin Park.

42. The complex interactions between the turtles and their environment is considered

A. an ecosystem **B.** a community

C. a population **D.** a habitat

Use the following information to answer the next question.

A wetland ecosystem

43. Which of the following items seen in the photo of a wetland ecosystem would be classified as abiotic?

A. Deer **B.** Trees

C. Grass **D.** Water

Use the following information to answer the next question.

Rose bush → aphid → ladybug → spider → robin → hawk

44. Which of the following roles does the spider fulfill in the given food chain?

A. Producer

B. Tertiary consumer

C. Primary consumer

D. Secondary consumer

Use the following information to answer the next question.

Sarah's little sister, Emily, has started a vermicompost bin in her classroom. A vermicompost bin uses red wiggler worms to break up food matter.

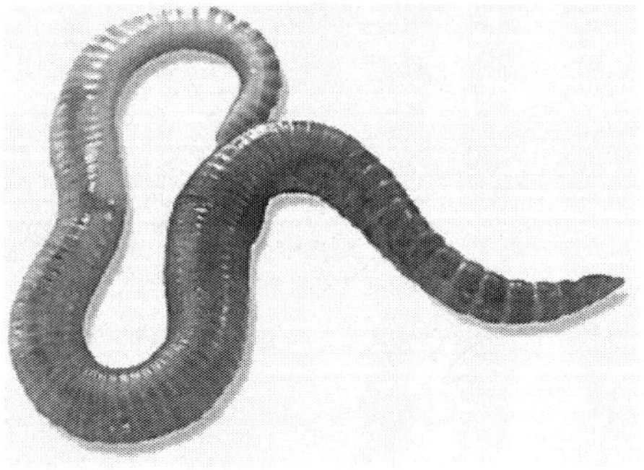

45. The role that the earthworms fill in the ecosystem is best described as

A. predators

B. producers

C. decomposers

D. primary consumer

46. Which of the following statements describes the **most important** role of the sun in a food web?

A. It supplies energy used by producers.

B. Its light allows consumers to find their food.

C. It is the main energy source for decomposers.

D. It provides warmth for both producers and consumers.

47. Which of the following sequences shows the order of the stages in the water cycle?

A. Respiration → Precipitation → Evaporation

B. Precipitation → Condensation → Respiration

C. Condensation → Evaporation → Precipitation

D. Evaporation → Condensation → Precipitation

Use the following information to answer the next question.

Mount St. Helens is best known for its destructive eruption in 1980, which left behind patches of newly formed ground.

48. Which of the following terms **best** describes the type of succession that occurs when plants appear on newly deposited ground following a volcanic eruption?

A. serial

B. primary

C. sequential

D. secondary

Use the following information to answer the next question.

A termite mound

The mound in the picture was built out of clay and saliva by termites in Australia. Most termite mounds are between two- and three-metres high, with the biggest known mound almost nine-metres tall. Termites are social insects that live together in the mound, and one mound can support hundreds to millions of termites. The main food source for termites is dead matter, and they are one of the few groups of animals that can digest wood.

49. The **most likely** reason that two identical termite mounds, located one kilometre apart from each other, cannot support the same number of termites is that

A. one mound is older than the other and can hold more termites

B. one mound meets the termites' need for space better than the other

C. the air quality is better at one location, so the termites prefer that mound

D. the amount of available food is different at each location, so one location can support more termites than the other

Use the following information to answer the next question.

Industrialization has impacted the environment in a number of ways. One of these impacts is depicted in the two cartoons below.

50. Which of the following environmental issues is depicted in both of these cartoons?

A. Climate change **B.** Deforestation

C. Urbanization **D.** Acid rain

ANSWERS AND SOLUTIONS — PRACTICE TEST 1

1. D	11. D	21. B	31. D	41. A
2. C	12. D	22. B	32. A	42. D
3. D	13. C	23. C	33. D	43. D
4. C	14. C	24. D	34. C	44. A
5. A	15. B	25. A	35. B	45. B
6. D	16. A	26. C	36. A	46. B
7. D	17. A	27. B	37. A	47. D
8. C	18. D	28. C	38. C	48. D
9. B	19. A	29. C	39. A	49. A
10. A	20. A	30. A	40. B	50. A

1. D

Heavy woollen clothes are worn to keep people warm during the cold winter months by preventing body heat from escaping. The correct answer is D.

2. C

Michelle's data, shows that the larger the volume of the ice block, the longer it takes for the block to melt. Therefore, the amount of time needed to melt an ice block is directly proportional to the volume of the ice block. As well, the longer the ice block is exposed to the heat source, the greater the amount of heat used. So, the heat needed to melt the ice block is directly proportional to the time it takes to melt, which is directly proportional to the volume of the ice block. Therefore, the amount of heat required for an ice block to melt is directly proportional to the ice block's volume. The correct answer is C.

Michelle did not measure the mass of the ice blocks for the experiment, so no conclusion can be made regarding the relation between the heat required and the mass of the ice blocks. The density of ice is constant, so the density of an ice block has no effect on the amount of heat it takes to melt it. Since the source of heat is the same in each case, the rate of heating is also the same. Therefore, the temperature of an ice block has no effect on the amount of heat needed to melt it.

3. D

A vacuum (empty space) between the two glass walls prevents heat loss because non-radiated heat requires some matter to transfer from one area to another. The plastic cap consists of only one layer of material without an intervening vacuum, so it conducts heat from the hot liquid to the outside air. The loss of heat from the liquid through the lid causes the temperature of the liquid to drop. The correct answer is D.

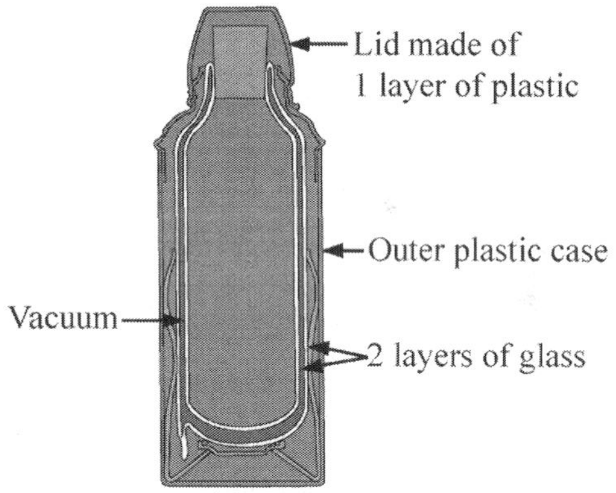

4. C

The particles of solids vibrate in fixed positions. When a solid is heated, the particles do not move from their fixed positions. Instead, they vibrate even faster. When the particles vibrate, they collide with the surrounding particles, transferring some of the heat energy to the cooler particles. Therefore, heat transfer occurs by conduction in solids. The correct answer is C.

5. A

Heat travels from a hot object to a cold object, not from a cold object to a hot object. It is temperature that is measured in degrees Celsius, not heat. Therefore, Jacob's statements 1 and 2 are incorrect. The correct answer is A.

The uneven warming of the atmosphere is responsible for many of the weather patterns on Earth. Winds and storms are created by the uneven heating of Earth's surface and atmosphere. This is because warm air moves by convection, rising up in the atmosphere, and cold air moves in to replace the warm air. Large birds, such as eagles, will find this warm air in the atmosphere and glide effortlessly for hours when in search of food. Therefore, Jacob's statements 3 and 4 are correct.

6. D

As the water is heated, the particles gain energy and start to move faster and away from each other. This creates larger spaces between the particles. As a result, the volume of the water increases. However, the amount of particles in the liquid remains the same, and the particles will be distributed evenly throughout the water. Thus, the correct image is

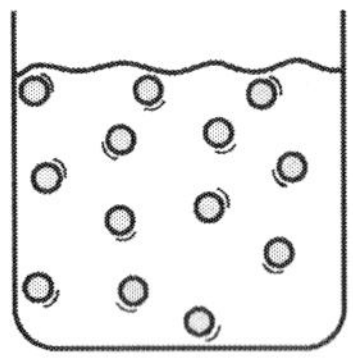

The correct answer is D.

7. D

The low temperature in the freezer causes the matter in the balloons to contract. Solids contract the least, and gases contract the most. Balloon 4, which contains helium gas, would shrink the most in the freezer, so it would have the smallest size at the end of five hours. The correct answer is D.

8. C

Metals are very good conductors. Copper is the only metal listed. Copper will cause the wax to melt the fastest.

Brick, wood, and plastic are not good conductors. It will take a long time for the wax to melt if one of these materials is used in the gap. The wax may also not melt at all. The material may prevent the heat from travelling through the bar to the end.

9. B

The candle heats the air above it, so the air becomes less dense and rises out the chimney opening that is closest to the candle. To replace the air that leaves through the chimney, cooler air comes down the second chimney opening. This is shown in the following image:

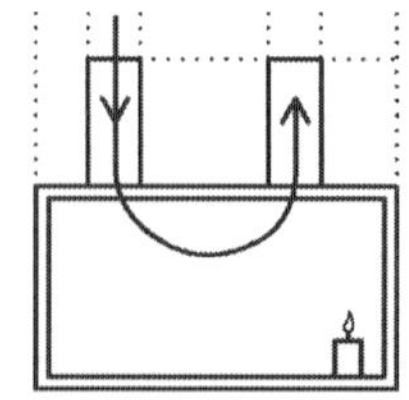

This creates a circular movement of air called a convection currents. The correct answer is B.

10. A

Dark-coloured material absorbs more radiant heat energy than light-coloured material does. Therefore, the black can absorbs more heat than the white can. The black can conduct the absorbed heat to the water inside of the can. The correct answer is A.

11. D

Greenhouse gases have the property of trapping heat radiated by Earth, preventing it from escaping into space. The sharp rise in the average yearly temperature from 1985 to 2005 was most likely caused by an increased amount of greenhouse gases. The correct answer is D.

12. D

A carbon tax is designed to tax all users of carbon-based fuels to discourage their use in an effort to reduce the emission of carbon dioxide, a significant greenhouse gas. While all of the given industries will likely be taxed, the industry that burns the most carbon-based fuel is the oil industry, which burns unusable parts of crude oil as it distills the crude to produce useful products, such as gasoline and diesel fuel. The correct answer is D.

13. C

The material used to make the boots for hockey skates needs to stretch and regain its original shape after stretching in order to be comfortable as the foot moves in the skate boot. Therefore, the most important factor is the plasticity of the material. The correct answer is C.

14. C

The force that causes a rope to stretch is a tension force. Once the rope reaches its maximum length, the tension force is used to lift the box. The correct answer is C.

Shear forces push two parts of a material in two different directions. A torsion force is exerted when the two ends of an object are twisted in different directions. A compression force squeezes a material together.

15. B

A load caused by an earthquake is the total force exerted on a structure by an earthquake. The load is a horizontal force on the structure. Since the force is horizontal to the structure, the magnitude of the load caused by the earthquake does not depend on the height of the structure. The correct answer is B.

The earthquake causes an acceleration of Earth's surface, creating a horizontal push and pull on the structure. This causes a horizontal acceleration of the mass of the structure. Therefore, the magnitude of the load caused by the earthquake depends on both the mass of the structure and the acceleration of Earth's surface.

A structure with stiff walls can resist the push and pull on the structure, decreasing the magnitude of the load caused by the earthquake. The stiffness of the walls will be determined by the building materials used for the structure.

16. A

Bridge 1 is an example of a truss bridge. A truss bridge is strong because the vertical beams resist compression forces and the horizontal beams resist tension forces. The triangle design spreads out both the compression and tension forces among the beams, increasing the overall strength of the bridge.

17. A

Earthquakes are more likely in coastal areas, so people often build houses with lighter wood because light-weight wooden walls cause less damage when they collapse. The correct answer is A.

18. D

The force that Jaya applied to the the ball of plasticine is a squeezing, or pushing, force. Compression forces crush a material by squeezing it together. The correct answer is D.

19. A

Shell structures have moulded shapes that enclose space. Both the bird's eggs and exoskeleton have moulded shapes that enclose space. Therefore, they are shell structures. The correct answer is A.

Frame structures are made up of parts fastened together. There is usually space between the components of a frame structure. The spider web and skeleton are examples of frame structures.

20. A

The centre of gravity can be thought of as the point in a structure where gravity pulls the structure downward. When a structure is symmetrical, its centre of gravity lies at its geometrical centre. The correct answer is A.

21. B

In order for the wind force to affect the sailboat correctly, the fan needs to apply the force in the correct direction. If the fan is in the correct position, then the angle of the sail needs to be adjusted to capture the wind force at the proper angle. The correct answer is B.

Increasing the magnitude of the wind force or the size of the sail will not result in the boat sailing straight if the wind force is not applied at the proper angle to the sails. Changing the direction of the wind force to the other side of the tank will result in the direction of the wind force being opposite to the side needed to propel the boat forward.

22. B

Gravity is considered an external force, along with wind and earthquakes. The correct answer is B.

Shear, torsion, and compression are all examples of internal forces.

23. C

Symmetry in a building increases structural stability. Decreasing symmetry by adding mass to only one side of the structure will decrease the building's structural stability. The correct answer is C.

Using approved materials, distributing the loads evenly, and reinforcing the base all increase the structural stability of a building.

24. D
The bridge was designed with girders that were not large enough to ensure that the bridge was rigid enough to withstand wind forces. Therefore this is an example of a poor design. The correct answer is D.

25. A
The solid materials in sewage can be filtered from the water component, allowing the water component to be reused. The correct answer is A.

Latex paint does not contain harmful components. The lead in lead-based paint cannot be easily separated from the paint mixture. Uranium is a pure substance, not a mixture.

26. C
The triangle frame indicates caution (e.g., flammable products), the octagon frame indicates danger (e.g., poisonous products), and the diamond frame indicates warning (e.g., corrosive products). The correct answer is C.

27. B
Megan's data shows that more salt dissolves in the acid as the temperature increases. The correct answer is B.

28. C
Mischa should use magnetism to separate the paper clips because only the paper clips will be attracted to the magnet. The correct answer is C.

The mixture is made up of only solid materials, so the methods of evaporation, filtration, and distillation are not appropriate.

29. C
When the temperature of a saturated solution is raised, more solute can be dissolved. If the temperature is then lowered, the solution contains more dissolved solute than its it should be able to hold. This is known as a supersaturated solution. Therefore, Todd creates a supersaturated solution.

30. A
The substance in a solution that gets dissolved is called the solute. In this case, the salt crystals are dissolved in the solution, so they are the solute. The correct answer is A.

31. D
Chloe grouped the materials into pure substances, solutions, and mixtures. She made a mistake by classifying rainwater as a mixture. Rainwater is a pure substance. The correct answer is D.

32. A

In a gas, the particles are spaced relatively far apart and can move about freely. The correct answer is A.

33. D

Pure substances have identical particles. Mixtures have different particles. The only pure substance listed is distilled water. Cheese sauce, orange juice, and apple sauce are all mixtures. Therefore, apple juice should be described as having different particles. The correct answer is D.

34. C

Crude oil is separated by distillation because its constituent liquids have different boiling points. The crude oil is heated quickly to a temperature past the boiling points of all of the liquids in the oil. It is then cooled in a distillation chamber in which the temperature differs at different places. This results in the vapour changing back into its component liquids at different heights along the chamber. The liquids are then captured into their own pipes. The correct answer is C.

35. B

The solvent is the component of the solution that is present in the greatest quantity. Thus, in the given solution, water acts as the solvent, since there is more water than any other liquid. The correct answer is B.

The quantity of milk in the given solution is less than the quantity of water. Honey will not act as a solvent in the given solution because the quantity of honey in the solution is very low. Sugar syrup is a solution containing sugar as the solute and water as the solvent. Therefore, sugar syrup cannot be considered as a solvent, since it is already a solution.

36. A

The unit mL, for millilitres, describes the volume of a liquid, not its concentration. The correct answer is A.

The units g/L, ppm, and mg/L reflect the concentration of a solute (grams, parts, and milligrams respectively) in a solvent (litres, per million, and litres respectively).

37. A

Solubility expresses how much solute can dissolve in a given amount of solvent at a given temperature. The correct answer is A.

38. C

Although computers have gotten smaller, they are replaced more often as technology becomes outdated. This causes the number of computers being produced to increase, meaning that the amount of natural resources used has not decreased. The correct answer is C.

39. A

Fair testing principles means that all the variables except the ones Julia tests (growth and fertilizer) are the same for each trial. Using the model ecosystem keeps variables such as temperature, humidity, and sunlight the same, so they do not effect the results of the experiment.

The affordability of the greenhouse, Julia's ability to check her plants at once, and the protections of the plants are all advantages of using a greenhouse, but they are not related to fair testing.

40. B

Hot and humid weather is not associated with droughts because humid weather implies that there is moisture in the air.

Increased fire risk, soil erosion, and increased pressure on fish habitats are all scenarios that are associated with droughts.

41. A

The flowers and insects are living, so the term that describes them is biotic. The correct answer is A.

Insects are not able to produce their own food, so they are not producers. The flowers and insects are two different species, so they are not a population.

42. D

An ecosystem consists of biotic (living) and abiotic (non-living) components. The correct answer is D.

43. D

Plants trap energy from the sun and transform it into food by photosynthesis in order to store the energy in their bodies. These plants are eaten by the primary consumers, which are then eaten by the secondary consumers, and so on. The energy stored by the plants transfers through a sequence of different species which is called the food chain. The correct answer is D.

44. A

Phytoplankton are small floating organisms that get their energy through photosynthesis. Organisms that make their own food through photosynthesis are called producers. The correct answer is A.

Decomposers break down dead and decaying tissue and recycle nutrients. Consumers are not able to make their own food, and they get their energy by eating other organisms. Primary consumers feed on the producers; secondary consumers feed on primary consumers.

45. B

Since frogs feed on spiders, an increase in the spider population will cause an increase in the population of frogs. The correct answer is B.

An increase in the spider population will have no effect on the coyote or deer populations. An increase in the spider population will cause the population of ants to decrease.

46. B

In the given food web, the crayfish feed on the snails. When the population of the snail decreases, the crayfish will be directly affected. The correct answer is B.

Since the trout, cyprinid, and white suckers do not feed on snails, the decline in the snail population will not affect them as much as it will affect the crayfish.

47. D

The term *condensation* describes the conversion of water vapour into droplets. The correct answer is D.

Evaporation is the conversion of liquid water into water vapour. Precipitation is the process by which the water droplets return to Earth's surface. Transpiration is the movement of water by plants.

48. D

Primary succession occurs on newly emerged land or a body of water that originally contained no living inhabitants. The correct answer is D.

Succession on previously settled land, such as forests, agricultural fields, or water-logged soil, is termed secondary succession.

49. A

There is only enough shelter for 2 500 deer. Even though there is enough food, water, and space in this area for more white-tailed deer, the population of deer that can live in the area is limited by the amount of shelter. As a result, since 1 000 white-tailed deer already live in the area, there is room for another 1 500 deer, (since 2 500 – 1 000 = 1 500). The correct answer is A.

50. A

Wolves are the main predators of the moose and caribou in the Yukon. Both moose and caribou populations were declining, so the government tried to reduce wolf predation, altering the natural food chain. The correct answer is A.

Wolves are very rarely a threat to humans or livestock in the Yukon, and reducing wolf numbers might actually decrease tourism, as wildlife is one of the main reasons tourists visit the Yukon.

ANSWERS AND SOLUTIONS — PRACTICE TEST 2

1. D	11. D	21. D	31. D	41. A
2. B	12. B	22. C	32. A	42. A
3. A	13. B	23. C	33. A	43. D
4. C	14. C	24. D	34. C	44. B
5. B	15. D	25. C	35. D	45. C
6. A	16. A	26. B	36. C	46. A
7. B	17. C	27. D	37. B	47. D
8. C	18. D	28. B	38. B	48. B
9. D	19. C	29. A	39. C	49. D
10. A	20. A	30. B	40. A	50. D

1. D

Diagram X shows a windmill. The wind turns the windmill, causing a generator to rotate, which generates electricity.

Diagram Y shows water moving. A device can be placed in the water that spins a turbine using the power of the moving water. This turbine would then spin a generator, which would then produce electrical energy. "Hydro" means water; therefore obtaining energy using the movement of water is hydroelectric energy.

Diagram Z shows solar panels on a roof. Solar panels capture the energy from the sun and convert it into electricity.

Chart D correctly identifies each of the energy sources in the diagrams.

2. B

When a solid converts into a liquid, an increase in its volume occurs. This is because the distances between the particles increase, and the particles become more loosely held. The correct answer is B.

Solids absorb heat energy in order to convert into liquids. As a result, the temperature cannot decrease during this process.

The intermolecular bonding gets weakened during the conversion of solids into liquids.
The intermolecular distance increases, and particles become loosely held.

Mass remains the same when solids convert into liquids.

3. A

A thermographic camera forms an image using infrared (heat) radiation. This shows where heat escapes from a room. The correct answer is A.

A digital camera does not form an image using infrared radiation and will not show from where heat is escaping from. A thermometer is not sensitive enough to detect one place in the room where heat is escaping. A thermostat detects the temperature in a room; it does not measure where heat loss occurs.

4. C

An electric space heater emits radiation in order to heat the air. The air near the heater becomes hotter than the air farther away from the heater.
This establishes a convection current, and the air inside the room heats up by convection. The correct answer is C.

5. B

Heat is a form of energy. This energy moves from one location to another by three different methods. These methods are conduction, convection, or radiation. Thus, each concept is directly related to the central concept of heat, so the concept map that best shows the relationship between these terms is:

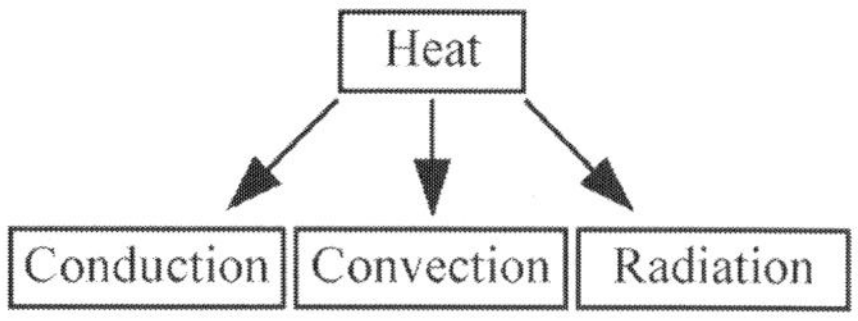

The correct answer is B.

6. A

The particles in matter move most slowly in a solid. As well, the particles in a solid are closest together. They just vibrate back and forth. The particles move faster in a liquid than in a solid because the space between the particles is greater. The particles move the fastest in a gas because there is more space between the particles in a gas than in a solid or liquid. Therefore, statements I and III are true. The correct answer is A.

7. B

Renewable sources of heat energy are sources that will not run out because they can be continuously replenished. Of Patrick's examples, the geothermal energy and sunlight are examples of renewable sources. The correct answer is B.

Coal and gasoline are considered non-renewable sources of heat energy because they are fossil fuels that were produced over millions of years. These sources cannot be replenished, meaning that they will eventually run out.

8. C

When a substance cools, the particles move with less energy. As the particles move with less energy, the spaces between them decrease. The arrows that show this are arrows O and N. The correct answer is C.

9. D

When the particles in the metal rod warm up, they gain energy and begin to vibrate vigorously. This allows heat to transfer from one particle to the next along the length of the rod. As the particles in the rod near the wax heat up, they pass on the energy to the particles in the wax. The wax particles then gain heat energy until the wax melts. When the wax melts, the pins fall. This process of heat transfer is called conduction. The correct answer is D.

10. A

Heat transfer by convection involves the movement of particles in liquids and gases. Mineral crystals are formed by the the cooling of solid rock by conduction. The correct answer is A.

Ocean currents are created when the warm water in the tropics rises to the surface and is replaced by the cold water from the polar regions. Thermals occur when the air that is warmed above land on Earth's surface is heated and rises. Many larger birds take advantage of thermal currents to glide effortlessly. Sea breezes occur when the warm air above the land rises and is replaced by the cooler sea air. These are all examples of convection currents.

11. D

Heat radiation travels as waves, which can easily pass through a vacuum. It does not require particles to travel. The correct answer is D.

Conduction occurs in solids. Convection occurs in liquids and gases. Both conduction and convection require particles.

12. B

When the gases in the atmosphere traps Earth's radiant heat, the temperature of the atmosphere rises. The amount of daylight depends on the positions of Earth and the sun, not the temperature in Earth's atmosphere. The correct answer is B.

Higher temperatures melt the glaciers at a faster rate. The melted water flows into the ocean, causing the sea levels to rise. Higher temperatures may also cause severe weather patterns. The melted water in the oceans may cause changes in wind patterns and temperatures, possibly causing severe climate changes. In some regions, the increasing temperatures may cause more severe drought conditions.

13. B

Trees are important in maintaining the atmosphere. They consume large amounts of carbon dioxide during the process of photosynthesis to make oxygen. When large areas of trees are burned or clear-cut, then less trees exist to consume carbon dioxide and produce oxygen. Therefore, the carbon dioxide levels increase, and the oxygen levels decrease. Burning the trees further affects these levels, as the process of burning uses up oxygen, and it produces carbon dioxide. The correct answer is B.

14. C

Products are ergonomically designed to increase their safety for human use. The correct answer is C.

15. D

The spring in the toy is compressed. When the lid opens, the spring straightens out, causing the jack-in-the-box to burst out of the box. The correct answer is D.

16. A

The weight of a structure is also called its static load; it is the constant and unchanging load experienced by a structure. The correct answer is A.

17. C

By increasing the thickness of the beam, the static load of the bridge also increases. This will decrease the amount of additional load that the bridge can support. Therefore, increasing the thickness of the beam will not increase the stability of the bridge. The correct answer is C.

Reinforcing the beam, building an arch under the beam, and using a stronger material for the beam will all increase the strength, or load capacity, of the bridge, resulting in a more stable bridge that can withstand greater forces.

18. D

To ensure structural safety, structures need to be designed to carry much heavier loads than they will actually have to hold. The load of 4 500 kg is three times more than the average load the balconies will have to hold. This load is much heavier than the load the balconies will have to hold. The correct answer is D.

A maximum load of 1 000 kg will not be sufficient because it is less than the amount of weight the balcony should hold. A maximum load of 1 500 kg will not be sufficient because it is exactly the top end of the range of weight the balcony should hold. A maximum load of 1 550 kg will not be sufficient because it only exceeds the range of weight the balcony should hold by 50 kg. This is not a sufficient safety margin.

19. C

Truss 3 will hold the greatest number of math textbooks. The sticks that cross in the middle add structural support to the truss. They also spread the compression force of the textbooks across the entire truss, which allows it to support more weight. The correct answer is C.

20. A

Frame structures have rigid frameworks made up of parts fastened together. A skeleton and a bicycle are examples of frame structures. The correct answer is A.

Solid structures are usually made from a solid piece of material with little or no space inside. A tree trunk and brick wall are examples of solid structures.

Shell structures have a moulded shape enclosing a space. A chicken egg and domed roof are examples of shell structures.

21. D

The centre of gravity is the point in a structure where its mass is evenly distributed. In a symmetrical structure, this is the geometric centre of the structure. In the middle of the plane there is equal mass in front and behind the centre of gravity, as well as above and below the centre of gravity. The correct answer is D.

22. C

Earth exerts a gravitational force on the tea bag, while the string exerts a tension force on the tea bag. The correct answer is C.

23. C

The magnitude of a force is measured in newtons. The correct answer is C.

Metres per second are the unit for velocity. Degrees measure temperature. Joules measure the magnitude of energy.

24. D

A static load is the constant and unchanging load that is experienced by the structure. In this situation, the static load on the bridge is the weight of the bridge deck itself. The correct answer is D.

A load that changes and moves is called a dynamic load. The force of the expanding metal, the weight of the moving truck, and the force of the wind are all changing loads.

25. C

Material strength and structure design, not symmetry, determine structural strength. The correct answer is C.

The mass in symmetrical structures is evenly distributed around the structure's centre of gravity. This increases the stability of the structure. Symmetrical structures also tend to be more aesthetically pleasing.

26. B

The soil foundation of a structure should be solid, not soft, to prevent the building from shifting. Therefore, a rock foundation would provide the most stable support for a highrise building. The correct answer is B.

27. D

The evaporation process uses a lot of energy to heat the sap so that the water evaporates. Energy production creates a lot of pollution, so the production of maple syrup creates a lot of pollution as a result of its energy use. The correct answer is D.

The evaporation process used to produce maple syrup only produces water vapour. There is no water or air pollution produced during evaporation. As well, the sap is removed without having to cut down the trees, so that they can be used again.

28. B

The solubility rate is the speed at which a solute dissolves in a solvent. In this case, solubility describes how quickly the sugar cube dissolves in the water. While using a smaller sugar cube will cause the sugar cube to dissolve faster in the water, this happens because less sugar needs to be dissolved, not because the solubility rate has increased. In fact, because less surface area is exposed, the rate of dissolving would actually be reduced. The correct answer is B.

By heating up the water, the water particles gain energy and will collide with the sugar particles more often to increase the solubility rate. By breaking up the sugar cube, Eric would speed up dissolving because he is exposing a greater surface area of sugar to the water. By stirring, the water particles collide more often with the sugar particles to increase the solubility rate.

29. A

Recall that evaporation is the process of turning a liquid into a gas. In the given scenario, water is a liquid, but sand is a solid. Sand will not turn into a liquid until it is heated to a temperature between 3 000°C to 4 000°C. Such temperatures can be created only under special circumstances. Therefore, when the sand and water are mixed and the mixture is boiled, the water will evaporate when the temperature reaches 100°C, but the sand will remain a solid. The correct answer is A.

30. B

A substance is classified as a mixture if it can be separated into constituent parts using physical methods. Mercury, like that found in thermometers, cannot be separated into constituent parts. It is a pure substance. The correct answer is B.

Air is a mixture of gases. Salt water is a mixture of salt and water; which can easily be separated by boiling the water. Concrete is a mixture of cement, gravel, and sand.

31. D

Brent's tea contains less tea molecules per amount of water than Stephanie's. This means his tea is more dilute. It could also be described as less concentrated, less saturated, or less potent. The correct answer is D.

32. A

Bronze is an metal alloy of copper and tin. Therefore, it is an example of a mixture. The correct answer is A.

Zinc, iron, and tin are all natural elements and can be classified as metals.

33. A

Condensation is the change from a gas, in which the particles move fast, to a liquid, in which the particles slow down but continue to move. This is similar to the music, which slows down but does not stop moving. The correct answer is A.

Evaporation is the change from a liquid to a gas; therefore the particles would move faster. Sublimation is the change from a solid to a gas; therefore the particles would move faster. Solidification is the change from a liquid to a solid; therefore the particles would slow down and stop moving, but continue to vibrate in place.

34. C

A solution is made of two or more materials that mix so that all or some of the materials cannot be seen. An example is stirring drink crystals into water. The water dissolves the drink crystals so that they cannot be seen, but they are still there because a sweet drink has been formed. When corn starch dissolves into water, cocoa powder into milk, and juice into ginger ale, only one of the substances will be visible. Therefore, column III contains examples of solutions. The correct answer is C.

A mechanical mixture is made of two or more materials that are mixed together without changing either substance. An example would be a salad that is made of lettuce, cucumber, and tomato. Columns I, II, and IV all contain at least one mechanical mixture.

35. D

Static electricity can be used to separate a salt and pepper mixture. Since pepper is lighter than salt, it takes less effort for pepper to overcome the force of gravity. Static electricity can then attract the pepper without attracting the salt.

Sand does not dissolve in water, so filtering the solution will remove the sand from the water.

Sugar dissolves in water, so evaporation can be used to boil off the water, leaving only the sugar behind.

Iron filings are attracted to a magnet whereas sand is not; therefore, magnetism can be used to separate this mixture.

36. C

Soft drinks contain liquid water as the solvent and carbon dioxide gas as the solute. The correct answer is C.

Air is a solution with nitrogen gas as the solvent and various other gases, such as oxygen and carbon dioxide, as the solute. Perfume contains liquid alcohol as the solvent and liquid essential oils as the solute. Salt water contains solid salt as the solute and liquid water as the solvent.

37. B

Recall that concentration is found using the following equation:

$$\text{concentration} = \frac{\text{weight of the solute}}{\text{weight of the solvent}}$$

To obtain a concentration expressed per 100 mL, the weight of the solvent is divided by 5. Therefore, the weight of the solute should also be divided by 5, resulting in a numerator of 10 g. Therefore, the correct expression of the concentration, per 100 mL, is 10 g/100 mL. The correct answer is B.

38. B

Water is called the universal solvent because it can dissolve many different substances. This is a problem because water can dissolve substances that then make it unusable. This means that the water is polluted. The correct answer is B.

Water cannot dissolve all substances. For example, oil does not dissolve in water. However, there are many solutes that do dissolve in water.

39. C

Integrated pest management is based on the principle that total elimination of insect pests is not often possible, very expensive, and often environmentally dangerous. If the farmer supports the use of IPM, he would not likely suggest multiple applications of the pesticide. The correct answer is C.

40. A

The zebra mussels out-compete the native mussel species for the food resources. The correct answer is A.

Zebra mussels settle on hard surfaces, so they are not clogging the channel like water milfoil. They only reproduce with their own species, so they are not out-competing for mates. They are filter feeders, not parasites.

41. A

The ability of an ecosystem to continue thriving is the ecosystem's sustainability. The correct answer is A.

42. A

An ecosystem is a system of complex interactions between living things (communities and populations) and their environment (habitat). The correct answer is A.

A community is all the species living in an environment. A population is all the individuals of one species living in an environment. A habitat refers to the environment in which an organism lives.

43. D

Biotic components are living; abiotic components are non-living. Of the given components, only water is an abiotic component.

44. B

In the given food chain, the spider is a tertiary consumer. It feeds on the secondary consumer, the ladybug. The correct answer is B.

45. C

Because the main food source for the red wiggler worms is dead material, the worms play an important role in recycling matter. This means they are decomposers. The correct answer is C.

46. A

Life on Earth depends on the continuous supply of energy from the sun. Producers use this energy to make their own food, forming the base for all food webs. The correct answer is A.

47. D

Since the water cycle is a cycle, it does not have a beginning or an end. However, the stages involved happen in a certain order. This is shown in the following picture:

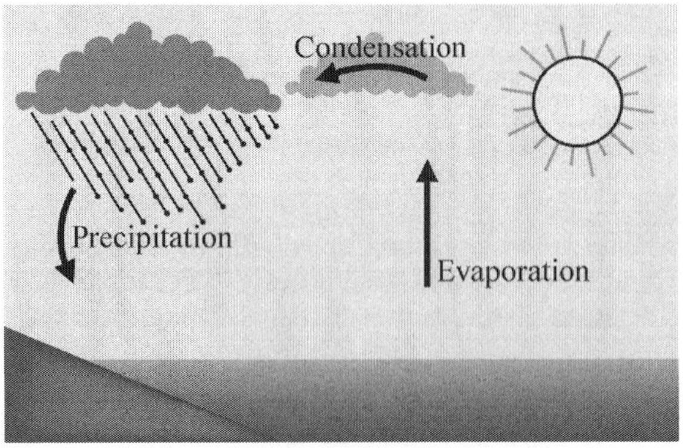

Of the given sequences, the only one that shows the correct order of the stages in the water cycle is: evaporation → condensation → precipitation.

The correct answer is D.

48. B

Primary succession refers to the first appearance of vegetation on a newly formed or exposed surface. The correct answer is B.

49. D

It is very possible that the available food (dead matter and wood) at the two sites is different. This is the most likely reason the two mounds support different numbers of termites. The correct answer is D.

The number of organisms an ecosystem can support is limited by the ecosystem's ability to provide food, water, space, and air for the organisms. If the mounds are identical, the age of the mound should not matter, and they should meet the termites' need for space equally. The mounds are only one kilometre apart, so it is unlikely that the air quality is very different between the two mounds.

50. D

Acid rain weakens trees by damaging their leaves, limiting nutrients available to them, and poisoning them. This is depicted in the first cartoon; the tree has lost almost all its leaves and is clearly not healthy. The second cartoon shows the trees at a negotiating table with factories. Acid rain is caused by emissions from factories. The correct answer is D.

Climate change is largely caused by emissions, but trees naturally process carbon dioxide through photosynthesis. Deforestation is the removal of trees, but the trees in the cartoons are still standing, just weak. Urbanization again relates to the clearing of forests, and industrial facilities are usually located away from urban centres.

Appendices

GLOSSARY

abiotic A non-living component of an ecosystem.

biotic A living component in an ecosystem.

centre of gravity The imaginary point within a structure where the force of gravity pulls down on the object.

climax community A community in the succession of an ecosystem, where the species are no longer changing.

compression A force that squeezes an object or the parts within object within it.

concentration The amount of solute (mass) dissolved in a certain amount of solvent (volume) in a solution. Written in g/mL or kg/L.

condensation The change of water in vapour form into liquid form.

conduction The transfer of heat from one substance to another by contact of the substances.

consumer A living thing that relies on another living thing for food.

convection The transfer of heat in a gas or liquid by the movement of the particles within the substance.

decomposer An organism that breaks down dead plant and animal material.

ecosystem All the living and non-living things in an area, and the interactions between them.

ergonomics The study of how the human body works when using objects or systems.

external force A force that acts on a structure from the outside; a load.

food chain A series of organisms in order of who eats whom.

force A push or pull acting on an object that can either cause a change in movement or a change in shape.

greenhouse gas A gas that contributes to the warming of Earth's atmosphere by trapping heat within the atmosphere.

heat A form of energy that transfers by a change in temperature.

insoluble A substance that will not dissolve into another.

insulate To use material that does not transfer heat to reduce loss or leakage of heat.

internal force A force that acts on a structure from within itself.

load An external force that acts upon a structure.

mechanical mixture A mixture that has visible different parts. Also known as a heterogeneous mixture.

mixture Matter that is made up of two or more pure substances.

organism Any single living thing. Examples of organisms are plants, animals, fungi, and protists.

photosynthesis The process by which plants make food for themselves.

pioneer community The very first group of plants to settle on a newly exposed or newly deposited surface.

precipitation Water that falls from the sky as rain, snow, hail, or sleet.

primary consumer The organism in a food chain that feeds directly on the producer.

primary succession The development of a pioneer community on a surface that has never had plants, such as newly exposed or formed surfaces.

producer An organism that makes its own food.

pure substance Matter that is made up of a single substance.

radiation The transfer of heat without the use of particles; the heat travels in the form of waves.

respiration The process of getting and using oxygen and removing carbon dioxide from the body.

saturated A solution in which the solvent cannot dissolve any more solute.

scavenger An organism that eats dead plant or animal matter.

secondary consumer An animal that eats the primary consumer in a food chain.

secondary succession The changes in a community that result from a disturbance, such as a fire or flood.

shear Two pushing forces acting in opposite directions within one structure.

soluble A substance that is able to be dissolved into another.

solute The substance in a solution that is dissolved and is present in smaller quantities in the solution.

solution A mixture of two or more substances that has only one visible part, also called a homogenous mixture.

solvent The substance in a solution that does the dissolving and is present in the largest quantity.

structure An object of any size that provides support.

sustainability The ability to keep going indefinitely.

symmetry The mass of the structure distributed equally around a line down its middle (the line of symmetry).

temperature A measure of the average kinetic energy of a system of particles that occurs in a substance.

tension A force that stretches and pulls something apart.

tertiary consumer An animal that eats the secondary consumer in a food chain.

torsion A force that cause an object to twist in shape.

transpiration The process by which water moves through plants and is released into the atmosphere.

unsaturated A solution in which the solvent is able to dissolve more solute.

NOTES

NOTES

NOTES

SOLARO Study Guides
Ordering Information

Student Notes and Problems
Workbook
Ordering Information

Student Notes and Problems (SNAP) Workbooks contain complete explanations of curriculum concepts, including examples and practice exercises

SNAP Workbook—$29.95 each plus applicable sales tax

Ontario SNAP Titles
Physics 12, University Preparation (SPH4U)
Physics 11, University Preparation (SPH3U)
Math 10, Academic, Principles of Mathematics (MPM2D)
Math 9, Academic, Principles of Mathematics (MPM1D)
Math 9, Applied, Foundations of Mathematics (MFM1P)

Total Cost

SOLARO Study Guides Ordered ________

SNAP Books Ordered ________

Cost Subtotal ________

Shipping and Handling
Please call for current rates ________

GST ________

Order Total ________

Payment and Shipping Information

Name ________________

School ________________

Telephone ________________

SHIP TO:

School Code ________________

School Name ________________

Address ________________

City: ________________

Postal Code: ________________

PAYMENT OPTIONS:

☐ By Credit Care VISA/MC

Name on Card: ________________

Number: ________________

Expirely Date: ________________

☐ By Enclosed Cheque

☐ Invoice School

PO Number: ________________

To order books, please visit
www.castlerockresearch.com

Volume pricing is available. Contact us at orders@castlerockresearch.com